# With Drama in Mind

## Real learning in imagined worlds

## Patrice Baldwin

Published by Continuum International Publishing Group
The Tower Building
11 York Road
London SE1 7NX

© Patrice Baldwin 2004

Reprinted 2007, 2008

ISBN: 978 1 85539 094 2

**Managing editor:** Carol Thompson

**Design and typesetting:** Kerry Ingham

**Illustrations:** Terry McKenna and Kerry Ingham


Printed in Great Britain by MPG Books Ltd, Bodmin, Cornwall

'When I examine myself and my methods of thought,
I come to the conclusion that the gift of fantasy has
meant more to me than my talent for absorbing
positive knowledge'

'I am enough of an artist to draw freely upon my
imagination. Imagination is more important than
knowledge. Knowledge is limited. Imagination encircles
the world.'

Albert Einstein ■

## ■ Author Acknowledgements

Thanks to Mary Clark my first drama teacher, who switched on the drama light for me in my early teens through Youth Theatre. Thanks to Rob John who has worked alongside me, continuously stimulating and challenging my own thinking and practice over many years, and to Jonothan Neelands who has also given me support, understanding and encouragement. And thanks to my dear friend Kate Fleming who has shown steadfast interest in my work and spurred me on to complete this book. Thanks also to National Drama, the leading professional association of drama educators for valued friendships and continuous opportunities to meet and work with high quality international drama practitioners. Thanks also to Alistair Smith for discussing drama and the brain with me, and to Steve Bowkett for agreeing to work with me to further explore story, thinking and drama practically and theoretically. Thanks also to Jim Houghton for giving me the opportunity to write this book and start building bridges and rainbows between educational worlds.

## ■ Picture Credits

The photograph of Chief Seattle (page 225) is reproduced by permission of MSCA, University of Washington Libraries (neg. NA893); *Love Conquers Fear* (pages 215 and 216) is reproduced by permission of Manchester Central Library, Local Studies.

# Contents

*...continued*

# PART THREE

■ Drama Units                                                                149

# PART FOUR

■ Photocopiable Resource Sheets                                              203

# **F**oreword

In this exciting and ground-breaking new publication, Patrice Baldwin draws on a wealth of experience and knowledge to provide an accessible, practical and inspiring guide to teaching drama in the primary school and transition years. She has worked as a teacher, headteacher and consultant and she is extraordinarily generous in distilling and sharing the lessons that she has learned from her own practical experiences of teaching drama.

This is also a very timely book. Patrice outlines a number of new government initiatives and priorities, which have re-valued the importance of drama both as a vital cross-curricular resource and as an important art form and subject in its own right. Patrice has also closely cross-referenced the teaching and learning potential of drama to other new and relevant initiatives which share a common ground of pedagogic principles and grounded theories about how best we can teach and learn. In each of the chapters in the first section of the book, Patrice carefully explains powerful theories and practices, which are beginning to find a place in primary schools. These include coverage of circle time, Philosophy for Children, creativity, multiple intelligences theories and others.

Patrice demonstrates both how drama can provide a practical means of enhancing and delivering these new initiatives and ideas, and also how in turn drama teaching and learning can be enhanced by an understanding of similar curriculum and pedagogic developments beyond the field of drama in education. In particular, Patrice draws our attention to important new understandings about how the human brain works in interaction with the environment and how we can use this research to improve the quality both of work in drama and in all our classroom encounters with children. This is, in my experience, the first book to make such close and practical use of these new understandings and potentially new pedagogic techniques.

There is a great deal to learn from this book. There is a thorough and rigorous use of appropriate theory and knowledge about human learning to support sound practical advice on how best to plan, manage and teach drama. Patrice is realistic about the challenges and concerns that many non-specialist teachers experience when beginning drama work, and throughout the book these teachers will find much to support and encourage them. Because of the close referencing to various guidance documents and research findings, they can also develop their experiences of teaching drama in the confidence that they are providing effective and appropriate learning contexts and pedagogic approaches for their pupils.

Essentially this book is a convincing argument of the need to go beyond the basics both in terms of the skills and knowledge contained in the curriculum and in terms of teaching and learning styles. What is advocated here is a more subtle and holistic view of human learning based on the idea of authentic achievement and personal growth. Patrice sees drama, in common with the other projects that she discusses, as being a humanizing means of unlocking the often hidden potential of every teacher and learner. Experienced teachers of drama will welcome this recognition, but also learn from their exposure to the other research, projects and pedagogic examples in the book. Non-specialist teachers who are drawn to the ideas of circle time or

Philosophy for Children, or to the importance of multiple intelligences theory, will find that drama can be a powerful way of realizing their own ideals for a broader and more humanizing curriculum that does not ignore the vitality of their pupils' imaginative and cognitive powers.

In addition, this book provides an essential toolkit of drama techniques and strategies that can be used in a wide variety of drama-related learning. There is sound and grounded advice on planning and managing drama that many non-specialists will welcome. In the final section, Patrice provides some stimulating schemes of work which are carefully annotated to guide the teacher. These schemes are also closely connected to the ideas and theories presented in the first section of the book, so that there is a very clear sense of 'theory in practice'. These schemes also reflect Patrice's skill in selecting and developing appropriate imaginative resources for pupils. She manages to design imaginative, creative and thoughtful schemes of work, which are also made accessible for a busy teacher. She carefully guides the reader through potential pitfalls and clearly indicates the learning potential at each stage of the drama.

It is hard not to be touched by Patrice's warmth and enthusiasm for drama. She really wants you to understand its place in the curriculum and the role it can play in developing a wide range of cognitive and imaginative skills. She offers you every encouragement and advice to help make a start on making drama part of the life of your classroom.

*Jonothan Neelands*
*Reader in Drama and Theatre Education*
*University of Warwick*
*March 2004*

# Introduction

'There is one thing stronger than all the armies in the world
and that is an idea whose time has come.'

*Victor Hugo* ■

'Imagine that what for drama practitioners was simply felt
to be so, might now be researched, and what was largely
instinct and belief, might now be verifiable. The good news
is that it probably is.'

*John Norman (1999)* ■

Young children from all cultures pretend. They create make-believe worlds that are stimulated by real or imagined experiences and, if they are fortunate, they will find adults who are adept at joining them in these make-believe worlds. Playful adults may be parents, carers, friends or possibly teachers and classroom assistants. Their reasons for playing make-believe with children may vary and, for teachers, the reasons may be rooted in an understanding that make-believe worlds are compelling places for children to be, within which they can be guided to learn in meaningful, memorable and enjoyable ways. Teachers who practise drama in education take all this one step further. They set about creating with children, sometimes quite complex shared, imagined and sustainable worlds which whole classes of children contract to enter alongside teachers. Within these shared, imagined worlds the children may have a play agenda and the teacher may have a learning agenda which can become synonymous in practice. Teachers who understand not just children and learning but also how drama works can make imagined experiences not only cognitively compelling and challenging but also aesthetically powerful and vivid.

It was from the seeds of dramatic play that drama in education grew and flourished, particularly in the 1960s and 70s, as teachers began to see the learning potential of creating and entering whole-class fictions. Dorothy Heathcote was a pioneer of this approach. The drama class worked co-operatively together with their teacher and committed themselves seriously as participants to an ongoing fiction. In the drama lesson they could pretend together to be a different people living in a different place and at a different point in time. Within the fiction infinitely possible plots could unfold, which the children owned with the teacher. Working in this way was (and still is) stimulating, motivating, enjoyable and compelling. It can also be thought provoking and deeply meaningful, linking memorable learning with emotion.

Drama soon became a vehicle for teaching creatively across the curriculum. For example, in history, drama could be used to help children to empathize through role with characters from the past and gain understanding of different viewpoints and historical events, bringing them alive and actively exploring them 'as if' they were there at the time. Often drama in education work was thematically based. A class might set off together on an enterprise as experts (anthropologists, botanists, geologists, archaeologists and so forth) on an imaginary voyage to an unexplored island and, through an ongoing drama, be keeping a ship's log (English), charting the voyage (maths), mapping the island (geography). All the while they would be solving imaginary problems together, maybe creating an imaginary settlement, meeting imaginary dangers together, making sense of imaginary relics, thinking and problem solving together, creating a story-drama. The teaching and learning flowed on the sea of children's ideas, with the teacher at the learning helm.

This 'whole-class' drama declined with the introduction of the statutory national curriculum, which led to more subject-specific teaching and a requirement to cover specific content at particular ages. Teaching soon became content centred rather than child centred. It became more difficult to organize learning to flow across curriculum subjects as detailed planning became a main concern and high stakes assessments and inspections checked curriculum coverage. National strategies weighted teachers attentions and timetables towards literacy and numeracy. However, some teachers successfully carried on using drama in education within their teaching of the newly prescribed curriculum and national strategies but nonetheless drama, and in particular whole-class drama, declined and became associated with the teaching of the 1960s and early 70s, which was being eroded and eradicated.

However, drama in education did not disappear. Some teachers felt it to be even more necessary as a way of bringing the new curriculum alive for children. After a while drama started to emerge or find synchronicity with new educational activities and movements such as Philosophy for Children (P4C) and curriculum areas such as PSHE. Soon drama in education was spawning new roots and names. 'Process drama', 'enquiry drama', 'issue-based drama' and 'context drama' started to emerge in conjunction with the burgeoning interest in thinking skills. Drama strategies have increasingly leaked into educational practice outside the context of drama lessons through teachers becoming aware of and using certain drama strategies as methodology – such as Mantle of the Expert, Hot-seating and Freeze-frame (see Part Two).

As thinking about thinking (metacognition) and the teaching of thinking has come to the fore in recent years, drama practitioners have begun to recognize that the stimulation, development and communication of thinking has always been at the heart of the drama process. Recently, enhanced understanding of the teaching of thinking skills by drama practitioners has sharpened process-based drama practice. Conversely, teachers engaged in the teaching of thinking skills are becoming increasingly aware of drama as a child-friendly and 'brain-friendly' medium with an established framework and methodology that supports the teaching of thinking.

Several years ago I attended a conference, at which a well-established and respected drama practitioner was talking about teaching and learning to an audience who were there to focus on the teaching of thinking. I realized that the methodology he was describing and exemplifying was drama in education and yet strangely, he did not once use the word 'drama'. At the end of his talk I said how pleased I was that he was promoting drama as a teaching and learning medium. He said, 'I advise you not to call what we do "drama"; call it "accelerated learning" if you want people to listen. As soon as you call it "drama" they will shut off.' I bristled in defence of drama. 'But it is drama that you are doing,' I protested. He agreed with me and said, almost conspiratorially, that it was also close to what was now being called 'accelerated learning', which was actively encouraged. He considered promoting the practice of drama in education more important than naming it. I appreciate now the many congruent aspects between accelerated learning and drama (see Chapter 1).

Around the same time I attended several courses about the brain and learning, including days on accelerated learning. I started to gain new knowledge and understanding about educationally relevant neuroscientific research, the theory of multiple intelligences, preferred learning styles, gender and the brain and so on. Again, what I was learning was powerfully resonating in relation to drama in education. I knew that drama was the most motivational of all subjects (Harland et al., 2000) but I was becoming increasingly aware why this might be so. It became clear that drama in education fitted with what was being referred to as 'brain-friendly' learning, like a glove. Drama is multisensory, visual, auditory, kinesthetic, tactile, multi-intelligent, emotionally linked learning. Drama relies on co-operation and through it we learn about ourselves as human beings and about others and the world we inhabit together. Drama is humanistic and concerned with the personal, social, moral, spiritual and cultural development of people.

This book is most certainly not about returning to the 1960s and 70s, within which much good and bad drama thrived. It is about helping drama to be understood in relation to our recent understandings about learning, thinking and the brain. It is about building theoretical and practice-based bridges between complementary educational worlds and movements. It is also about understanding where drama fits into and supports the existing curriculum and that of the future. And most importantly, it is about trying to support learning-focused, process-based, child-centred practice for the benefit of children first, and then teachers.

This book aims both to help drama practitioners understand more about the brain, thinking and learning, and to help those who are interested in the brain, thinking and learning understand more about drama as a learning model and methodology. I am a drama specialist with a particular interest in learning and the brain. I am not a neuroscientist. If it transpires that there are any errors in this book I apologize in advance.

This book is timely. It is published at a time when teachers are being officially told that they should be teaching for creativity (QCA, 2003a) at a time when they are being asked to focus more specifically on teaching and developing speaking and listening and, within that, drama (QCA, 2003b and c), and at a time when Arts Council England have republished a second edition of *Drama in Schools*. It is also published at a time when schools are being encouraged to take back the freedom to organize the planning and teaching of the national curriculum and the national strategies in their own way, including teaching across subjects and in ways that are active and learning-centred rather than teaching-centred (DfES, 2003).

# How to use this book

## ■ PART ONE

This section explains what is meant by drama in education and how and why drama and dramatic play enable learning. It considers dramatic play and drama in the light of what neuroscientists have discovered in recent years about the way the brain functions most effectively and how it is wired for learning, particularly through play (including role play) and talk. It explains the important role of adults in helping sustain and develop children's natural learning skills and suggests how teachers might do this. Part One presents drama as a holistic, multisensory, multi-intelligent, cognitive and affective, shared learning experience that can be made accessible to the majority of children. Links are made between drama and current research on dialogic talk. Connections are also made between drama methodology and several recently emerged child-centred educational movements which focus on developing children's thinking for learning as well as their emotional well-being.

## ■ PART TWO

This section names and explains some of the main tools in the drama teacher's toolbox. Drama for learning has a well established methodology and strategies which can be of benefit to any teacher as a means of developing children holistically as thinkers and creators. Part Two lays out clearly some of these strategies and conventions. It explains what they are, what they do and how to go about selecting appropriate drama strategies. It also suggests how strategies might be best mixed, matched and developed in order to make thinking and learning multi-intelligently more accessible.

## ■ PART THREE

Part Three offers a series of drama units. These exemplify the ways in which drama strategies and forms can be brought together to produce a coherent and enjoyable unit of drama work that can stimulate teaching and learning across the curriculum at various key stages. The units of work are presented in columns that make clear which drama strategy is being used and why, as well as giving helpful instructions to the teacher as to how to set up and carry through the various activities. The drama units give evidence to the claims made in Part One, that drama is an accessible medium for all teachers.

## ■ PART FOUR

Photocopiable sheets are provided that offer optional additional support to clarify and extend thinking for learning. The sheets are generic and adaptable for a range of purposes both within the lessons, after the lessons or for teachers to use in ways unrelated to drama. The resource sheets take some of the key drama strategies explained in Part Two and link them to simple, visual frameworks, which can then support the organizing and recording of the emerging and evolving thoughts shared within the drama.

# PART ONE

# **D**rama in **E**ducation

## ■ In this chapter we consider:

■ the spectrum of teachers' and children's perceptions and understandings as to what is 'drama in education' or 'drama in schools';

■ influences that have led to a shift in drama teachers' attitudes and practice in relation to the national curriculum and the re-emerging emphasis on a more humanistic and creative, learner-focused curriculum;

■ the shifting impact on practice of the dichotomy between drama as 'process' and drama as 'product';

■ underpinning links in theory and practice between drama, circle time and Philosophy for Children.

*'In everyday life, "if" is an evasion; in drama "if" is the truth.'*
*Peter Brook* ■

## ■ What do children and students think drama is?

If you ask children and students what they think drama is, their replies will of course depend on their past experiences and present understanding but they usually mention 'putting on plays' and 'acting'. Young children have usually had some involvement with a Christmas play, even if only as audience or spear carrier or as the shepherd in the nativity with the tea towel on their head, and to most children drama will be synonymous with performance – with a product, rather than a process. That is because, for many children, the school production has been their main, or only, school experience that has been labelled 'drama' and taking part in or even seeing a performance is usually memorable. It may never have occurred to children that there is something else they have been naturally involved in since around the age of two years, and that is making up their own dramas, initially alone and later with playmates.

Try asking children of any age (or even adults) these three questions:

■ Do you ever pretend to be someone else, even though you know that you are not really?

■ Do you ever pretend that you are somewhere else, when you know that you are not really?

■ Do you ever pretend that something is happening, when it isn't really?

**PART ONE**

Most children will answer that they do at least some of the above and I tell them that this is one of the reasons that I know they will be so good at drama – they are doing it already and have been practising their drama skills for years! They have been engaging with imagined settings and developing plots through role play and often doing so in groups! Young children readily agree that they play pretend games together, create imagined worlds and live out pretend scenarios within them. They have been stimulated and motivated to spend considerable amounts of time in this sort of activity for years, sometimes with an adult involved but more often, not. While doing this for reasons that will be explored later in this book, they have also unwittingly been practising and developing the skills that are central to drama and theatre. Carrying out this type of dramatic play as a whole class with the teacher accepted as a co-participant and guide is the basis of drama in education – or in other words, drama for learning in schools.

If you ask 'What is drama?' to a child or student who has benefited in schools from drama for learning lessons, then the replies will inevitably indicate a broader definition and deeper understanding of drama (Harland et al., 2000).

*'It makes you sort of look at the world from a different perspective than if you hadn't done drama...[We] have been doing something on the last woman hanged – you can see the side that she should have been hanged and that she shouldn't – you get behind just the everyday good and bad.'*

*Year 10 pupil* ■

*'I would say that I think that one of the advantages [of drama] is that it gives me a bit more experience about what the wide world, the outside world, is like and so essentially, hopefully makes it a bit easier to fit in and understand how it works and the way things happen in it.'*

*Year 10 pupil* ■

## ■ What do teachers think drama is?

Teachers also vary greatly in their understanding of what drama in schools involves or could involve. Again it will depend on their previous experience of drama in schools and what training they have received. Many teachers link drama with predominantly script and performance ('theatre') but many are also aware that drama in schools can be much more than this, and that drama has a methodology that can be used for teaching and learning.

Many teachers will have tried out a bit of hot-seating and maybe some improvisation without necessarily having had any drama training. Others (usually for personal rather than professional reasons) will have avoided anything connected with drama. And there will be some teachers for whom drama as a methodology is a central feature of their teaching. Working in role with children attracts, interests and excites some teachers and fills others with trepidation and insecurity.

The more teachers learn about drama for learning the more they realize that drama is not just the Christmas play and the occasional bit of hot-seating, but a compelling teaching and learning medium that needs to be available to all teachers. Ask a drama specialist what drama is and a much broader definition of drama and its purposes will usually be forthcoming (NFER, 2003).

> 'I see drama as a means of people engaging with the world around them... and in that way hopefully develop them to analyse and communicate interactively with what is around them, and to question and to sometimes enjoy praise. To do that you have to give the tools of drama, because the power in the drama comes when the people in the drama actually feel it as well as think it and then they say, "Oh gosh, yes"...'
>
> Head of Drama in a secondary school ■

> 'It (drama) is something that is a life inside their head: it's an imaginative life, a creative life...'
>
> A drama teacher ■

## ■ Drama – process or product?

Over the last 30–40 years, those teachers that are drama practitioners have had an ongoing and fairly fruitless debate about drama in schools, and 'theatre'. During that time drama in education – or drama for learning – has changed both qualitatively and quantitatively. In the 1960s and early 70s drama was child centred and process centred rather than art form and product centred. There was a debate that was almost a rift between drama-in-education practitioners (drama for learning) and teachers of theatre. Process based drama-in-education practitioners were giving or sharing ownership of evolving dramas with the children. They utilized the children's ideas to create a shared fiction together and through drama methodology supported them to learn about themselves as people, as well as to actively learn across the curriculum. Attention was focused on the level of the children's feeling engagement with the 'as if' experience. Little attention was paid to the theatrical elements and form in terms of quality during drama-in-education experiences. It was primarily about lived, imagined experience for the participants. Performance was almost a dirty word and audience was an irrelevance. The word 'pretend' was frowned on as this might lessen engagement with role. Children were told that they *were* the characters they were playing. Most drama-in-education practitioners were not overly concerned about any theatrical elements of the work, since attention to them would have interrupted the process. Many of the practitioners in primary schools in particular were teachers who were not necessarily drama or theatre trained and yet they were highly successful at using drama as pedagogy as they understood dramatic play and children. When drama as methodology was linked to developing thinking and learning it became of relevance to all teachers. When it was defined as teaching theatre, it tended to stay in the hands of specialist drama teachers and became confined mostly to the drama studio or hall.

Theatre practitioners who were performance focused were not happy that drama in education (drama for learning) was being referred to as 'drama'. They focused on developing theatrical skills for performance to an audience. Sometimes the performance was devised with children, and drama strategies might support this process. However, they disassociated themselves with drama-in-education practitioners who focused on drama for learning rather than learning for drama; on the development of children rather than the development of drama itself. Drama in education focused on process, and theatre practitioners focused on product, and in the 1960s, 70s and early 80s the different camps did not explore the immensely fertile middle ground.

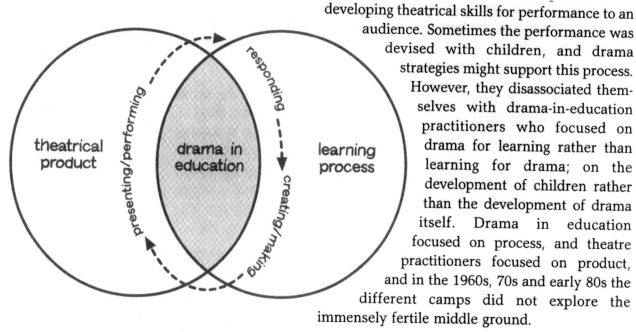

## ■ What is drama in education now?

Drama in education practice has evolved since the early 1990s and now makes greater and more polished use of theatrical conventions and forms, while maintaining working in role. Many drama-in-education practitioners now pay more conscious attention to the theatrical elements of their work and realize that the same drama strategies and devices that can be used to support children's learning, role play and meaning making may also be used to devise theatrical performance and vice versa. Increased attention to the theatrical elements within drama for learning lessons can strengthen pupils' engagement with their role and help focus and tag the learning as well as developing the child's understanding of how theatre works. Drama lessons can bridge the worlds of dramatic play, drama for learning and theatre, in order to access, make and communicate meanings.

Drama in education has evolved into drama for learning, an active, interactive and reflective, shared, creative learning experience based on working in role. What is created through the drama for learning process sometimes ends up being rehearsed and presented later for interpretation and response by an audience, but this may not be an intended outcome of the process. Performances or presentation of work by pupils is more likely to be to and for each other within the drama lessons themselves as a means of sharing understandings and moving the class drama on. Within drama-in-education lessons the children are invited to shift back and forth, both as participants and as each other's audience, throughout the evolving drama. They are makers, performers and responders within the same drama at different times, while the teacher sculpts the learning.

*Drama and theatre have their roots in early dramatic play*

The reasons for these significant shifts in drama-in-education practice may be partly linked to a realization that drama-in-education practitioners and theatre practitioners have much common ground and much to offer each other's practice and yet research carried out by the National Foundation for Educational Research (2003) into arts education in secondary schools indicates that the process–product paradigm remains relatively more pronounced for drama than for any other art form, with teachers often still falling at either end of the process–product spectrum.

## ■ What and where is drama in the national curriculum?

The place of drama within the national curriculum for primary schools particularly, has strongly influenced the way that practice has developed. When the national curriculum came out in the early 1990s, teachers were expecting drama to be given separate subject status as an art form in its own right alongside music and art. It didn't happen. Drama was not initially made statutory. Many theatre practitioners were quick to blame process-based drama practitioners for blurring the identity of drama as a subject but before long both drama and theatre practitioners were struggling together to maintain the very existence of drama in schools in any shape or form. Drama was soon disappearing off timetables as the first content-laden, assessment-focused, statutory national curriculum was squeezed into the timetable.

Some drama practitioners were pleased that drama was not a national curriculum subject because it meant that it had escaped prescription. Without a statutory curriculum for drama, teachers could cover what they wanted in drama if only they could find some time in which to do it. Unfortunately, most primary teachers did not find that time, and drama as a subject rapidly declined.

When the national curriculum was reviewed, drama was made part of the statutory English curriculum as part of speaking and listening. Some drama teachers were pleased that it was now at least part of a statutory core subject. There was a short lived and mistaken assumption that drama would now have to be taught. However, the English curriculum soon effectively became the National Literacy Strategy which was for several years only defined as reading and writing. With drama as part of speaking and listening, it continued to be sidelined or ignored completely by most primary schools, despite being supposedly a compulsory part of English. It is only recently that attention has been paid again to the development of speaking and listening and, within that, drama.

Some drama-in-education practitioners carried on throughout, working with drama methodology to teach the national curriculum and particularly as a medium for the teaching of literacy and even managing very occasionally to teach discrete drama. Others felt that drama methodology was no longer permissible as teachers were now being told for the first time how and what they should teach in English and inspections were ensuring that they did. Drama in education declined further (as training time or courses were now less available).

Where drama in education continued to be practised as a pedagogy, it adapted and evolved in ways that fitted in with the emerging national curriculum requirements and educational demands of the day. Learning intentions were being made more specific and drama lessons were less able to flow with the children's ideas and had to fit more strictly within lesson times. Lessons became shorter, had greater pace and were linked to national curriculum subject matter. It became increasingly unusual to see sustained, ongoing, cross-curricular, drama-based projects that were developing and sustaining the children's own ideas and were not constrained by lesson timetables. Covering the content of the curriculum was seen as problematic if drama was allowed to wander too far off the teacher's learning objectives through following children's ideas elsewhere.

Drama strategies continued to be used as teaching and learning strategies in various subjects, particularly literacy, but the development of drama in its own right was lost in most schools and drama as a subject started to disappear from primary school timetables altogether. Recent research (NACCCE, 1999) reports that drama now exists on the timetable as a subject in less than 50 per cent of primary schools and is the least taught arts subject in its own right, but it also shows that drama as a medium for teaching other subjects is once again on the increase.

Recent (2003) but very different publications from the QCA and Arts Council England (see Introduction) are likely to result now in more drama happening in schools.

## ■ Where is drama in the broader, holistic and humanistic curriculum?

The new national curriculum and its high stakes assessments in two subjects soon left many teachers feeling uncomfortable about the time available for developing the whole child. Teachers had less time to simply talk with pupils and relate to them on a personal level. Schools were imparting content and there was a felt need to develop children as thinkers. New subjects and areas started to emerge that to some extent addressed this and gave time to listening and developing children as rounded human beings – for example, Personal, Social and Health Education (PSHE) and Citizenship were introduced. Circle time and Philosophy for Children (P4C) became popular, as did other ways of teaching thinking.

At the same time, inspectors were being asked to report more broadly on children's social, moral, spiritual and cultural development and schools began widening their taught curriculum and seeking ways of providing a greater human and emotional focus. Drama as a methodology is frequently used within these 'new' humanistic curriculum areas that have emerged and in some instances has developed from the same roots.

## ■ Drama and circle time

Circle time has emerged successfully as a humanistic, child-centred, whole-class activity alongside the statutory national curriculum. Circle time models were originally used in industry and have now been adapted and developed in many primary schools as part of personal and social education. The circle is a shape much used within drama lessons, and circle time, like drama, is based on a supportive and safe group-work with commonly understood and agreed rituals, active listening and group ground rules.

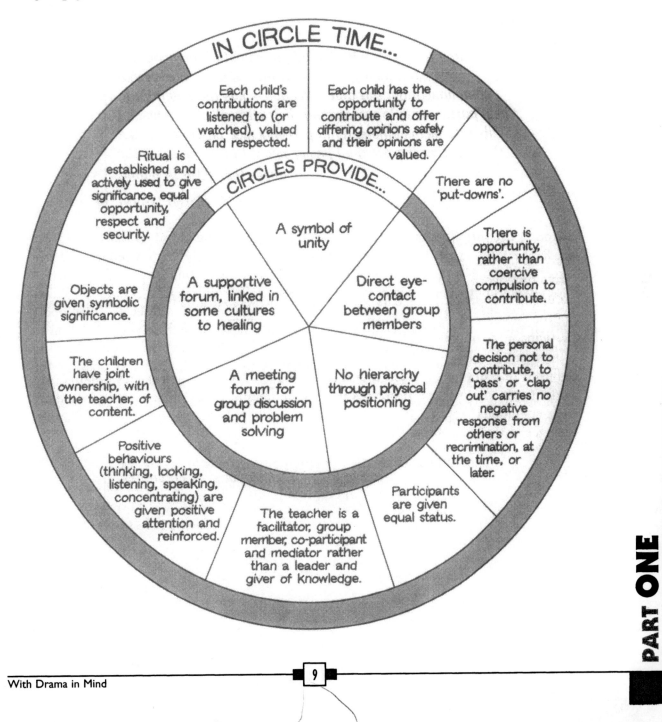

IN CIRCLE TIME...

Each child's contributions are listened to (or watched), valued and respected.

Each child has the opportunity to contribute and offer differing opinions safely and their opinions are valued.

Ritual is established and actively used to give significance, equal opportunity, respect and security.

CIRCLES PROVIDE...

There are no 'put-downs'.

There is opportunity, rather than coercive compulsion to contribute.

A symbol of unity

A supportive forum, linked in some cultures to healing

Direct eye-contact between group members

Objects are given symbolic significance.

The children have joint ownership, with the teacher, of content.

A meeting forum for group discussion and problem solving

No hierarchy through physical positioning

The personal decision not to contribute, to 'pass' or 'clap out' carries no negative response from others or recrimination, at the time, or later.

Positive behaviours (thinking, looking, listening, speaking, concentrating) are given positive attention and reinforced.

The teacher is a facilitator, group member, co-participant and mediator rather than a leader and giver of knowledge.

Participants are given equal status.

Circle time, like drama, can be used to explore issues and feelings of personal and current relevance to the children but in drama this takes place within a shared fiction and the children are operating in role. In order for this to work in either circle time or drama, a set of ground rules need to be agreed with pupils and the clear contract for circle time is almost identical to that of a drama contract (see page 84.)

Drama, unlike circle time, requires the children to share in the creation of a fiction, so it needs an additional contract rule:

■ **The children agree to try to support the make-believe and not do anything deliberately that will break others' belief in the shared fiction.**

Children understand the importance of this drama contract rule because it links to their previous agreements with playmates about what is required to sustain dramatic play and pretend worlds together.

The similarities between drama and circle time are not surprising as circle time has been developed and made popular in schools by Jenny Mosely, who is a trained drama teacher.

> *'The drama process – with its unique potential to encourage spontaneity, creativity, imagination, non-verbal communication, fun and reflection – has the potential to help participants to understand their current situations and liberate them sufficiently to perceive new possibilities and then develop the personal power needed to bring about the changes they wish to make.'*
>
> Jenny Mosely (1996) ■

Through the introduction of circle time, many schools have put in place a perfect seedbed for the growth of whole-class drama. Jenny Mosely acknowledges that her circle time work is based on the work of Dr Jacob L. Moreno, the founder of active group-work approaches such as psychodrama and socio-drama (see Chapter 3). These approaches use a range of established drama forms and strategies to support participants to understand, explore and develop a sense of themselves in relation to others and to acknowledge and accept responsibility for their own actions. Moreno believed that drama provided a unique medium through which it was possible for participants to move real problems into the 'here and now' and access and develop their spontaneity and creativity in ways that could then lead them to make positive changes in their real lives.

> *'Spontaneity as a creative function endeavours to create the self and an adequate environment for it.'*
>
> J.L. Moreno (1946) ■

A key difference between drama and circle time is that in drama the child is being asked to work in a distanced way through adopting a role. In circle time the children's personal attitudes and opinions are publicly presented and remain personally attached to the child. Drama, like dramatic play, provides a powerful and unique, playful yet serious, social forum which is distanced safely from the child through role play. Children in role can try out a range of attitudes, viewpoints and opinions on the drama group, that are then attributable to the fictitious characters presented, rather than staying attached to the children themselves. In role they can actively experience and feel first hand the group's response to their thoughts and actions of the fictitious character they represent. The characters revealed through role play in drama do not come from thin air but from the children's real and imagined previous experiences; from their real and imagined selves. In drama the children perceive themselves as members of the drama group, which is essentially a social group.

## ■ Drama and Philosophy for Children (P4C)

P4C is based on the work of Matthew Lipman (1991) and originated in the USA. It has become increasingly popular in UK schools through the work of Karin Murris, who has brought back and developed Lipman's work to include the use of picture books to support philosophical enquiry with children. P4C is based on the belief that all children are natural philosophers. The supporting methodology gives opportunity for children to be supported to think philosophically through class discussion about ethical and moral issues that are of relevance and importance to them.

Like P4C, drama also offers a whole-class framework and supportive structure and methodology through which classes can explore moral and philosophical issues and can enquire and discuss together. Drama provides a forum for philosophical enquiry in role.

In P4C the group, which is usually the whole class, becomes a 'community of enquiry'. Its aim is to enable children together to explore alternatives, consider evidence objectively and logically and voice reasons for their personal beliefs and, at the same time, to develop 'reasonableness' and independence. Children are supported by the teacher to follow disciplined lines of enquiry and ask and answer focused questions in order to elicit individual and group opinions and beliefs about various issues. Their answers have to be actively listened to by the group. Children are required to ask their own philosophical questions and to think critically about their own opinions and those of others in the group. Like drama, it requires children to follow a whole-group contract or set of conventions and will only work well with the class fully engaged. It relies on, encourages and develops dialogue, co-operation and mutual tolerance and respect.

### Community of Enquiry conventions include:

- The teacher is a guide and facilitator, not a leader.*

- Everyone listens to the speaker with respect.*

- Everyone responds to the speaker either verbally or internally.*

- Responses are to the person who is speaking and not to or through the teacher.*

- Responses to the speaker are prefaced with 'I agree' or 'I disagree'.

- Reasons are always given to support agreement or disagreement with the speaker.

- Everyone's shared thoughts are valued and considered as possible truths, rather than as right or wrong.*

- People may 'pass' if they are thinking but not ready or willing to speak.*

- People take turns.*

*\* Congruent with drama conventions*

### In P4C the teacher's role is to:

- select a suitable stimulus that will promote enquiry;*

- establish the conventions of the community of enquiry;*

- steer discussion through comments and questions that are intended to encourage clarification – for example, 'I think that you are saying that...';*

- encourage group engagement with the speaker – for example, 'Can anyone else say what they think... (name of child)... is saying to us?';

- Draw out implication through comments and questions – for example, 'So are you suggesting that this would lead to...' and 'If what you say is true, does that mean that...?'.

*\* Congruent with the drama teacher's role*

### In P4C the children's role is to:

- actively listen to each other with respect; *

- build on and develop each others' ideas; *

- challenge each other to give reasons for views and opinions; *

- identify assumptions;

- follow lines of enquiry; *

- conform to logical thought patterns. *

*\* Congruent with children as drama participants*

The drama group and the P4C group both operate collectively and supportively with similar operational contracts that are in place from the outset. The Drama Contract (see page 84), is very similar to the Community Conventions of P4C shown opposite.

The drama teacher, like the P4C teacher, selects a suitable initial stimulus, which will promote and support the class to deal with philosophical issues, human conflicts and dilemmas through whole-group enquiry. Drama, like P4C, uses ritualistic structures to mark the value and significance of contributions, facilitate active listening and to clarify. The drama teacher uses established yet flexible strategies, conventions and forms, as well as discussion, to keep the drama group fully and actively engaged with each others' contributions and ideas as well as to focus the enquiry and support creative and critical thinking.

Drama offers a unique type of Community of Enquiry within which participants are enquiring from within a communal and evolving fiction.

Stories, poems or picture books are frequently used as the initial stimulus in both P4C and drama. Story is a medium that children hook into. Many stories contain significant moral or ethical issues and dilemmas for the characters within them. Through the introduction of well-chosen stimuli the teacher encourages children to be curious, to ponder, to wonder, to think and to formulate worthwhile philosophical questions.

In P4C the children offer their own opinions. In drama the child presents their character's opinions and viewpoints and only the child needs to know whether it is also their own personal viewpoint. They can try out philosophical reasoning through role play before deciding whether to own it. Drama also enables children to create and live out their own story-dramas that may (with the skilled intervention and guidance of the teacher) give rise to or answer moral and ethical issues. Issues arising from the children's own dramas are bound to be of direct relevance and concern to them.

In P4C the philosophical questions are raised and considered formally. In drama, philosophical questions can also be raised and explored formally through the careful selection of strategies.

Within drama, key moral and ethical issues for consideration can be:

- **arrived at** through strategies such as Improvisation;

- **held still** through strategies such as Freeze-frame, Still Image, Tableau;

- **opened up** through strategies such as Thought-tracking, Hot-seating, Conscience Alley, Forum Theatre;

- **developed and extended** through strategies such as Storytelling, Improvisation, Small Group Playmaking;

- **reflected on** through strategies such as Flashback or Storytelling.

(See Part Two for further information on using these strategies.)

PART ONE

Any philosophical question can be explored and considered through drama. Linked to the drama units in this book, philosophical questions might include:

- Is it acceptable to imprison someone who is a public nuisance without having a trial? (*Drama Unit 1*)

- Is it justifiable to hit a bully... or is fighting always wrong? (*Drama Unit 3*)

Within drama lessons the notion of a Community of Enquiry can operate at two levels. The class itself is a real community but the drama may give opportunity for the children to operate simultaneously as pretend members of fictitious communities – for example, a Native American community (Drama Unit 5) or a storytelling community (Drama Unit 1) or even a community which is entirely of their own creation (Drama Unit 4).

## ■ Creativity through drama across the curriculum

Concurrently, and since 1999 specifically, there has been a growing acceptance that creative thinking now needs focused development within education.

When the national curriculum was reviewed and amended in 2000 one of the reports intended to influence that review was by the National Advisory Committee on Creative and Cultural Education (NACCCE). This government-commissioned report, *All our Futures: Creativity, Culture and Education* (1999), stresses the need to develop creative thinking and behaviour and to find and promote teaching for and with creativity in education. The value of teaching in and through drama was recognized within part of the report.

> *'OFSTED data on pupil response indicates drama to be at the very top in motivating learning. Such data underlines the value of a broad and balanced curriculum that incorporates opportunities for pupils to learn within and through arts subjects, and within and through focused creative and cultural contexts.'*
>
> *DfEE (1999)* ■

Recent Ofsted research into creativity, *Expecting the Unexpected* (2003), is littered with good examples of teaching for creativity through drama in both primary and secondary schools.

There was a growing concern among teachers that, with a prescriptive and repetitive curriculum that was literacy and numeracy led and which promoted specific ways of teaching, children's creativity might not be having sufficient time or opportunity to develop. Developing creativity is recognized as important not only within the development of rounded and fulfilled people, but also in relation to the prosperity of creative industries. Since *All our Futures*, the DfES has been keen to provide teachers with examples of teaching that promotes pupils' creativity while still teaching the national curriculum. Following on from recommendations within the NACCCE report, the Qualifications and Curriculum Authority started a three-year project (2000–2003) to find and promote teaching for and with creativity across the curriculum at Key Stages 1, 2 and 3. Their findings were published in the report

*Creativity: Find it, promote it!* (2003a). Selected lessons were gathered, throughout a year initially, that were considered to be high-quality case studies of teaching for creativity. These were sifted, collated and later disseminated by the QCA via their website (www.ncaction.org.uk). Drama is evident in many of these lessons as a creative teaching and learning medium across a range of subjects, not just within English lessons.

More recently *Excellence and Enjoyment – A Strategy for Primary Schools* (DfES 2003) has summarized some of the findings from this project.

> *'Teachers found that when they actively planned for and responded to pupils' creative ideas and actions, pupils became more curious to discover things for themselves, were open to new ideas and keen to explore those ideas with the teachers and others. Promoting creativity is a powerful way of engaging pupils with their learning.'*
>
> *DfES (2003)* ■

*Excellence and Enjoyment* also has defined good teaching and learning (page 29) and drama as a methodology is congruent with its principles:

■ Ensure every child succeeds.

■ Build on what learners already know.

■ Make learning vivid and real.

■ Make learning an enjoyable and challenging experience.

■ Enrich the learning experience.

■ Promote assessment for learning.

It refers to:

■ Working inclusively.

■ Developing enquiry and creativity.

■ Group problem solving.

■ Matching teaching and strategies to a range of learning styles.

■ Building learning skills across the curriculum.

■ Making children partners in learning.

Drama as a teaching and learning medium has much to contribute to each and all of the above. It is an inclusive learning medium that encourages and develops enquiry and creativity, and group problem solving is central to it. It is accessible to a range of learners and offers strategies that match a range of learning styles. Drama can be used to enhance and develop learning across any curriculum area and the children and the teachers are partners in the learning. It is motivating and enjoyable and involves challenging and supporting children to succeed individually and together. Children bring to it what they know as a starting point and, through action and imagination, make the learning vivid and real.

**PART ONE**

# Drama and the Brain

## ■ In this chapter we consider:

- how 'facts' about the brain may have advanced our understanding of drama for learning;

- the basic structure and functions of the brain and the significance of imitation, mimicry and imagination in learning;

- how dramatic play and drama is synonymous with the way that the young child's brain is stimulated and wired to learn and how it integrates the cognitive and affective;

- the ways in which both teachers and pupils may respond to drama if they perceive it to be potentially stressful;

- the teacher's role as a mediator of imagined experiences, supporting the learning process;

- some links between drama lessons and accelerated learning.

*'The creative artist is an observer whose brain works in new ways making it possible to convey information about matters that were not a subject for communication before.'*

J.Z.Young (1987) ■

*'Brain research in time will have a profound effect on how we teach in schools.'*

Rita Carter (1999) ■

*'Knowing why, leads to other discoveries, new applications and further refinement... We are beginning to understand why some teachers are effective.'*

J.T. Bruer (1993) ■

*'Insights into the human brain will have a profound impact, not just on us as scientists but also on the humanities, and indeed they may even help us bridge what C.P. Snow called the two cultures – science on the one hand and arts, philosophy and humanities on the other.'*

Professor Ramachandran (BBC Reith Lectures, 2003) ■

In recent years there has been a considerable growth in our understanding about how the brain functions and how we learn. Many models of 'brain-friendly' or 'brain-based' learning have emerged based on this new information. Drama-in-education practitioners have become increasingly aware why drama for learning has been working and have been able to refine practice to maximize its potential. Drama practitioners have been using a methodology for learning that they have known works and yet only in recent years have begun to discover more about why it works. The more we understand about the brain and the more we discover about the ways in which children learn most effectively, the more light this throws on how to better develop drama as a learning process. It also helps us understand the natural advantages that drama, rooted in dramatic play, has as a well established 'brain friendly' learning medium.

## ■ Ten things you need to know about the brain

1. 90 per cent of our knowledge about the brain has been learned in the last 15 years.

2. Vast areas of the brain's functions are still not understood – especially about nature/nurture, genetic inheritance, sex differences and so on.

3. The brain is about the size of a large fist and weighs about three pounds. It is a hugely complex multi-processor capable of processing, for example, 36,000 visual clues per hour.

4. We do not run or control the brain – it functions through a complex of chemical and electrical stimuli. Remember the last time you tried to remember something, failed and gave up – only for the information to pop into your head later without any effort on your part? The brain is busy and, if the environment is appropriate, it will continue to work on the problem.

5. We use all parts of the brain often but only five per cent of its capacity.

6. The electrical rhythms of the brain change every 90 minutes or so.

7. The brain works by growing or connecting neural networks. We can grow it in the sense of developing its capacity to make connections, principally by providing appropriate stimuli in the right environment.

8. The entire triune brain system works as one – it is chemically and electronically programmed to create the illusion of unity. Different parts of the brain, however, focus on different functions – for example, the neocortex deals with novelty, patterns and meaning, while the limbic system deals with pleasure and feeling.

9. The brain provides a mechanism for survival and is a natural learner – the more connections it can make, the more able it is to react to life-threatening situations.

10. 90 per cent of learning is non-conscious – it happens with no conscious effort on our part. Next time you are tempted to disagree when someone states the critical importance of non-verbal communication in teaching behaviour, remember this.

**John Norman (1999)**

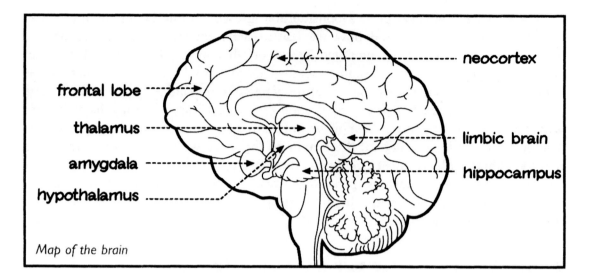

*Map of the brain*

## ■ How our brains respond to stimulus

It is helpful when considering pupils' responses to the drama experience, to consider how the human brain responds to sensory input – and, particularly, threat. Based on the work of Antonio Damasio and Joseph LeDoux, Robert Sylwester (1995) writes about two pathways in the brain. He calls one the reflective response system and the other the reflexive response system. In *The Brain's Behind It* (2004), Alistair Smith refers to the first system as the 'high road' and the second as the 'low road'.

The *reflective* response system involves circuitry between the thalamus, hippocampus and neocortex to provide time for sensory input to be analysed and synthesized in the following way: First, sensory input comes via the thalamus, which links the brain and the external world. Next, the link to the hippocampus enables the brain to check if there are already stored memories associated with the new input, thus enabling the neocortex to recognize basic patterns. Then, moving from the rear of the cortex to the frontal lobes, the sensory data is analysed, synthesized and interpreted, and a response is finally planned and executed.

As the name implies, the reflective response system is slow in order to allow for reflection. It is involved in activities such as reading and discourse. While it is helpful in a library it is not always helpful on the plains of Africa where the current structure of our brain evolved. There, the time taken to reflect could make the difference between survival or death. Fortunately for our survival there is an alternative system:

The *reflexive* response system is primarily responsible for our emotional response to sensory data. It involves a direct link between the thalamus and the amygdala and hypothalamus. The amygdala attaches emotional significance to sensory input. Sylwester suggests this reflexive system focuses on three key survival issues:

■ *Do I eat it?* (the fight response)

■ *Do I run away from it?* (the flight response)

■ *Do I mate with it?* (the gene pool response).

To this list we can add a fourth issue:

■ *Do I seek safety in numbers?* (the flocking response).

If the answer to any of these basic questions is 'yes' then the body gets involved via the hypothalamus, which is the link between the brain and the internal world. Blood pressure rises, heart rate increases, adrenalin flows and major muscle groups contract ready for action. This is the essential difference between cognition and emotion – in emotion the body gets involved (our language reflects this when we use phrases such as 'a broken heart', 'it brought a lump to my throat' and 'I was gutted'). Joseph LeDoux calls this system 'the fast and dirty route'; 'fast' because reflection is inappropriate when faced with a threat, and 'dirty' because, in the absence of reflection, it does not discriminate.

While the reflexive response system was necessary in the face of a pride of lions on the plains of Africa, it is not so useful in the drama studio! But children bring this system into the drama lesson just as they bring their now redundant appendix and with it comes the fight, flight or flocking responses.

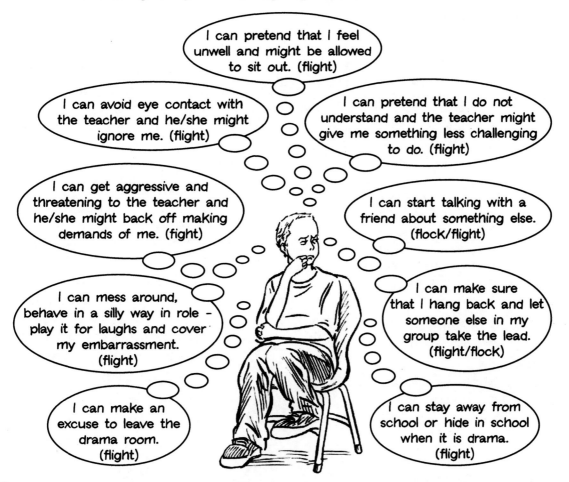

During drama lessons children need to know that they will not be placed under threat by being put in any embarrassing situations in front of their peers and against their will. This is why there are built-in 'safe' and agreed ways of entering and holding back from the drama within drama lessons and ways for pupils to take time out if necessary. A drama contract (see page 83), drawn up by the teacher with the children, combined with the sensitivity of the drama teacher, should ensure that each child is able to manage the level of perceived threat. This will enable the children to stay present and probably participate, without feeling that they have to flee from the drama or resort to damaging or disliking the drama experience. Only when the drama participants feel safe can they relax and focus their attention on the drama.

Some teachers can feel threatened and stressed at the idea of doing drama with children. Recent research (NFER, 2003) suggests that it is the art form least taught in primary schools as a subject on the timetable in its own right. The reasons for this are multi-fold but one is that many teachers believe that they lack the professional or personal confidence to teach it. Many have themselves had bad experiences of drama in the past, either as participants or as teachers, and they feel emotionally vulnerable in drama lessons. A nervous teacher at the start of a drama course recently was heard to say, 'I can't believe I've been brave enough to come on a scary course!' Her written evaluation indicated that she had left reassured and positive about drama as she had been kept safe throughout the practical drama experience. When drama tends to be avoided by teachers it is due to notional barriers that have been created in teachers' minds and which need to be overcome unless children are to continue to be denied drama. Teachers fearful of teaching drama may give avoidance reasons that can also be categorized in relation to primitive 'fight, flight and flock' responses.

Good process-drama teaching involves willingness on the part of the teacher to shift from the most common and familiar styles of teaching and to relinquish a significant degree of lesson ownership and even content to the children. It does not require teachers to let go of their learning objectives or be unsafe. It requires the teacher to become a co-participant and facilitator of learning rather than a giver of knowledge. It asks that the teacher alters the traditional teacher/pupil relationship, often through working as a teacher in role, and that the teacher accepts the often relatively lower status shift, for a while, that Teacher in Role can involve. Drama is seen by many teachers as risk-taking teaching and therefore can raise their stress levels or, put more positively, it can be seen by teachers as exciting, unpredictable teaching, vital and of-the-moment teaching that motivates and engages children, is stimulating to teachers themselves and is learning focused.

Most teachers need to feel safe in their teaching. Prescribed teaching methods have contributed to and supported this. But moving to and just beyond the edges of a teacher's professional comfort zone with the agreement and support of the class is a learning experience for both and can pay dividends in terms of developing a teacher's practice. Besides, if teachers have a basic understanding of how drama and its strategies work, then they have little need to feel drama lessons might be unsafe. If nothing else, the lesson can be halted at any time and reflected on through discussion with pupils.

## ■ Teacher as mediator

The role of the adult in dramatic play, and the drama teacher within drama lessons, is facilitator, mediator and fellow contributor. The child is motivated to be involved as the process is mainly experiential rather than instructional but the drama experience can lose its learning potential unless mediated by a teacher who can offer structure and help focus pupils' thinking and support their meaning making.

The abilities required by drama teachers are:

- to listen well;

- to know when to contribute as a co-participant and when to hold back and wait;

- to support children to recognize, develop and communicate their own ideas;

- to develop a creative climate of generating and sharing ideas while maintaining the self-esteem of all children, whatever their apparent level of active contribution;

- to empathize with participants both in and out of role;

- to establish, respect and maintain the safe distance between the role and the child;

- to work confidently as a fellow participant alongside children, without anxiety about teacher status and class control;

■ to select safe, yet challenging drama strategies and aesthetic forms which are appropriate to focused learning;

■ to offer active and reflective strategies which support increased cognitive and affective understanding;

■ to offer a range of culturally understood, aesthetic forms for representing and communicating their individual and collective ideas to others;

■ to help children to recognize their own abilities as drama creators and performers as well as responders to drama.

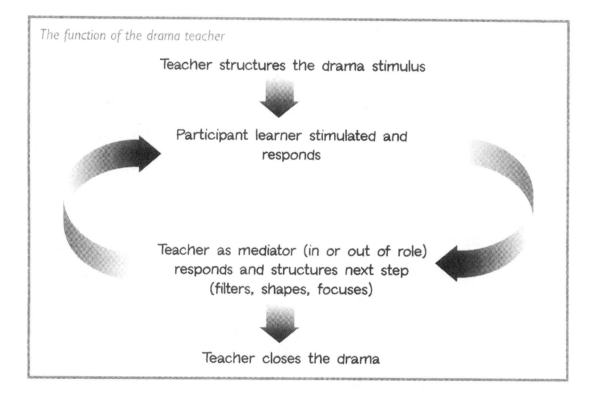

*The function of the drama teacher*

Teacher structures the drama stimulus

Participant learner stimulated and responds

Teacher as mediator (in or out of role) responds and structures next step (filters, shapes, focuses)

Teacher closes the drama

## ■ Instrumental enrichment (IE) or structured cognitive Modifiability

Dr Reuven Feuerstein (1980) has considered and developed the role of the teacher as a mediator in learning. He worked in Israel with Jewish adolescents who had been traumatized and were failing to achieve within conventional education systems. Feuerstein suggested that these pupils were failing because they had not had the benefit of adults as mediators of learning experience, able to support the children to shape and help them make sense and meaning of their experiences. Until they had a mediator the children's responses to experience were lacking structure and comprehension. Feuerstein created a system of instrumental enrichment (IE) that accelerated these pupils' progress markedly – for example, 90 students made up three years' progress on average when taught using Instruments of Enrichment for only one year. Feuerstein's system of IE is now used in some schools, and recently in South Africa particularly, where it is being used with many black children in an attempt to make up for prior educational disadvantage.

Within whole-class drama-in-education lessons the teacher is available throughout as a mediator of the learning, maybe particularly powerfully so when in role alongside the children. The drama teacher is constantly providing structures and focus to the creative and learning experience during the drama process, through the skilled use of timely, well chosen and well presented drama strategies and conventions which could be considered as 'instruments'. The teacher uses strategies as instruments to support and sustain the children's engagement with the learning, providing opportunity for the conscious holding of moments for consideration, supported review and reflection.

## ■ Feeling and emotion

Drama has clear links with emotions. In relation to the way learners' emotions and feelings link with learning and the brain, teachers need an awareness of the following:

1. There is no single view of what emotion is or where exactly in the brain it comes from.

2. Emotions are things that happen to us rather than things we will to occur. We have little direct control over our emotional reactions.

3. The common view of the brain function connected to specific areas of the brain is now being questioned. This view which held that the limbic brain is the centre of all emotion is in dispute.

4. While this view of the limbic brain as the most important processor is still powerfully current, it is also very clear that many brain systems are part of the emotional brain and might be involved in the processing of different kinds of emotion.

5. New research is showing that a small organ in the forebrain called the amygdala (Latin for 'almond'), which is part of the limbic brain, may have connections to parts of the brain that bypass the neocortex – the area most concerned with higher functions of thinking and reasoning. By implication then, emotional arousal has the power to dominate and control thinking (try telling yourself that you should not be depressed, for example!).

6. Most emotional responses are triggered by stimuli that are processed unconsciously; the stronger the stimulus, the more powerful the response.

7. Subjective emotional experience – that is, a specific feeling – results when we become consciously aware that an emotional system in the brain is active from the various indicators available to us.

8. The various indicators include changes in skin temperature and heart rate and somatic and visceral reactions – bodily feedback arising from hormones and peptides moving to the brain. These 'long distance messengers' give us those gut feelings which are very familiar. Some other areas of research are exploring the idea, not that we cry because we feel sad, but that when we cry we feel sad (cause not result) – thus emphasizing the vital importance of physical feedback and arousal.

9. A central part of the system of unconscious emotional response is the connection of short- and long-term memory which allows us to process and identify the feeling – thereby bringing it into the arena of conscious emotional feeling.

John Norman (1999)

PART ONE

Drama links visual images and emotion. Vision and emotional response become linked when a message is sent to the amygdala, the gateway to the limbic system. Looking at a photograph of a loved one for example may result in a strong, spontaneous emotional response. Remembering a strong visual image from a drama can also can re-evoke emotional responses and memories. Theatre and drama (as all visual arts) set out to deliberately evoke and tag significant emotional responses to stimuli, including visual, aural and kinesthetic stimuli. In drama, the imagined experiences are nonetheless felt and integrate cognitive, affective and aesthetic experiences. During whole-class dramas significant dramatic moments can be focused on and tagged for participants through the use of visual image, light and dark, sound (spoken and heard) and silence, movement and stillness.

## ■ Neural pathways and networks

Areas of the brain are connected by cells called neurons. There are billions of neurons and many will never be used. The neurons develop dendrites, which transmit information to other neurons. They also develop axons, which enable information to be received from other neurons. Connections, or neural pathways, between neurons (synapses) are established and become stronger the more they are stimulated and used. If neural pathways or synapses (connections) are not used, after a time the neurons will be 'pruned' and die off. New neurons can continue to be produced in certain brain areas, including those associated with learning and memory (the hippocampus). Neurons communicate with each other through electro-chemical activity which scientists can now observe using brain imaging techniques. Neurons in different areas of the brain can be seen to 'fire up' and interconnect, as the brain links and processes information through the interaction of action, thought and emotion. Neural pathways become networked in relation to different multisensory stimulation and the pathways most frequently stimulated and used over time are enabled to connect more quickly.

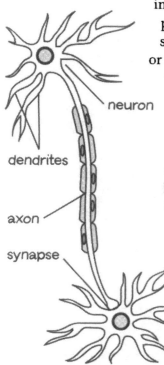

neuron

dendrites

axon

synapse

Many learning experiences are primed to occur during what neurologists refer to as particularly sensitive periods for 'synaptogenesis' (the connecting of neurons and establishment of neural pathways for learning). These sensitive periods for learning are believed to exist mainly within the first five years of a child's life and missing sensitive periods for synaptogenesis can cause problems with learning later. This key sensitive period from age one to five includes the time when dramatic play is most prevalent (from around the age of two). It is no coincidence that this is also the time when children's brains are most sensitive to the learning of language; the activities are inter-related.

Children are making sense of the world around them through acting and re-enacting real and imagined experiences. They are verbalizing in make-believe worlds, generating, rehearsing and practising the language required. They are also experiencing the emotional thrill of role play, of feeling 'as if'. Children's dramatic play stimulates and uses many different parts of the brain, just as drama does, simultaneously exciting visual, auditory, spatial and motor functions.

Play apparently gives us bigger and better brains. Research (Iwanuik et al., 2001) suggests a link between the brain size of different species and the amount that each species plays between birth and maturity. Young children need ample opportunity to learn through the route of play, including make-believe play.

Dramatic play prepares the brain for learning as the child is:

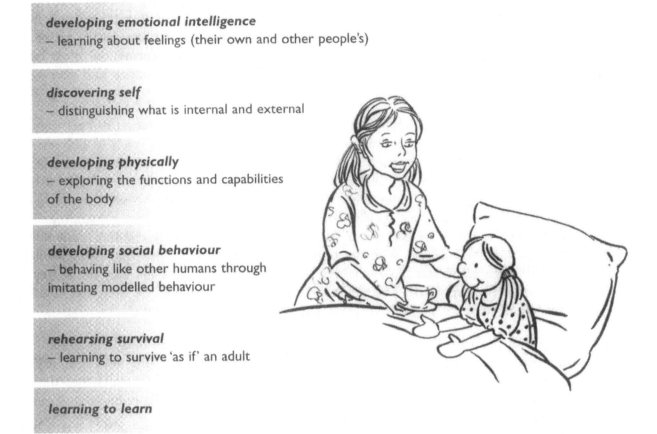

*developing emotional intelligence*
– learning about feelings (their own and other people's)

*discovering self*
– distinguishing what is internal and external

*developing physically*
– exploring the functions and capabilities of the body

*developing social behaviour*
– behaving like other humans through imitating modelled behaviour

*rehearsing survival*
– learning to survive 'as if' an adult

*learning to learn*

Dramatic play stimulates the brain and can sustain the interest of young children over relatively long periods of time, well beyond the times that many educators claim that young children can concentrate. This is because the activity is directly linked to the interests and needs of the child.

## ■ Imitation and mimicry

> *'One of the hallmarks of our species is what we call culture.*
> *And culture depends crucially on the imitation of your*
> *parents and of your teachers, and the imitation of complex*
> *skills may require the participation of motor neurons.'*
>
> *Professor Ramachandram (BBC Reith Lectures, 2003)* ■

PART ONE

Imitation and mimicry, sometimes referred to as 'the first learning style', have links with both dramatic play and drama. Observations have been carried out into what is happening in the brains of monkeys when imitation and mimicry occurs or is suppressed. Giacomo Rizzolati (1990) discovered that some of the same motor command neurons, which he refers to as 'mirror neurons', are fired when a monkey watches an action, as when the monkey actually carries out the action. In a sense, the monkeys are rehearsing the action in the mind, getting ready to carry out the action, without actually carrying it out. According to Professor Ramachandran, in order for the brain cells to fire while the body is not actually carrying out the action, a 'virtual reality internal simulation' and 'internal mental transformation' must be taking place. The monkey is reading the actions of the other monkey and gearing itself up to carry out the actions.

There is a part of the brain then that is dedicated specifically to imitation and mimicry. When we are watching an action, our own brains are alerted to be ready to also send a message to our bodies to carry out that action. However, another part of the brain, part of the pre-frontal cortex, suppresses that action and normally holds us back from actually carrying it out. Otherwise we would go through life incessantly actively imitating those around us, which would be rude, limiting and time consuming. It would also be repetitive and serve little ongoing purpose. Young children gradually learn to selectively engage with the actions of others through observing them, while inhibiting the immediate need to physically respond and copy what they are seeing. Imitation and mimicry in humans is thus kept in check while we read and make meaning of what we are observing and store that which is meaningful.

If areas of the brain that are used to do a task are also used when imagining doing it, then this has important implications for the value of dramatic play and drama. It suggests that there is a neurological value in pretending, in imagining and acting out. In drama, participants are carrying out actions 'as if' they are really doing them and as neural pathways need to be used or lost, then using them in drama becomes purposeful. Dramatic play could be seen as a form of 'virtual reality internal simulation' (Professor Ramachandran) as well as an external one. One wonders, if scientists were to observe brain images in children that were pretending and dramatic playing, would mainly the same neurons be firing up as if the children were actually carrying out the actions in real life? Does dramatic play have a purpose linked to rehearsal and strengthening the neural pathways, thus enabling neurons to be used rather than lost?

*Observing triggers the imagination and activates neural pathways that link to the observed action*

The ability to internally model the actions of others, to be able to imagine oneself doing the observed task, and thereby to activate or fire responses within the brain in a similar way while not really carrying out the task, links learning and imagined experience. If this is the case, then should schools be more focused on stimulating and developing learning through imagination, including the use of role play and re-enactment?

> *'Research suggests that children under the age of four or five may not have fully developed the cognitive skills that facilitate learning from formal instruction. Such research has led some to question the value of formal education at an early age and to suggest that a focus on social interaction, play and exploration might be more valuable.'*
>
> Sarah-Jayne Blakemore (2000)

> *'The best available evidence suggests that teaching more formal skills early in school gives children an early academic advantage, but that this advantage is not sustained ... an early introduction to a formal curriculum may increase anxiety and have a negative impact on children's self-esteem and motivation to learn'.*
>
> Caroline Sharp (2000)

Asking young children to sit and listen for long periods of time seems particularly inappropriate as we learn more about the brain and how children learn through play, through adults modelling and through multisensory and imagined experience. It could be that formal education too early might be seen as a form of neural deprivation at a sensitive time for the establishment of neural pathways that are paving the way for learning. Formal education prevents young children from moving around, playing and talking for long periods, yet all these things are necessary key activities congruent with the way the brain is wired to learn.

Judith Rich Harris (1998) suggests that more advanced mimicry and imitation is learned within peer groups, who provide models of behaviour through play, for and with each other. This occurs once the dramatic play is social and shared, and the peer group (rather than the parent) increasingly influences the play and the child. It is a step towards the growth of independence from the parent. Drama is one way in which children can work socially and educationally with the whole class as a peer group.

To return to the subject of mirror neurons, it is interesting to make another connective leap and to consider mirror neurons as possibly significant in relation to people's responses as audiences of theatre and screen drama. Are mirror neurons fired when we are watching drama and is this linked to why watching drama can be so engaging and emotionally moving? Do we on some level actually imagine that we are the characters emotionally as well as in a suppressed and subliminal physical way? Are humans who are watching characters' actions on stage or on television (or on computer and video games) responding neurologically 'as if' they are themselves carrying out the actions, intentions and movements they are observing, and also responding emotionally to some degree?

PART ONE

*Observing drama encourages empathy and identification with characters*

In theatre it could be that the speech and actions of the actors are observed and listened to by the audience and responded to in a way that is inhibited by part of the pre-frontal cortex and controlled by theatrical convention. The audience is invited to respond personally, cognitively, affectively and silently to what they see but without being able in most forms of theatre to physically move. The audience opportunity for externalized response is delayed and comes later through applause, review and retelling and, with children, often through re-enacting. Young children at first actively join in with what they are watching on television (for example, talking to television presenters) and then gradually learn to inhibit their responses and recognize the distance. They learn to suppress and to delay re-enactment and play out what they have seen later, maybe in the playground, and they engage with the experience both physically and emotionally.

Professor Ramachandran suggests that in humans, as the mirror neuron system became increasingly sophisticated, it led to 'an explosive evolution of this ability to mime complex actions, leading to the cultural transmission of information that characterizes us as humans'. Theatre is an important means of cultural transmission. It is also simultaneously an important means of encouraging empathy.

## ■ Drama and accelerated learning

The work of Alistair Smith is now widely known. He has utilized recent knowledge and understanding of the brain and recent educational research to draw up a model of learning which links to motivation and achievement. He promotes a process-based model of teaching based on understanding how children learn best and has called his model 'accelerated learning'. The Accelerated Learning Cycle has four stages, shown below.

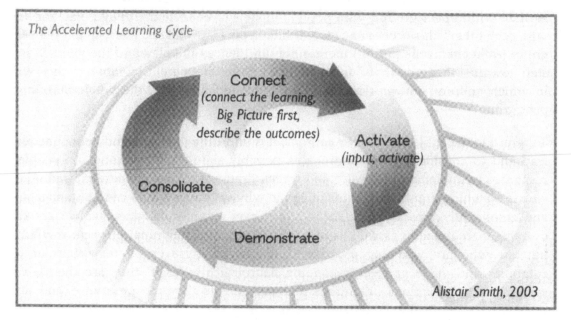

The Accelerated Learning Cycle

Connect
(connect the learning, Big Picture first, describe the outcomes)

Activate
(input, activate)

Consolidate

Demonstrate

*Alistair Smith, 2003*

Drama is also a process-based model of teaching and, although drama lessons do not necessarily follow the Accelerated Learning Cycle exactly, they share many of the features of the accelerated learning process. Drama will 'hook' the children by linking with learning through imagined experience and playfulness, which is a natural way in which the brain is wired to learn. However, in accelerated learning the Big Picture is offered first and in drama this is not necessarily so. It is more likely that it will emerge as the drama evolves and the Big Picture of the whole drama and its meanings unfold.

The drama lesson uses a series of strategies that offer access to learners with different preferred learning styles. The activities will be rooted in what interests them, will be multisensory, experiential and will shift between individual, group and whole-class activity. Children in drama lessons do not sit for long periods; they move around, shift pace and type of activity, separating and combining visual, auditory and kinesthetic activity, exploring meaning and tagging learning multi-intelligently.

In drama:

- Learning is based on what the children already know and bring to the drama.

- The teachers provides frequent and consistent feedback (in and out of role).

- Strategies are used that enable the pre-processing of thinking about the drama and what will happen next.

- Participants are enabled to review what has gone before.

- Strategies are used that enable participants to keep pre-processing questions that the learner/drama participant wants answered.

- Links are made between content and process, explicitly encouraging thinking about thinking (metacognition).

- Learners are encouraged to develop self-knowledge.

- Individual, group and whole-class performance outcomes are set up.

- The content is chunked down through a sequence of 'bite-size' strategies.

- Children are often enabled to affirm their own performance targets.

- Strategies and theatre forms act as planning templates for the structuring of thinking and outcomes.

- Outcomes are differentiated.

- Visual, auditory and kinesthetic modes of presentation, communication and expression are utilized.

- Long-term memory is accessed.

PART ONE

■ Input can be generated, presented or repeated using a range of strategies and forms – for example, storytelling, Freeze-frames, movement and so on.

■ Active listening is required both in and out of role.

■ There are structured opportunities for reflection, assimilation and review both in and out of role.

■ The range of multi-intelligences are used and developed.

■ There is a balance of activities over time.

■ The range of drama activities enable access to learners with a range of preferred learning styles.

■ The learner gains an understanding of the drama process and why different forms and strategies are used.

■ There is a frequent shifting between individual, paired, group and whole-class activity.

■ Learners learn to make choices and evaluate their performances.

■ Learners demonstrate and communicate their new understanding and knowledge and meanings, using a variety of drama forms such as Still Image, performance and storytelling.

■ There are demonstrations through performance within the lesson, including the 'performance' of the teacher as model.

■ A spiral of reflection is encouraged.

■ There is opportunity through improvisation, presentation and performance to offer 'models' of success.

■ Reviewing techniques and strategies enable the children to consider key moments from within the drama in a multiplicity of ways.

■ A range of memory and recall-focused strategies are used, such as, Eavesdropping and storytelling.

(See Part Two for explanations of the strategies mentioned in this list.)

# Dramatic Play and Learning

## ■ In this chapter we consider:

■ the links between dramatic play skills and drama skills;

■ ways of supporting the development of dramatic play skills within classroom settings;

■ the role of the adult as co-participant in early dramatic play for learning;

■ dramatic play as an inclusive or exclusive social activity;

■ how emotionally charged dramatic play and drama link with our long-term memories;

■ the links between psychodrama, socio-drama and drama in schools;

■ the necessity to maintain safe boundaries between reality and make-believe.

*'I play my games of real believe, I play them every day'*

Peter Dixon (2002) ■

*'A child does not symbolize in play, but he wishes and realizes his wishes by letting the basic categories of reality pass through his experience, which is why precisely in play, a day can take half an hour and a hundred miles are covered in five steps.'*

L.S. Vygotsky (1978) ■

*'Cancel your subscription to Infant Genius Monthly, throw away your flash cards and play together the three of you: the baby, you and the cardboard box.'*

*'Children find out about their world through play. Through sensory interaction the structure of the motor and sensory motor strip changes. The best learning is like play.'*

Alistair Smith (2004) ■

**PART ONE**

Early on, babies mirror their mothers' expressions. Their mimicry and imitative responses are reinforced by parents and carers who reward the child with their attention, smiling and repeating expressions, sounds and actions and thereby provide positive feedback.

As the child develops physically, learns to crawl, stand and walk, he/she moves on to acting out a wider range of activities and behaviours for which the significant people in their lives initially act as models. To begin with, imitation and mimicry of parents and carers is carried out in their presence and alongside them. Children gradually become more able to remember speech and actions and to carry them out when the parent is no longer present. They use what has been observed, heard and experienced in real life as the basis for practising, and later generating, their own actions, speech and imagined experiences. This moves the activity beyond just imitation and mimicry into a creative and imaginative activity which has an outcome that is clearly of value to the participant; an activity which reveals their increasing cultural knowledge, skills and understanding.

Children will become increasingly empowered and life skilled within their imagined worlds. They will pour imaginary cups of tea, drive pretend cars, pretend to do the shopping and so on. When Mum or Dad is cooking tea, the young child may well be playing at doing the same. The empathetic adult might decide to join in the make-believe play, receiving and drinking pretend cups of tea and possibly chatting in role with the child. Sensitive adults are alert to the opportunities that such playing with children in role can offer. Joining in is often pleasurable for adults and they are motivated to do it. It is a bonding experience between the adult and child and gives important messages to the child about the value that the adult places on their play. It also opens up real opportunities for supporting learning.

*Adults joining in with role play links closely to Teacher in Role*

Aware adults will see opportunities to talk with and teach their children from within these imaginary and enjoyable contexts. At a simple level, the adult who asks for three lumps of sugar in a pretend cup of tea may see a real opportunity for counting together within the child's pretend world. This is the very root of good drama in education – an empathetic adult in role (within school this would be the teacher or learning support assistant) in an imagined world with a child, facilitating the practice of real skills within contexts meaningful to the child. The fictional contexts (the play) are jointly owned. It is no accident that the word 'play' is a word that is part of drama vocabulary.

Gradually the young child gains an increasing and necessary sense of separateness from the model adult. They begin to *pretend* to be their role models at times of their own choosing and become increasingly able to sustain their dramatic play. Adult co-participation is not necessary but is often welcomed as long as the adult does not hijack the fiction and move it too far away from areas of interest to the child. Sensitive adults will get a sense of, and respect, the child's imagined world before entering it. Young children's play tends to be rather repetitive and somewhat ritualistic when they are left to their own play but, with a perceptive and involved adult, it can be moved sensitively into an exploration of what is not yet known. This is congruent with the principles of good drama lessons, which explore through role play rather than simply re-enactment.

At first, the child's play is rooted strongly in the real world that they are trying to make sense of, but as they begin to listen to and play out stories they become able to seamlessly incorporate aspects of reality, fantasy and fiction into their increasingly imaginative drama worlds.

## ■ The skills of dramatic play and drama

While dramatic playing, young children are not only practising life skills but also drama skills. Dramatic play involves:

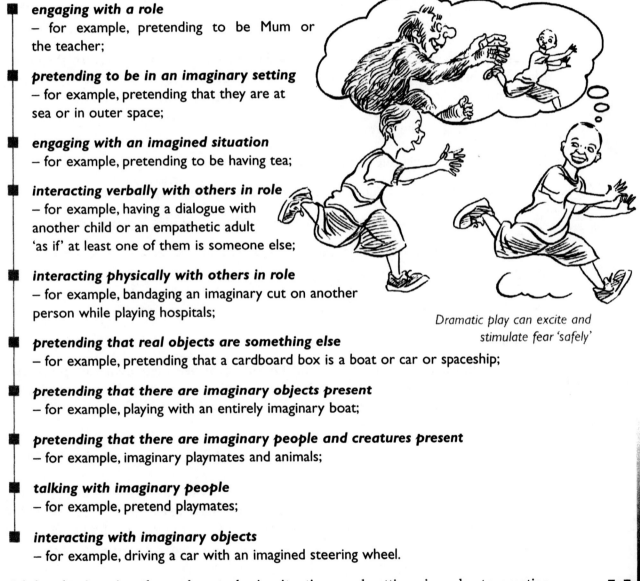

- *engaging with a role*
  – for example, pretending to be Mum or the teacher;

- *pretending to be in an imaginary setting*
  – for example, pretending that they are at sea or in outer space;

- *engaging with an imagined situation*
  – for example, pretending to be having tea;

- *interacting verbally with others in role*
  – for example, having a dialogue with another child or an empathetic adult 'as if' at least one of them is someone else;

- *interacting physically with others in role*
  – for example, bandaging an imaginary cut on another person while playing hospitals;

*Dramatic play can excite and stimulate fear 'safely'*

- *pretending that real objects are something else*
  – for example, pretending that a cardboard box is a boat or car or spaceship;

- *pretending that there are imaginary objects present*
  – for example, playing with an entirely imaginary boat;

- *pretending that there are imaginary people and creatures present*
  – for example, imaginary playmates and animals;

- *talking with imaginary people*
  – for example, pretend playmates;

- *interacting with imaginary objects*
  – for example, driving a car with an imagined steering wheel.

Adults also imagine themselves to be in situations and settings in order to practise real skills and to rehearse success – such as practising a speech to an imaginary audience in advance. Fantasizing and/or enacting fantasies may be a form of adult dramatic play, which may be shared with a partner in order to stimulate and excite.

**PART ONE**

## ■ Role-play areas

Most early years classrooms have role-play areas. These are spaces within which entering imagined worlds is facilitated through a planned environment that has a learning focus. The area may be designed to represent for instance a home, a hospital, a shop, a travel agents, a restaurant. These are usually popular spaces for young children and some ownership of the space is offered when children are invited to contribute to the discussion and planning of such areas or to bring in objects for the area. The teacher will of course consider objects and props, that he/she wishes to place within such areas, with consideration for the potential learning. For example, a teacher might decide to put a telephone in a hospital corner in order to encourage verbal make-believe and put a writing pad near it to encourage emergent writing. The teacher might provide different coloured pretend medicine bottles for teaching and assessing the children's knowledge of colours, a tray of bandages of different widths and lengths to give opportunity for matching activities, dolls of different skin colours to raise awareness of cultural diversity and so forth.

Children usually need some time to get used to the novelty of newly refurbished role-play areas before empathetic adults join in their make-believes. The role of the adult upon entering the role play is to create challenges from within the fiction.

The teacher might role play:

■ a patient who is difficult to communicate with;

■ a doctor who wants a detailed verbal report of a patient's symptoms;

■ a hospital florist who cannot write and needs help with writing message cards;

■ a hospital matron who will be inspecting the ward for tidiness;

■ a visitor who is seeking a lost relative;

■ a patient who has lost their memory;

■ the hospital cook who is planning a menu.

There are times when children should be left to devise their own role plays and dramas and times when the teacher or learning support assistant can enter sensitively with a learning agenda and raise the learning stakes.

## ■ Whole-class activities to support and encourage make-believe

There are many playful make-believe activities that teachers can invite young children to participate in alongside them, which take place outside the role-play corner. These activities can reveal to the teacher whether or not a child has acquired and developed a range of dramatic play skills and is prepared to work co-operatively and sometimes verbally with an adult in a shared fiction.

The following activity sequence can enable teachers to assess early drama skills as well as give children drama skills practice. The activities are rooted in the child's known world, in real activities and experiences familiar to the child, but they shift the known into make-believe contexts.

1.  Imagine that there is a lump of modelling clay in front of you. Do not touch it yet! It is about the size of a tennis ball. In a moment I am going to ask you to pick it up and play with it for a while, feeling it change shape in your hands. Pick your lump of clay up now...

2.  Well done. I could really imagine that lump of modelling clay when I looked at some people's hands. Now I want you to put it down while I explain what I would like you to do with it next. In a moment I am going to ask you to make it into a sausage shape. I wonder how you might decide to do that? Pick up the clay again and make it into a sausage shape now.

3.  Good, I could see that some of you were really concentrating on what you were doing then. Now I want you to make it into a sausage shape again but this time I want you to find a different way of doing it.

4.  Now roll the imaginary clay back into a ball shape and hold it still while I explain the next challenge to you. Now I want you to make the lump of modelling clay into a model of a person. Think carefully about what you will need to do first... and when you are ready, start making that model of a person.

5.  Now turn to your partner. Take it in turns to show your model to your partner and describe it to them. Tell them exactly what it looks like. Listen to your partner's description and if you want to know more, you can ask them questions. If they describe their model well, you might be able to visualize it (imagine a picture of it in your mind).

6.  Now I want to see how clever you are at telling your partner how you made the model. What did you do first? There is not one 'right' way to make a model person. There are lots of different ways. I wonder how you did it? What did you do first. Start telling your partner what you did now.

(This activity can be extended so that one child then gives the other instructions as to how to make the same model, while the listener carries out the instructions with imaginary modelling clay. Or, they can progress to making one model together!)

The activities above presuppose that the child has had real experience of playing with modelling clay. If not then it will need to be provided. The activities are designed to be increasingly demanding and can tell a teacher whether the children are able and willing to:

■ accept and use an imaginary object;

■ listen and follow instructions;

■ apply imagination to a task;

■ interact verbally with another person in a shared make-believe situation;

■ co-operate and communicate with each other visually, verbally and kinesthetically.

These are the pre-requisite skills that children need in order to take part in whole-class drama. Most children bring these skills to school from the outset. Those who do not will need plenty of opportunity to carry on developing make believe and acquiring and practising these skills both inside and outside the classroom.

PART ONE

Any experienced real activities known to children can become the basis of a pretend activity. Other activities (which can be carried out individually or with a partner) could include:

- wrapping a pretend present for someone;

- doing an imaginary jigsaw;

- painting an imaginary picture with pretend paints;

- building a tower from pretend wooden building blocks;

- folding an imaginary newspaper in half and half again.

Many make-believe activities can be carried out at tables and do not require much space. They can be carried out in a spare few minutes as well as within planned lessons and used as a means of encouraging children to co-operate, listen and concentrate, as well as to develop their drama skills.

## ■ Make-believe within circle activities

There are many circle activities that offer practice in the skills of make-believe and shared fiction making. For example:

1. Ask the children to pass a stick (or ruler) around the circle. Ask them to use the stick for a few moments as anything but a stick – for example, a pretend toothbrush, comb, lollipop, microphone. Each child should say 'Thank you' when the stick is passed on to them. They may pass the stick on without using it if they do not want to contribute. They may repeat something that someone else has already done if they wish (enabling active involvement even if the child has no ideas of their own or if their idea has been carried out already.)

2. The same activity can be carried out using different objects – a ball or a scarf perhaps. Alternatively, a chair or box may be placed in the centre of the circle and children take turns to use it as anything other than what it is.

3. Ask a child to help you carry an imaginary box into the centre of the circle. Has any child got an imaginary key that will open it for you? Inside the box can be:

    - Storydust that can take everyone together to storyland for a visit and possible adventure. The dust is used ritualistically to get there and back. They create the ritual with you.

    - Imaginary objects that can be taken out of the box and passed around and that have different physical properties – for example, sticky, slippery, heavy, sharp, small and so on.

    - An imaginary storybook which only has the first page complete.

    - An imaginary key or keys that will open something... but what?

    - Dream dust that gives you pictures in your mind.

Each of these drama activities establishes a framework that becomes known, ritualistic and safe and which can act as a springboard for the children's own ideas, which are very simply performed. Children have opportunity to contribute but need not. However they are expected to stay present and 'pass' if they wish.

Through such whole-class, imagined activities the teacher is introducing children gradually to the idea of being part of a collective whole-class make-believe. It is intended also to be a bonding and inclusive imagined experience for a class. Such activities indicate to a teacher whether the class can work co-operatively in this way, as this will be necessary for whole-class drama.

## ■ Dramatic play and the tribe

While dramatic playing together, children are, among other things, rehearsing and practising surviving and living in social groups. In order to do this they move from playing alone to playing dramatically with others. They create together imaginary worlds that can mirror aspects of the real world as they collectively perceive it. They replicate and create situations within which they can practise skills linked to survival and find out more about becoming an effective human being.

*Dramatic play can be inclusive or exclusive*

Dramatic play groups will quickly exclude children who hamper or spoil this important form of play and do not follow the implicit rules of make-believe which sustain it. Exclusion by peers from such play is a powerful social control device and children will usually be prepared to modify their behaviour and conform in order to be included in this important group learning activity. In drama lessons too, particularly when children are used to drama and know its rewards, peer pressure sometimes operates in order to sustain the fiction. Children get irritated with those whose behaviour threatens their drama experience.

The child that has difficulty getting on with others in social situations will not suddenly be able to play harmoniously once a situation is imagined rather than real but will have opportunity to practise and develop their social skills as long as the group accepts them into the fiction. In successful group dramatic play situations children will learn to relinquish personal control increasingly to each other in order to sustain the dramatic play. Most children want to be accepted as part of the group or class tribe and, where a group or class fiction exists and is valued, most children will behave in ways that ensure that they remain part of it.

Having friends to play with, belonging, being accepted by others, is a strong preoccupation of children as they move into and through schools. Children who find themselves excluded continually from dramatic play (or who exclude themselves), are experiencing significant social exclusion and are being increasingly disadvantaged in a multiplicity of ways. They need access to their peers to develop many areas of learning for life.

## ■ Dramatic play – the stages of development:

1. **Solitary dramatic play**

   For example, the child in the hospital corner who is in his own make-believe world and shows no interest in playing with anyone else.

2. **Parallel dramatic play**

   For example, the child who plays alongside another child (or an adult), appearing to be in the same make-believe as their 'partner' but they do not have anything much to do with each other.

3. **Paired dramatic play**

   Two children play together. They can sustain a shared make-believe for increasing amounts of time. They each are benefiting from the imagined and shared experience and so compromise in order to sustain it. It falls apart sometimes as they disagree over shared ownership of the storyline, the relative status of their roles and disparity with levels of engagement and commitment to the fiction. These are the same things that can lead to class dramas falling apart. An empathetic adult as the partner can help work through some of these problems and be part of a successful paired dramatic experience.

4. **Small group dramatic play**

   Small groups evolve of about four children and play within the same agreed make-believe, maybe breaking off into sub-groups at times. The sustainable groups are usually not greater than four children. The same problems emerge as above but sometimes with the additional rifts that sub-grouping can cause. The children are learning to compromise about their personal ownership of the fiction but they are gaining membership of a group. Teachers and learning support assistants within small group dramas as fellow participants can offer good models and help support successful group dramatic play.

5. **The whole-class drama**

   Although large group dramatic play can emerge naturally with children, the whole-class drama is only likely to happen if it is established by a teacher. In a sense it is a very advanced form of teacher-initiated dramatic play which is inclusive and deliberately learning focused. There is shared creative ownership of the evolving drama but the teacher is scaffolding and framing the experience through the use of drama strategies which are theatrical.

Imaginative and dramatic play is an important indicator, which is linked to the development of children across many areas, including, most significantly, cognitive development. The child who is having difficulty playing and, as part of this, is having difficulty with dramatic role playing, is likely to be having difficulties with learning also. Teachers know that if children cannot play in imagined worlds, if they cannot embrace the idea of 'What if?', then it is likely that they have some form of learning difficulty and conversely, that children who play well and can enter into pretend and 'What if?' situations, tend to be those that learn best. There are well-established and direct cognitive links between play, learning and understanding (Bolton, 1979).

## ■ Adults' memories of dramatic play

Can you suggest reasons why you played this make-believe game?

Do children today still play the same dramatic game or its equivalent?

Can you can remember an example of your own dramatic play as a child?

Can you recall any particular emotions associated with this play?

Most teachers can recall an example of their own dramatic play with clarity and give reasons why they think they played and repeated certain dramatic games. They can also recall associated emotions. Interestingly, women seem to remember more easily than men. Certain patterns emerge. Men most often give examples of super-hero and adventure games such as building dens, that are quite physically demanding and competitive. Women often recall riding pretend 'horses' and games that are caring and more co-operative, such as 'libraries' or 'schools'.

*'I used to play "surgeries". I really wanted to be a doctor when I grew up and I used to have a big first aid kit that I had gathered and have other children as my patients...I still wish that I had become a doctor really.'*

Patricia (age 50)

PART ONE

The emotions that adults have associated with childhood dramatic play activities are happiness, followed by excitement, contentment and fun. The purposes include:

■ to copy behaviour;

■ to feel grown up;

■ to entertain;

■ to ease frustration or boredom;

■ to escape

■ to impress.

Negative emotions associated with recalled dramatic play are less frequent but included anger, disappointment and frustration, mainly because the dramatic play was not working.

## ■ Children's memories of dramatic play

Asking children to recall their early dramatic play memories is also revealing. At around the ages of eight to eleven children are still close enough in age to recall early dramatic play quite vividly and yet are sufficiently distanced from it to be reasonably objective and able to articulate their feelings about it and its functions. The children's perceived function and purposes for their dramatic play can be categorized as follows:

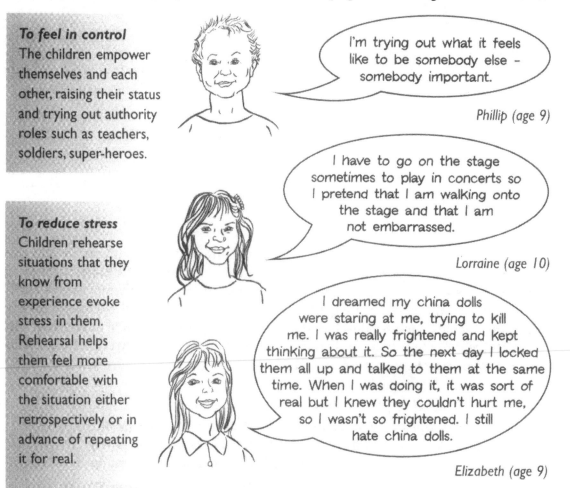

**To feel in control**
The children empower themselves and each other, raising their status and trying out authority roles such as teachers, soldiers, super-heroes.

> I'm trying out what it feels like to be somebody else – somebody important.
>
> *Phillip (age 9)*

> I have to go on the stage sometimes to play in concerts so I pretend that I am walking onto the stage and that I am not embarrassed.
>
> *Lorraine (age 10)*

**To reduce stress**
Children rehearse situations that they know from experience evoke stress in them. Rehearsal helps them feel more comfortable with the situation either retrospectively or in advance of repeating it for real.

> I dreamed my china dolls were staring at me, trying to kill me. I was really frightened and kept thinking about it. So the next day I locked them all up and talked to them at the same time. When I was doing it, it was sort of real but I knew they couldn't hurt me, so I wasn't so frightened. I still hate china dolls.
>
> *Elizabeth (age 9)*

Children also play out entirely imaginary situations that cause them stress – for example, those that they have dreamed and which have over-stimulated them.

**To raise levels of stimulation**
When children are feeling bored or lonely, they pretend that something interesting is happening. This stimulates them and helps them to shift moods.

> I get bored and pretend that I am playing with an imaginary friend.
>
> *Tina (age 9)*

**To socially include or exclude**
Dramatic play, once it becomes social, may involve adopting or developing rituals and rules that the players will recognize and adhere to. The play itself can reflect and become a forum for elaborating on real life situations and issues.

> We used to play a game about riding horses. We didn't like Gemma, so we used to call our pretend horses the same name as her real horse and whip them. She used to get really upset and run away, which is what we wanted.
>
> *Jessica (recalling a game she played at age 8)*

## ■ Dramatic play as survival practice

The human brain is wired up for survival rather than direct instruction and dramatic play often involves practising primitive survival skills in a pretend world without adults. This sort of play might take the form of being alone on a desert island, lost in a forest, hunting and gathering, building dens and shelters and so forth.

> I play a game in the woods near my house. I've played it for years. The first time I played the game, I was feeling a bit nervous at being alone in the woods. I started thinking about what it would be like if I had to live there by myself and I started to build a den. After that I went into the woods quite a lot and pretended that I lived there and that I had left home. I still play it sometimes.

Repetitive dramatic play about being 'alone in the big wide world' is common and rehearses how it might feel to be successful at living independently in the future. Many children's stories and films successfully hook into and explore children's anxiety and fascination with the idea of living without adults (for example, *Lord of the Flies* and *Home Alone*).

*Tina (age 9)*

Observation of 'pretend' play can be very revealing. Professionals such as psychotherapists, child psychiatrists and family therapists sometimes observe or join in children's dramatic or 'small world' play to gain insight into the child's thinking and past experiences. Through the dramatic play, much is revealed as they re-enact, elaborate, extend or devise, making further sense and meaning of lived and witnessed experiences. A cognitive therapist can help a child to re-engage with a lived experience through dramatic play and support them to think about past experiences in different ways. Psychodrama is one means of doing this.

# ■ Psychodrama

It is important to mention that psychodrama is a specialist area that should never be the intended domain of the classroom drama teacher but of a trained director of psychodrama. It is a therapeutic discipline, used in a variety of contexts and requires not just drama expertise but also psychotherapeutic expertise. Like circle time it is based on the work of Jacob Moreno. It focuses on groups supporting individuals to move towards increasingly healthy responses to simulated real life situations enacted with the support of the group. This approach can be seen as having links with Forum Theatre (see Part Two).

On rare occasions a teacher will unintentionally unlock, through drama, unhealthy and disturbing pupil responses that link psychologically to the real life of the child. If this occurs it will be because, for that child, there has been a boundary breakdown between real and imagined worlds and characters, and the drama is no longer safe for them unless a director of psychodrama is leading. The child should be sensitively withdrawn from the drama for 'time out'. There are healing strategies that can be used but inexperienced drama teachers would be best advised to withdraw the child and to offer opportunity to talk with the teacher out of role.

# ■ Socio-drama

Socio-drama, like circle time, brings alive and gives form to the group's values and beliefs, before challenging them, with the possible aim of enabling the reconstruction of those beliefs and values. It involves simulating real situations that often involve social and peer pressure – such as teenage pregnancy, bullying and substance abuse. The group members may witness or learn different ways of perceiving and responding to various social situations. Forum Theatre has strong links with socio-drama.

> 'It (drama) makes you work together, definitely makes you
> work together and try to make the best you can with the
> people you have got, the people you are working with. You
> have got to take a bit of initiative. Say there is someone in
> your group who won't work with anyone else in the group
> apart from one or two people, you are going to have to say,
> "How about we do this?" And if they disagree, then say
> "Well what do you want to do?"'
>
> *Year 7 pupil* ■

# ■ The boundaries of reality and make-believe

*'The world of pretend is the world of make-believe (making beliefs!). The child can do the task safely.'*

Steve Bowkett (2003) ■

The make-believe world of dramatic play is a fictitious world and it is important that children recognize this. As long as children know that they are pretending, and that the members of the group within which they are operating are also pretending, then they can feel safe. This 'willing suspension of disbelief' underpins both dramatic play and drama. Boundaries between make-believe and reality must be recognized and maintained by the group for the well-being of participants. People who are unable to differentiate between reality and make-believe are mentally unwell.

Young children however are learning the boundaries and can sometimes get the distinction between reality and make-believe blurred. This can be quite frightening. Adults, including teachers, are often inconsistent about the ways in which they deal with reality with young children. For example, trusted adults, parents and teachers encourage children to believe in Father Christmas and the Tooth Fairy and yet in other areas are keen to ensure that children recognize what is real and what is pretend. Just as young children watching television believe the characters are real and wave to them, so some confused adults write to the characters of soap operas.

Drama teachers in role must make it clear to children when they are 'in role' and when they are not (see page 97). It can be disturbing to young children when the familiar is changed. If, without warning or explanation, a teacher pretends to be someone else and starts to behave differently, this is likely to generate anxiety in a child. However, if the child understands that the familiar adult is pretending and is entering a shared world of make-believe with the child, then this is stimulating – if the child is in agreement. Drama is about 'a *willing* suspension of disbelief' and not about breaking down boundaries between reality and pretend, with children unclear about whether what an adult is saying to them is true or not. Dramatic play and drama are about moving willingly and with agreement, back and forth across recognized boundaries, not about dispensing with them.

# **D**rama and **I**ntelligences

## ■ In this chapter we consider:

- drama as a teaching and learning medium that recognizes, utilizes and develops the full range of Howard Gardner's multiple intelligences;

- the notion that drama can be used as an effective methodology for the assessment of 'intelligence' across a wide range of subjects and areas;

- the way that drama provides opportunities for individual, group, private and shared reflection and supports the development of reflective intelligence;

- drama as a cognitive and affective vehicle for recognizing and developing emotional intelligence;

- what children say about drama and emotion.

*'An intelligence is the bio-psychological potential to process information in certain ways in order to solve problems or fashion products that are valued in a culture or community.'*

Howard Gardner (10th International Thinking Conference, 2002) ■

*'One's intelligence is the sum of one's habits of mind... humans don't get ideas; they make ideas.'*

L.B. Resnick
(quoted by A. Costa at 10th International Thinking Conference, 2002) ■

*'It is not having knowledge that matters but how you use the knowledge that matters... you can't teach wisdom but you can teach for wisdom... to be wise is not just to say wise things – it is to do them.'*

R.J. Sternberg (10th International Thinking Conference, 2002) ■

*'We are faced with the paradoxical fact that education has become one of the chief obstacles to intelligence and freedom of thought.'*

Bertrand Russell ■

What we consider intelligence to be and whether or not we see it as modifiable and measurable, influences significantly the way that we structure teaching, the curriculum and the education system itself. There has been a shift in our understanding of human intelligence away from something that is genetically based, towards something that is modifiable through effort and being developed continuously throughout our lifetimes.

## ■ Drama and multiple intelligences (MIs)

> *'I believe that if people have different profiles of intelligence we cannot simply ignore the fact. You can't have a uniform school system in which everybody is taught the same thing in the same way.'*
>
> *'It's hard to assess how people's minds work... what we can do is observe what children are doing; any teacher who's really awake watching kids in a classroom designed to encourage the use of multiple intelligences will learn a lot about how they learn.'*
>
> *Howard Gardner (TES interview by Karen Gold, July 2002)* ■

> *'For the most part, academic psychology has been blind and deaf to the arts.'*
>
> *Howard Gardner (10th International Thinking Conference, 2002)* ■

Howard Gardner, a psychologist at Harvard University, has suggested that humans have a multiplicity of intelligences, that each person has their own individual profile of intelligences and that for different people, certain intelligences may be their central intelligences, which can be their main gateway to learning.

Gardner(1983) originally claimed there were seven intelligences:

1. *Linguistic* (for example, poet or writer)

2. *Logical-mathematical* (for example, scientist or logician)

3. *Spatial* (for example, architect, pilot or surgeon)

4. *Bodily-kinesthetic* (for example, dancer or footballer)

5. *Musical* (for example, composer or musician)

6. *Interpersonal* (for example, leader, counsellor – aware of others' feelings)

7. *Intrapersonal* (reflective individual, aware of own feelings)

Gardner has since extended his original list to include two more intelligences:

8. *Naturalistic* (for example, Charles Darwin – an ability to classify the environment)

9. *Spiritual* (for example, Nietsche – existential intelligence, raising the big questions such as 'Why are we here?')

The number of intelligences is not important. What is important is that teachers and pupils are aware that all learners have different intelligence profiles, preferred learning styles and gateways to learning. This leads teachers to an appreciation of pupils' preferred learning styles. It helps children to understand that how they may learn best can impact positively on their vision of themselves as a learner. It is not a question of teaching only in the pupils' preferred ways but of ensuring that learning is accessible to all pupils and planning for multi-intelligent learning. It may be that many children who are deemed to have learning difficulties are not being taught in ways that accord with their intelligence profiles and that enable them to learn.

Teachers will still want to develop the broad range of individual pupils' intelligences. People may have a high IQ according to traditional intelligence testing but poor intelligence in other areas – for example, inter- and intra-personal intelligence. Good interpersonal intelligence is often a better indicator of success in life than high IQ, which has been traditionally so prized in education.

Teachers themselves have individual multi-intelligence profiles and preferred learning and teaching styles. Unless teachers consciously consider developing a range of teaching styles beyond their central style, then they may fall into teaching in repetitive ways that continuously disadvantage the same types of learner.

Since the introduction of the national curriculum and the National Literacy and Numeracy Strategies, teachers have adopted fairly uniform teaching styles. Learners with strong verbal or mathematical intelligence have benefited from a curriculum that has been particularly literacy and numeracy focused and geared towards high stake assessments in English and mathematics. Often children as young as five have been sitting still for relatively long periods of time, listening rather than learning literacy and numeracy multi-intelligently and actively. Girls have consistently out-performed boys. Maybe girls, who tend to have a more developed verbal intelligence than boys, have been advantaged by the ways that literacy has been taught. Maybe standards of boys' literacy would rise if they were taught multi-intelligently.

## ■ Dramatic play and drama as multi-intelligent learning

If we accept that dramatic play is an effective and natural learning medium, and then match what it involves against Howard Gardner's range of multi-intelligences, we may have an enhanced understanding as to why it is so effective. Both dramatic play and drama utilize, integrate and develop simultaneously a broad range of intelligences and are therefore a gateway to learning for pupils with a range of preferred learning styles.

Drama as a teaching and learning medium utilizes and develops the range of multi-intelligences in an integrated way, offering multisensory access to learners with different preferred learning styles. Drama strategies and conventions take account of and develop the range of intelligences. They offer multi-intelligent access to information, ideas and concepts and gives opportunity to participants to make, respond, express and communicate meanings and ideas multi-intelligently through a range of aesthetic forms, through the creative juxtaposition of images, movement, words and sounds.

## Learning styles:

**Linguistic –** Dramatic play and language develop congruently. Drama usually involves spoken language both spontaneously through improvisation and in performance. Drama integrates the spoken and written word, most commonly through play-scripting, and develops understanding of text and sub-text.

**Logical-mathematical –** Problem solving is central to the drama process. Most dramas involve pupils as characters with problems to solve in role. Presenting and performing also involves a variety of problem solving.

**Spatial –** The use of physical and personal space between characters both practically and symbolically (in relation to meaning) is of importance in drama. This is true within lessons and for staging productions.

**Bodily-kinesthetic –** Some dramatic play is very physical. Drama involves using and understanding the effects of contrasting movement and stillness. It requires and develops physical control of the body and its gestures and movements. Some types of drama such as physical theatre and dance-drama are particularly physically focused and demanding.

**Musical –** Music is used frequently in drama as a stimulus or as an accompaniment to create atmosphere or to tag the emotional experience aurally. Music is sometimes composed within drama lessons as an integral part of the drama itself.

**Interpersonal –** Social interaction and co-operation, the ability to work with others, is a central feature of successful dramatic play and working in and through drama. Listening well to each others' ideas, gauging co-participants' needs, empathizing, appreciating different viewpoints and responding sensitively to them, is key to successful drama making.

**Intrapersonal –** The arts are closely linked with recognizing, understanding and developing one's personal feelings and responses and working with one's 'self'. Dramatic play helps develop a sense of 'self'. Drama involves accessing personal feelings and emotions and then using them to guide behaviour through role, initially in imagined worlds, and then later, in the real world.

**Naturalistic –** Drama can focus on the development of naturalistic intelligence or use it in the devising of dramas.

**Spiritual –** Drama involves and inspires reflection and contemplation (partly though ritual) on the human condition and identity. Drama clarifies life situations and then supports the imagination, enabling the individual to rise above the boundaries of these situations, supporting growth and transformation.

**PART ONE**

## ■ Assessment in drama

> '*Assessment, not creativity, remains the driving force behind learning, with what is now a token arts curriculum subjected to an inappropriate process of standardization. The National Association of Head Teachers has warned the government that it is producing "a philistine nation". It is probably easier to govern. It is certainly easier to assess.'*
>
> *Sir Peter Hall* ■

The way that intelligence is discussed and the way it is assessed by cultures is influenced by what different cultures value and perceive intelligence to be.

> '*Our culture has valued the language/logical mode of intelligence, the law professor mode, and the more you resemble the law professor, the smarter you will be seen to be. If Bobby Fischer hadn't lived in the 20th century, in a place where chess was valued, he wouldn't have been called smart.'*
>
> *Howard Gardner (TES interview by Karen Gold, July 2002)* ■

Different cultures place different value on the arts and, within that, drama. In Western culture we do not assess and judge the intelligence of children primarily by their artistic or dramatic skills. Howard Gardner suggests that many people regarded as intelligent in Western culture would not be regarded as such in a culture which valued musical or painting skills above words. Gardner himself places value on the arts in learning, and possesses significant musical intelligence himself.

Gardner argues that we need to move away from standardized testing and both teach and assess according to pupils' intelligence profiles and preferred learning styles. He believes that assessment should be based on genuine problem solving and the creation of products and that methods of multi-intelligent assessment should be devised that offer choice and enable pupils to show what they genuinely can do and understand.

Drama could be assessed multi-intelligently or used as a multi-intelligent medium of assessment in other subject areas. It is often used as a means of assessing pupils' speaking and listening skills but what is said by children in their drama lessons reveals much about pupils' knowledge and understanding in other areas. Watching pupils working together in drama enables teachers to assess social and personal skills. The way that their drama work is refined, rehearsed and communicated through presentation also enables the assessment of drama and theatre skills. The drama process (formative) needs to be considered and not just the product (summative) if we are assessing drama in schools.

It is not appropriate to assess drama through mainly verbal and written tests about drama. These test pupils' ability to talk and write rather than their ability to participate in and create meaningful drama. This is a particular danger with drama being placed within the English curriculum. For assessment systems to be valid they need to be matched to the nature and content of what is being assessed, not influence the way it is taught. If not, then in an assessment-driven education system the test or exam is likely to negatively affect the teaching practice.

## Reflective intelligence

David Perkins (1995) suggests that intelligence has three components:

- fixed neurological intelligence (as assessed in IQ tests);
- specialist intelligence, knowledge and experience gained over time;
- reflective intelligence about self and one's mental habits of mind.

Reflective intelligence is particularly important in relation to:

- making personal choices
- solving problems
- creative thinking
- learning in new contexts
- knowing yourself as a learner.

Reflection helps pupils to understand not only what they have learned but how they have learned. It helps them consider how what they are learning and experiencing fits with what they already know and what they want or need to know next. He suggests that reflective intelligence relies mainly for its development on opportunities outside school and most often in the home.

## Reflection in drama

Drama can give an in-school forum for the use and development of reflective intelligence through providing structured opportunities for individual and group reflection, with the teacher alongside as a reflective and supportive mediator and reflective co-participant. Drama has strategies that are specifically aimed at supporting or guiding individual and shared reflection at significant points in the drama – for example, Freeze-frame, Thought-tracking, Forum Theatre, Conscience Alley and so on (see Part Two).

## Emotional intelligence (EI)

*'There are many ways in schools of enabling young people to discuss and express their feelings and emotions. Among the most important are the arts... there is a difference between giving direct vent to feelings and the creative processes of the arts... the process is not simply one of discharging feelings – though it may involve that – but of giving them form and meaning.'*

NACCCE (1999)

*'The old paradigm idealized reason as free from emotion. The new paradigm urges harmony of head and heart. To do well in life we must first understand exactly what it means to use our emotions intelligently.'*

Daniel Goleman (1996)

PART ONE

*'Emotional intelligence is a way of understanding and shaping how we think, feel and act...Our emotions are affected by our thoughts and by our physical bodies and at the same time those emotions affect our thoughts and our physical bodies. There is no separation between these three parts of us.'*

Catherine Corrie (2003) ■

*'Emotional intelligence is recognizing a feeling in your body and taking charge.'*

Noreen Wetton (Healthy Norfolk Schools Conference, 2003) ■

*'...the intrapersonal intelligence – knowledge of the internal aspects of a person; access to one's own feeling life, one's range of emotions, the capacity to effect discriminations among these emotions and eventually to label them and to draw upon them as a means of guiding one's own behaviour. A person with good intrapersonal intelligence has a viable and effective model of himself.'*

Howard Gardner (1993) ■

*'When we turn our mind's eye inward to our emotions, we find them at once obvious and mysterious. Yet they are the states of our brain which we know best and remember with the greatest clarity.'*

Joseph LeDoux (1996) ■

The term 'emotional intelligence' is a fairly new one in educational parlance and links to the ideas of Daniel Goleman, who argues the importance of developing pupils' emotional intelligence. Goleman considers that anger, sadness, fear and other negative emotions can have damaging effects on our well-being and therefore our lives, and can also have a negative impact on a child's ability to learn. Children learn best when they are in a state of rational and emotional balance, or what Goleman refers to as 'flow'.

We know that body and mind are linked physically, cognitively and emotionally and teachers need to recognize and support the integrated development of all three areas within their teaching and to seek safe and positive ways of doing so.

Thinking and acting rationally (cognitively) but without reference to emotion (affectively) can have negative consequences, as can reacting and acting emotionally without applying rational thought. Emotional intelligence enables children to make good decisions and act in positive ways, with reference to their own well-being and the well-being of others. This is a very important life skill.

Developing emotional intelligence helps children to know, understand and manage their emotions through reflecting on them and linking them consciously and rationally to their actions. In drama, the actions may be pretend but nonetheless the decisions and consequences of decisions played out draw on and have resonance within the real world of the child. Emotional intelligence is personal but it is gained partly with reference to understanding the impact and effect of one's own emotions on others and taking some responsibility for that. Drama provides a supportive forum for checking out that impact in a distanced way with the teacher there to mediate the experience, often from within a role.

> *'Imagining what it is like to be someone other than yourself is at the core of humanity. It is the essence of compassion...'*
>
> **Ian McEwan (The Guardian, 15 September 2001, following 9/11)**

Drama offers a stimulating and rich opportunity to discuss and understand our own emotions, attitudes and beliefs through observing, empathizing with, feeling and exploring the emotions of characters both portrayed and interacted with in role. In drama there is a safe and distanced opportunity to recognize and talk about emotions together.

When a child is playing a character of their own creation within a class drama they are having to consider how to react and act as another person. To do this successfully they will need to draw on what they know and have actually experienced emotionally. They will need to link real and imagined emotional experiences in order to develop a plausible character. Although the child will develop the character through working in role they will be consciously or unconsciously feeling and responding as themselves within the drama and this may support the development of their emotional intelligence as it will be a teacher and class mediated experience.

When children are devising drama there is opportunity for trying out a range of ways of reacting as a character and discussing with other people which is most constructive. Characters' actions and the consequences of actions can be considered rationally and emotionally with others, acted, re-enacted and reflected on individually and together with peers and with the teacher as a mediator.

Drama also gives opportunity for the modelling of constructive interactions and relationships – modelling caring relationships and conflict resolution strategies for example. Observing or enacting characters who are behaving with emotional intelligence can give children fresh ways of acting and talking in emotionally charged situations, of observing and trying out what the positive impact might be on them and on others if they respond in different ways. Conversely, considering why emotionally unhealthy characters are behaving as they do and replaying scenes in which we can see how the outcomes could be different for that character also informs us emotionally (as in Forum Theatre, page 137). A good drama lesson can be a safe forum within which participants can be guided and managed to become increasingly aware of emotions, can be helped to recognize and name them and can enact and rehearse taking control of them competently and intelligently. This may be done in role but the feeling through engagement with role is real and the learning is transferable.

Drama is a place for feeling and trying out emotions in a controlled way, for being guided in reading the emotions of other people and gaining more understanding of the impact of one's own and others' emotions. Participants are not held personally responsible once outside the drama, for the actions and feelings of the characters they create and portray within the drama. In drama, children can pretend to be emotionally competent, practise becoming more emotionally competent and thereby be supported to actually be more emotionally competent. Emotional competence has a 'feel-good' factor, which is intrinsically motivating.

The development of emotional intelligence is supported through drama by:

### Self-talk and self-awareness

- Drama strategies support inner dialogue and give structured opportunities to voice it.

- Working in role heightens awareness of self through distancing from and returning to 'self'.

### Recognizing social cues

- Drama is a social activity and focuses on analysing and acting on cues.

- Problem solving and decision making are applied to feelings

- All dramas have problems to be solved together and decisions for characters to make.

- Drama strategies give opportunity to make emotions and thoughts explicit and shared and to then make and reflect on intelligent decisions collaboratively.

### Understanding other perspectives

- Working in a range of roles and interacting with others in role is a powerful way of actively engaging with other people's perspectives, which encourage ongoing consideration of our own.

### Positive attitudes

- Research by Harland (2000) suggests that participation in arts (including drama) in schools, leads to a positive atmosphere and environment and enhanced enjoyment.

### Non-verbal behaviours (eye-contact, gestures and so on)

- Drama involves a significant focus on reading non-verbal messages and portraying and communicating them through gesture, eye-contact, movement, positioning and so forth. The non-verbal and verbal messages are juxtaposed for greater clarity of meaning.

### Verbal behaviours (listening, positive responses, assertiveness)

- Drama relies on and develops active listening and response. It supports and gives opportunity for inference and the understanding of sub-text and the meaning and emotions lying behind spoken and written words.

*Adaptation of Mel Rockett and Simon Percival (2002)*

Harland has researched, among the effects and effectiveness of the arts, the emotional effects of drama as perceived by secondary school pupils. The pupils voiced in a variety of ways an awareness that drama helped develop their emotional intelligence and also recognized the therapeutic and intrinsically rewarding aspects of drama, as shown in the comments opposite.

'Drama has helped me to feel calmer in some ways, not being worried about these sorts of thing, a good way of taking away some tension.'
(Year 7)

'If you act something out you tend to feel like, "Ah, this person is rather like me", like, she does this and that, and you begin to know more about yourself.'
(Year 9)

'Within drama if you do a particularly good piece of work, you feel really good about yourself. You think, "Oh yeah, that was me, I did that!"'
(Year 9)

'Sometimes it [drama] helps you to understand yourself and how you feel and how you look, see what's different about yourself.'
(Year 9)

'In drama you get to express your feelings, so you should be able to understand what people are going through.'
(Year 8)

'In drama you kind of forget yourself. Even if you have got troubles or something like that, you can just be somebody else.'
(Year 7)

'We did about this girl. Her parents were completely ignoring her. So, there was neglect, and we learned about how people feel about neglect, being ignored completely. When we did that, it just so happened that my mum and dad had this really big argument, and me and my brother were getting a bit neglected. So, it helped me understand how it felt at home.'
(Year 9)

'Once you have spoken to someone in drama you can go out and have a conversation with them.'
(Year 10)

'Well, it's nice, kind of, to express yourself as a different person because you take on, like, their feelings and what they think and stuff.'
(Year 9)

'It gives you a chance to like do some empathy, putting yourself in another person's shoes. And it has an effect on you that you can understand the way people feel when they do drama and the way they express themselves and the things they say and how they feel about certain subjects.'
(Year 8)

'It's made me come closer to my feelings. Before, I wanted to use, like, hand gestures and my facial expressions and things like that. Before, I just expressed things by mouth, by talking, but later I learned ... I know how to use my body.'
(Year 8)

**PART ONE**

# Drama and Thinking

## ■ In this chapter we consider:

- the synchronicity of drama for learning and the teaching of thinking;

- the ways in which drama methodology can be employed within recent main approaches to the teaching of thinking;

- the clear links between the process of high quality thinking and the process of drama for learning;

- that drama strategies can be used to scaffold, support and make explicit individual and shared thinking;

- what children say about drama and thinking.

*'The opportunities for developing thinking skills through socially mediated activities should not be underestimated. Such socially mediated activities cannot be left to chance but need to be designed by the teachers drawing on knowledge of children's thinking processes, pedagogy and content.'*

*'Developing thinking recognizes that cognitive competence is increasingly viewed as being distributed – dependent on physical, social and symbolic support for development and enhancement.'*

Carol McGuinness (1999) ■

*'Before this century is out, no curriculum will be regarded as acceptable unless it can be shown to make a contribution to the teaching of thinking.'*

John Nisbet quoted in Carol McGuinness (1999) ■

*'Your children are not your children. They are the sons and daughters of life's longing for itself...*

*You may give them your love but not your thoughts. For they have their own thoughts.*

*You may house their bodies but not their souls.*

*For their souls dwell in the house of tomorrow, which you cannot visit, not even in your dreams.'*

Kahlil Gibran (1926) ■

Drama provides a motivating forum for the development of pupils as active and interactive listeners, speakers, thinkers, movers and image makers – that is, as active learners, not as passive recipients simply trying to remember and then recall someone else's passed-on thinking or knowledge or simply re-enacting someone else's existing story.

Learning how to learn and becoming better at thinking involves specifically thinking about thinking (metacognition), and being aware of different types of thinking and ways of structuring or supporting thinking for different purposes. *How* pupils learn, and not just *what* they learn, is important in shaping their ability and willingness to learn and carry on learning, to perceive themselves as thinkers and lifelong learners. Pupils need to be helped to acknowledge, develop and celebrate a perception of themselves as good thinkers. Drama classes provide a 'thinking community' which creates and celebrates its individual and shared thinking through collective imagined experience and performance.

Teaching *thinking* involves teachers in:

- setting challenging tasks that encourage and support pupils to think in a sustained way about an issue or problem that may not have just one answer;

- encouraging pupils to gain understanding of a range of thinking patterns;

- encouraging pupils to use and build on what they already know to make sense of new information;

- thinking together through collaborative talk and active listening;

- teacher intervention when appropriate to ask questions, challenge, support or extend pupil thinking;

- debriefing pupils on their solutions to a task and their strategies for carrying it out;

- helping pupils to make connections between the thinking involved in the task and other contexts in order to encourage transfer of knowledge and skills.

*Based on the Key Stage 3 National Strategy key messages about 'Teaching Thinking' (DfES 2002).*

Teaching *thinking through drama* involves:

setting a series of open and closed challenging tasks, which engage the pupils and encourage them to employ different types of thinking for different purposes. The series of tasks, which are framed through strategies, can be focused on individually and as contributing to the evolving whole-class drama. All pupils are given ongoing opportunities to actively and interactively explore imaginary issues, think creatively and critically and problem solve individually, in pairs, groups and as a whole class;

using drama strategies that encourage pupils to gain an understanding of thinking patterns such as considering in a balanced way the pros and cons of particular courses of action through the use of Conscience Alley or actively listening to and contributing to a character's thoughts through Thought-tracking (see Part Two);

PART ONE

- stimulating, supporting, guiding and encouraging pupils to consider and use what is known to them already in order to connect, imagine and create something original together;

- planning to use strategies and conventions flexibly to support pupils to listen actively, think alone or together, talk collaboratively, move and present together;

- intervening and mediating either in role (Teacher in Role) or out of role, in order to ask questions that support, challenge, extend or promote pupils' individual and collaborative thinking. Using a range of teacher in roles (see Part Two) offers immense flexibility for both close and distanced intervention and mediation;

- supporting reflective thought as to what has been learned both in and, through the drama – for example, guiding reflection on their 'as if' experiences and their solutions and responses to issues, actions, problems and events within the drama as well as giving direct feedback sometimes;

- encouraging pupils to talk together about how to do the tasks set and afterwards, to talk about how they did the tasks. Also to consider the thinking skills employed at different stages of the process as well as to consider that there may be different ways to think through and around the same task;

- helping the pupils to make connections between the thinking involved in different parts of the drama and with their thinking in 'real life' contexts, in order to encourage the transfer of knowledge and skills. Although the pupils are distanced from the problems and issues within the drama (through working in role), the knowledge and skills gained and developed are transferable;

- enable pupils to support, share and value each others' thinking during the drama process and in response to performance.

Drama strategies can be used out of the context of drama lessons as teaching and learning techniques and can offer an effective methodology for stimulating and giving opportunity for participants to share and develop specific thinking skills.

Wigan LEA's 'Arts Reasoning and Thinking Skills' project (2002), based on the Cognitive Acceleration in Science Education (CASE) model, contains examples of the teaching of specific thinking skills in thinking skills lessons that use a range of drama strategies. Wigan LEA have developed a folder of arts-based lessons aimed at developing specific types of thinking through various art forms at Key Stage 3, including drama. These are not drama lessons through which the teaching of thinking is infused; they are thinking skills lessons, which use drama methodology. Their primary aim is to develop thinking skills through the medium of drama rather than develop drama skills, although it has been claimed that in the thinking skills lessons, drama skills are to some extent being developed (or at least practised) also.

An alternative approach to developing thinking skills through drama is to develop whole-class drama lessons that have the development of thinking skills as a specific focus embedded within them but which also focus on the development of drama. Swartz and Parks (1994) describe the teaching of thinking through different subjects as 'infusion'. They claim that the infusion approach improves pupils' thinking as well as enhancing the learning of any content. This approach is exemplified within the drama units in this book. It more easily enables meaningful drama to flourish and give contextually engaging reasons for thinking.

Swartz and Parks analysed and categorized the different type of thinking skills as follows:

- Sequencing and ordering information
- Sorting, classifying, grouping, analysing
- Identifying part–whole relationships
- Comparing and contrasting
- Making predictions and hypothesizing
- Drawing conclusions
- Giving reasons for conclusions
- Distinguishing fact from opinion
- Determining bias and checking the reliability of evidence
- Generating new ideas and brainstorming
- Relating cause and effect
- Devising a fair test
- Defining and clarifying problems
- Thinking up different solutions
- Setting up goals and sub-goals
- Testing solutions and evaluating outcomes
- Planning and monitoring progress towards a goal
- Revising plans
- Making decisions
- Setting priorities
- Weighing up pros and cons.

Within drama lessons it is likely that some of these types of thinking will be required and developed more frequently than others. It is useful for teachers planning and shaping drama lessons to keep the range of thinking skills in mind in order to ensure that they structure the lesson in ways that give opportunity for children to practise and develop a range of thinking skills within the drama. Overuse of the same drama strategies set up in the same way repeatedly will elicit the same types of thinking and speaking opportunities. However, an awareness of the types of thinking opportunities that have not been facilitated can enable the teacher to adapt activities and strategies, in order to focus within the drama on specific types of thinking. This can be done without sacrificing the holistic and aesthetic drama experience and the development of drama itself. It is possible to infuse the development of drama and of thinking without hampering the drama process and without leaving the focus and development of specific types of thinking to chance.

*The National Curriculum* handbook (DfEE and QCA, 2000) makes it clear that thinking skills should be developed across all subjects within the national curriculum. It categorizes thinking skills as:

■ Information processing

■ Reasoning

■ Enquiry

■ Creative thinking

■ Evaluation.

Within drama, all these categories of thinking skills are employed and developed both out of role as the drama is being set up, and within role as the drama is happening.

Within whole-class drama, children are:

■ *Processing information* and selecting from what they know in order to create and sustain their role. As the drama unfolds they are processing what is occurring in the evolving drama in order to make sense of it in relation to what they already know.

■ *Reasoning* out of role, with others, as to what to select for presentation and performance and how to best present it effectively. Also reasoning within role as a character, as the drama progresses.

■ *Enquiring* of characters in role during the drama in order to gather information and to deepen and sustain engagement with the evolving fiction. Also linked enquiry out of role – for example, in historical dramas, when gathering authentic information in order to inform the role and the drama.

■ *Thinking creatively as individuals* in order to generate and develop roles, and thinking creatively with others in order to generate, create and develop the drama itself.

■ *Evaluating* in role throughout in relation to the unfolding fiction and their place within it. Also evaluating out of role – for example, evaluating their own performance and that of others.

Resnick (1987) claimed that high quality thinking is not difficult to recognize, although it is difficult to define. The characteristics of high quality thinking he defined are very much synonymous with high quality process drama.

| High quality thinking: | High quality drama: |
|---|---|
| ■ is not routine – the path of action is not fully known in advance | ■ is not routine. The way that the drama will develop is not known in advance by anyone, including the teacher, as it is linked to pupil responses and ideas which cannot be predicted. The pupils' share ownership of the drama and its direction with the teacher as fellow participant |
| ■ tends to be complex – the total path is not visible from a single viewpoint | ■ offers the opportunity to make public and consider a variety of different imagined viewpoints throughout, that collectively build an increasingly complex and multifaceted picture of the constantly evolving drama. Creating and appreciating different viewpoints and perspectives are central to the development of dramas |
| ■ yields multiple rather than unique solutions | ■ has a path that need not be linear. Multiple solutions can be considered and explored in turn or simultaneously. The drama can move back and forth in time to view, re-view and re-think key moments from new perspectives gained through active, imagined experience |
| ■ involves nuanced judgement and interpretation | ■ creates opportunities for meanings to be explored and arrived at through the integration or juxtaposition of verbal, visual and kinesthetic activity. This provides a flexible and accessible means of exploring and expressing nuanced judgements and interpretations |
| ■ can involve the application of multiple criteria which may conflict with one another | ■ involves problem solving and resolving dilemmas creatively both in and out of role. This requires the application of multiple criteria that may conflict with one another |
| ■ involves uncertainty – not everything about the task at hand is known | ■ involves uncertainty at a level that is safe and manageable and is therefore motivating and engaging. It is dynamic and evolving. Participants know that not everything about the task at hand is known in advance. They are exploring and creating together, what is not yet known to them |
| ■ Involves imposing meaning – finding structure in apparent disorder | ■ requires the teacher to scaffold the drama experience in ways that enable the participants to actively find, make and communicate their own meanings. As the pupils become increasingly conversant with the strategies employed by the teacher to do this, they become increasingly able to structure and order their own imagined experiences |
| ■ is effortful – considerable mental work is needed for the kind of elaborations and judgements required | ■ is active and interactive. It requires continuous engagement and mental effort by participants at varying levels and is both cognitively and affectively demanding |

*Based on Carol McGuinness (1999)
and Patrice Baldwin and Kate Fleming (2003)*

## ■ Pupils' voices about drama and thinking

'Your imagination can just run riot [in drama and art]. It's just doing stuff that you'd never thought of doing before.'
(Year 9)

'In drama we look at why people have done things. It's like psychology - look at why somebody, like maybe a wife who's been beaten - hurt her husband. We look at why she did it, look deeper into it.'
(Year 9)

'You can't actually do drama on your own and you learn that it's the fusion between my idea and your idea that makes something good, and that's probably a life skill isn't it?'
(Year 8)

'In drama you are acting out a role play and you have to think about the composition of the piece where you stand. You have got to think about whether, who should say what and so on.'
(Year 9)

# **D**rama, **C**reativity and **I**magination

## ■ In this chapter we consider:

- the synchronicity of the drama process and the creative process;

- drama strategies as flexible and adaptable tools for the free-flow of ideas or for focus at different stages of the creative drama process;

- the links between the drama process and creative outcomes;

- some simple class activities that stimulate the imagination and share make-believe;

- the positive correlation between drama methodology and what we know about the way that children create and learn best;

- the role of the drama teacher as facilitator of children's own imaginations and creativity;

- what children say about their own creativity and how teachers can enable and support it.

*'...as imagination bodies forth*
*The form of things unknown, the poet's pen*
*Turns them to shapes, and gives to airy nothing*
*A local habitation and a name.'*

William Shakespeare, A Midsummer Night's Dream

*'First (creativity) always involves thinking or behaving*
*imaginatively. Second, overall this imaginative activity is*
*purposeful: that is, it is directed to achieving an objective.*
*Third, these processes must generate something original.*
*Fourth, the outcome must be of value in relation*
*to the objective.'*

NACCCE (1999)

**PART ONE**

'"*Creative play*" – *seeking to see the world afresh – is at times a fight against the fascination which familiar associations and directions of thought exert on us. Young people need to be encouraged to understand the importance of this type of "play".'*

Professor Lewis Minkin ∎

*'The creation of something new is not accomplished by the intellect alone but by the play instinct acting from inner necessity. The creative mind plays with the objects it loves.'*

Carl Jung ∎

*'Creativity itself...deliberately venturing into unknown territory, is an intrinsically essential part of the education process. It requires practice. Repeatedly risking failure is an essential part of the creative process... Creative activities give young people the chance to experience that sense of fear, of "not knowing" in a supportive environment, while acquiring transferable skills, while reflecting on any and every aspect of the lives they live – and while creating something.'*

CAPE UK (conference briefing paper) ∎

There are many definitions of creativity abounding but these now include a definition from the National Advisory Committee on Creative and Cultural Education, who define creativity in *All our Futures: Creativity, Culture and Education* as:

*'Imaginative activity that is fashioned so as to produce outcomes that are both original and of value.'*

NACCCE (1999) ∎

In drama the individual and collective imaginations of the class are stimulated and then fashioned, through the use of drama strategies, to produce intrinsic and extrinsic outcomes that are original and of value to the participants, and are sometimes of value to an external audience.

The *Oxford English Dictionary* defines 'to create' as 'to bring into existence'. In drama the work is brought into existence by first stimulating the initial interest of the children and then keeping them on task with a will to create. Working in whole-class drama the children are acutely aware that the drama does not yet exist and that they are together bringing it into existence. This is part of the hook for children – the unknown elements, the risk-taking, the dynamic nature of it.

In drama it is important that the initial stimulus gains interest. This stimulus might be, for example, an artefact, a piece of music, a story, children's event or issue that

With Drama in Mind

is of interest and relevance to them, or an interesting visual image. Children are curious and a drama stimulus that offers some initial information but leaves much open for imaginative exploration, for active wondering, will stimulate creative thinking. Too much information given may not stimulate creative thought. Knowledge itself is not sufficient.

> *'Thinking – feeling – acting is an elegant dance between aspects of mind and body – conscious, subconscious, imagination and memory.'*
>
> Steve Bowkett (2001) ■

Imagination is key to creativity which always involves playing with ideas, connecting what is already known and linking and using it in new ways and contexts. Creativity cannot happen in a vacuum. It relies on the ability to play with existing knowledge and ideas in a way that generates and creates new ideas that are original to the thinker. Some of the ideas being played with are juxtaposed, held and developed and others are discarded on the way. Drama encourages the mingling, merging and discarding and re-shaping of real ideas offered by the participants within fictional contexts.

Children will require some existing knowledge and understanding of the medium of drama as well as knowledge of the drama's subject matter in order to be able to think and link together knowledge, thoughts, ideas and imagination in ways that will stimulate creative and critical thinking and create new drama. The participants are stimulated to use their individual and collective imaginations to actively consider 'What if?' through working in role, thinking and behaving 'as if' together.

Drama enables participants to distance and free themselves through working in role so that they can work on problems together that mirror real life problems. Working in role with others enables participants to be less wedded to their existing perceptions and more open to generating, linking and integrating new ideas. They have less personally at stake. Working in role invites participants to unblock fixed positions and patterns of thinking and actively play with ideas – to take 'safe' risks in role.

Creative thinking within school drama lessons usually has timetable constraints but the flow of ideas stimulated by a challenging drama may stay with a child at an unconscious and intuitive level beyond and between lessons. Creative thoughts and ideas may surface and resurface consciously at other times and incubate between lessons, being then able to be fed back in to the next lesson. Although a lesson has finished, the imagined experience stores significant associated thoughts and feelings and may carry on working on the drama unconsciously. Ideas and associated images may flood back into the conscious mind unexpectedly, even a considerable time after the drama lesson.

A child who took part in a series of drama lessons, based on the Viking invasion of Lindisfarne, wrote a poem about it (unprompted) months later, inspired by listening to a piece of music for the first time. The class teacher informed me that the music evoked memories and feelings experienced during the drama lesson of several weeks earlier. The music was not connected to the lesson as such but the child linked it in his mind and it inspired a creative outcome later.

Creativity does not necessarily benefit from unlimited time and space in which to think at all stages. It would also be rather impractical in many schools. Imposing time constraints and deadlines on children creating drama at certain stages in the drama process can give the right level of pressure to prompt an outcome. During process drama lessons it is likely that creative thinking will occur and that the quality of thinking will impact on the presentation, performance or other outcome. A well-judged time constraint can step up the pace and the level of challenge spurring the children to respond, get on with trying things out practically and take creative risks. Conversely, an ill-judged time constraint may lead to anxiety and disorganization that will be sufficient to hinder the creative thinking process and may leave a sense of frustration or failure.

A constraint can stimulate or stunt creative thinking. Limiting props rather than over-providing costumes, artefacts and other resources, can also help or hinder creative thinking in drama – for example, 'The only piece of costume or prop you can use in this scene is a scarf... It can become whatever you want it to be... Use your imagination... improvise... what could this scarf become?' Some children may be held back by this limitation and others inspired. Without more (or less) support for some children it will remain forever a scarf! Any object or shape can stimulate imagination and there are many activities that the teacher can set up to invite playful creative thinking and establish a culture in which playfulness and creativity are valued.

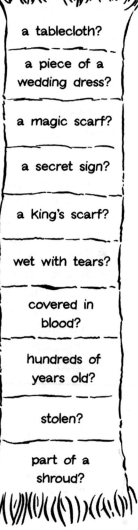

This scarf could be...

a tablecloth?

a piece of a wedding dress?

a magic scarf?

a secret sign?

a king's scarf?

wet with tears?

covered in blood?

hundreds of years old?

stolen?

part of a shroud?

■ **The Chair Game**
Seated circle with a chair in the centre. In turn the children have opportunity to enter the circle and use the chair as anything other than a chair. They decide what the chair will be – for example, a typewriter, television, newspaper, supermarket trolley.

■ **The Slap-stick**
Pass a stick or baton around the circle. When each child receives the stick they thank the giver and then use the stick as anything other than a stick – for example, a toothbrush, comb, flute, ruler.

This activity can be done with a variety of different objects – such as a ball, a cardboard box or a roll of tape, for example. Participants may pass the objects on without using them if they wish.

■ **The Statue Game**
In pairs, the children take it in turns to make their bodies into an interesting still shape. The partner views the shape and quickly responds to it, using it in some way – for example, pretends to chip at it as if it is a statue, or pretends to hang a coat on it as if it is a coat stand. The shapes should be responded to quickly.

Recent research by the QCA (2003) into teaching for and with creativity across the curriculum suggests that children learn best when they:

■ learn through practical experimentation and problem solving;

■ use role play and dance, for example, as a method of exploring ideas;

■ use visual skills and materials;

■ are able to discuss ideas in small groups and work together.

Drama is congruent with the way that the QCA claims children learn best:

■ Creating drama involves a high degree of experimentation and problem solving individually and in groups both in and out of role.

■ Role play as a way of exploring ideas is at the root of drama.

■ Drama is a highly visual medium and often uses props and materials.

■ Making and reading visual images is an important aspect of drama.

■ Drama strategies can separate or integrate visual, auditory and kinesthetic learning and form.

> *'Giving pupils the opportunity to choose ways of working and to shape the process, the direction of the work or the outcome led to more creative behaviour.'*
>
> *QCA (2003)*

> *'Teachers who inspire creativity have a clear idea of what it means to be creative… they model the creative process for their pupils, with all the attendant risk-taking this can involve.'*
>
> *Ofsted (2003)*

The teacher can help or hinder creative thinking in drama. The drama teacher structures the lesson framework in a way that sets out to scaffold and step, and even model at times, the creative process for all children. The children are offered a considerable degree of ownership of both the content and direction of their drama. The more they become used to working in drama, the more the children gain an understanding of the drama form and the more able they are to select their own forms.

In August 2003 Ofsted inspected schools in relation to their success at developing creativity in pupils. The report, *Expecting the Unexpected*, recognized that drama promoted creativity in many of the lessons observed.

> *'In many of the art and design and drama lessons observed, high levels of creative work were associated with pupils' ability to observe, analyse and use – often with authority – different codes of representation. Where this was not the case – where self-expression was given too high a premium – the work was often shallow and undemanding.'*
>
> *Ofsted (2003)*

**PART ONE**

The drama teacher selects strategies that stimulate and support creative thinking without constraining it and adapts the strategies in such a way as to make them accessible to all pupils, whatever their preferred learning style, while offering an appropriate level of challenge. If the drama teacher sets too high a creative challenge then stress about not understanding, feeling unable to complete the task and looking foolish in front of peers will mean that engagement and creativity will be inhibited due to anxiety. There is risk to the 'self' in speculating and offering tentative, half-formed ideas publicly – and yet half-formed ideas are the seeds of creative thinking. If the drama activities and tasks are not within the grasp of the children then they may simply become frustrated, lose interest or misbehave in a diversionary way, which will break the drama and inhibit creativity.

Conversely, drama tasks that are undemanding and lacking in challenge will lead to the participants losing interest and, therefore, motivation. The children will switch off through boredom. Sometimes very prescriptive teacher-directed drama lessons where young children are effectively no more than puppets in the teacher's drama can lead to boredom and lack of concentration.

When drama is based around what interests the children and they know that they together own the way the drama takes shape, then their sustained interest is assured and the seeds of creativity are watered. If children's ideas are valued and used, then they will feel that ideas are worth having and that they are rewarded. If their ideas are sought, valued, encouraged, developed, presented and celebrated, then they will be inspired to keep the ideas coming, to try to have and offer many ideas – and many ideas are important to the creative process.

In drama lessons the individuals within groups share their ideas and make them available to each other in order to develop their whole-class drama. A free-flow of shared ideas contributes to the number of ideas that may be drawn on and linked as the drama evolves. This is a healthy and constructive shift in emphasis from children being possessive about their ideas and jealously claiming and guarding them. They are working creatively towards a shared outcome

A drama lesson may produce a multiplicity of creative outcomes. An original thought contributed during the drama process might be considered to be a creative outcome in its own right just as much as a performance piece or product may be. Many children enjoy showing or sharing their drama work with others through presentation and performance. This can be exciting and enjoyable. It gives a clear creative purpose to the work and encourages and relies on sustained effort. For many, the knowledge that their work, their 'creative outcome', will be presented or performed to an audience is motivating (even if that audience is each other within the drama itself). However, participating in a drama performance or the prospect of doing so can also provoke anxiety, and teachers therefore need to ensure that children are moved to the edge of their comfort zones but not beyond them.

The QCA research (2003) on creativity in education indicates that:

> *'Pupils responded in a particularly positive way when they were put in the role of the teacher and had to explain to their peers or support a younger child's learning.'*

Links can be made between this and the Mantle of the Expert strategy (pages 107–110) where children are empowered to be 'the one who knows' and, while respected 'as if' real experts, they approach some 'real' enterprise. This challenges them to use their present knowledge, understanding and imagination and to pretend to be someone else creating and imparting knowledge and advice to someone who is pretending to be in 'real' need of it.

> *'Creative learners need:*
>
> ❑ *a wide array of contexts within which to apply their skills and knowledge;*
>
> ❑ *teachers or guides who can expose them to strategies for thinking about the connections between their experiences.'*
>
> **Seltzer and Bentley (1999)**

Drama is rooted in imagination and the imagination can provide a limitless number of imagined contexts within which children can create and practise real skills and use real knowledge to claim imagined knowledge and acquire and rehearse imagined skills (Mantle of the Expert). The drama strategies that the teacher employs support the connection of real life and imagined experiences.

Creative ideas, behaviours and outcomes for pupils are not arrived at by teachers who simply light the blue touchpaper of a creativity firework called 'Drama' and stand back. Teachers need to observe and actively listen in order to decide in which direction the drama might flow. They can then decide how and when to intervene in or out of role in order to support the pupils in making connections that will encourage their creative and critical thinking.

Some drama strategies such as improvisation support a free-flow of ideas, while others seem more obviously to encourage specific focus and depth rather than breadth of thought. Most drama activities require both a free-flow and focus of thought at different stages of the creative drama process – for example, Small Group Playmaking (pages 135–136) in which:

1. The group may start by brainstorming ideas as to theme, characters, setting and opening situation.

2. They may then bring the scene to life, improvising and thereby generating and creating speech and actions together.

3. They may create and try out different ways of playing the same scene.

4. The improvisation can then be re-viewed and re-played with selected speech and actions rehearsed further.

The drama teacher needs to know when to give thinking space and enable free-flow and when to intervene with a contribution or question that will move their creative thinking and the drama forward. The skilled drama teacher who is tuned in to both the children and the drama, can gauge what is the most beneficial teacher move to make and how best to support creative thinking.

The creative thinking involved in the drama process is of value in itself and may or may not lead to an outcome or created product that can be shared and appreciated by others, such as a presentation or performance. When there are outcomes in drama lessons they will always be original as they use the children's own ideas that are generated live in the lesson. Teachers may embark on the same drama lesson with different classes of pupils and the creative thinking and created outcomes can still be original to the participants. Even a play at the theatre is original every time it is performed as it is a dynamic, interactive and live experience that cannot be replicated exactly.

Creating a product, however, is not necessarily the same thing as being creative. Creative thinking implies a quality of thought, which often has a particular 'eureka' moment which links to a breakthrough in thinking and maybe influences the direction of the drama.

Talking with children about what they consider supports or hampers their own creativity and what they think creativity is can tell teachers much about the conditions that they require in order to think and work creatively.

## ■ Creativity – the pupil's voice

Ask children the following questions about creativity and listen to their guidance for teachers and educators. The voices below are from children whose teacher was involved in the 2003 QCA research project on creativity in education (www.ncaction.org.uk).

**What do you think creativity is?**

- 'When you let your hopes and worries go.'
- 'Doing new things and expressing your feelings in music or art or drama.'
- 'Working together and sharing your ideas and imaginations.'
- 'When you are allowed to be messy – it's fun.'
- 'When you see things in your mind and can show them.'

**How do you know when you are being creative?**

- 'When you feel you have made something of your own that no one else has made.'
- 'When you feel goodness inside you.'
- 'When you use your imagination.'
- 'It makes you smile and be happy inside.'
- 'When I need to show what I have in my head.'
- 'You do your best and you learn.'

**How do teachers help you to be creative?**

- 'Tell you that you are an artist.'
- 'Tell us to use our imaginations.'
- 'Help us to get our own ideas.'
- 'Inspire us with nice comments.'
- 'I don't know!'

**What could teachers do to help you be more creative?**

- 'Give us more time so we can think better.'
- 'They could be more inspiring and fun.'
- 'They need to help us more.'
- 'We just don't have enough time to think.'
- 'Letting us do what we want instead of telling us what to do.'
- 'Listen to us more.'
- 'Use some of my ideas.'
- 'Let us finish.'

# Drama, Thinking and Talk

## ■ In this chapter we consider:

- the curriculum link between speaking, listening and drama;

- drama as a context for meaningful talk for different purposes and of inter-thinking;

- the teacher as a dialogic partner and model in role;

- the rules of talking and thinking together in and out of drama;

- what pupils say about drama and talk;

- how different drama strategies can be used to scaffold and support talk for different purposes and enable processing time;

- a possible cognitive and affective vocabulary for stages of the drama process.

> *'Language is a flexible toolkit for collective thought... an inter-thinking tool!... We create a Megabrain by linking ourselves together and the whole is greater than the sum of its parts...'*
>
> Neil Mercer ('New Perspectives on Spoken English in the Classroom', QCA conference, 2002) ■

> *'It is by combining talk and action with thought that children, especially young children, most effectively learn.'*
>
> Robin Alexander (2000) ■

Drama within the present national curriculum has been placed within 'speaking and listening' as an aspect of English. Most dramas involve spoken language both in their devising and in presentation. The drama lesson is a forum for talk and a socially mediated activity within which language is a key means of sharing and shaping thinking. It also is a forum in which talk can be integrated or juxtaposed with image, movement and sound.

The teacher scaffolds a range of opportunities for talk throughout drama lessons and is able to offer a range of purposes for talk in and out of role, in different size groups and in a variety of imagined contexts. The teacher is also able to be a talking partner, a mediator and a model for talk within and about the drama. The use of language by teachers and the language interactions between pupils and teachers is of key importance in drama lessons.

Language is both a means of social communication and a tool for cognitive development. Communication and cognitive skills are being developed within the social, whole-class drama lesson. The teacher's use of language both inside and outside the drama, plays a vital role in enabling and supporting the pupil's own use of language and can support, challenge and extend their inter- and intra-thinking – in other words, their internal and shared thinking. The drama teacher is able, through taking on roles him/herself, to offer an enormous variety of models of speech, to encourage verbal interaction and 'dialogic talk' and to use different types of language for a wide range of purposes. Drama gives children unique collective opportunities to talk as either themselves or 'as if' they are other people in imagined familiar or unfamiliar settings for a multiplicity of imagined purposes. Language is not only a way of communicating thinking, it is a means of exploring and clarifying it and is itself a medium and shaper of thought.

The Russian psychologist Vygotsky (1978) suggested in the 1970s that language helps us to learn to think in various ways as well as to communicate. He suggested that 'intermental' experiences influence the ways in which individuals think 'intramentally', that thinking together influenced individuals' thought. He also suggested that verbal interactions between learners with supportive and knowledgeable members of the child's community will influence significantly the development of thinking. That community today could perhaps be taken to include communities of enquiry such as those that drama is able to offer, and supportive members could include teachers.

Talking together enables 'inter-thinking'. Neil Mercer has been leading a team at the Open University since the late 1980s, which has been investigating children's collaborative talk. Teachers have been active participants in this research, which has been mainly focused on Key Stage 2. The early research studied children's collaborative speech during computer based problem solving but the research has been extended into different curriculum areas, including English. Observation and analysis revealed that children's talk in groups without any supporting framework was not very productive. They were not very likely to engage with ideas in any sustained way, share information well or reason. Incidences of exploratory talk were low.

> 'In exploratory talk:
>
> ☐ pupils and teachers engage constructively with each others' ideas;
> ☐ contributions build on previous comments;
> ☐ relevant information is offered for joint consideration;
> ☐ there is speculation;
> ☐ people give reasons for their views and seek them from others;
> ☐ reasoning is visible in the talk.
>
> Additionally:
>
> ☐ proposals may be challenged but reasons given
>    and alternatives offered;
> ☐ knowledge is made publicly accountable.'
>
> **Neil Mercer ('New Perspectives on Spoken English in the Classroom',
> QCA conference, 2002)**

What Mercer suggests certainly rings true in relation to exploratory talk within role play corners. The children's talk is not likely to be sustained and particularly productive without an empathetic adult who is able to listen, interact verbally in make-believe, model, guide and support sustained talk. This same adult role as dialogic partner is taken forward into drama lessons.

The 'Thinking Together Project' (DfES, 2002) aimed to enable children to become better 'inter-thinkers' and to enable teachers to teach inter-thinking. A programme of 'thinking together' lessons was developed and implemented. These involved an agreed contract, or ground rules for talk, which are very similar to those of drama.

'Thinking together' ground rules for talk are that everyone should:

> □ *'be actively encouraged to contribute;*
> □ *offer opinions and ideas;*
> □ *provide reasons for their opinions and ideas;*
> □ *share all relevant information;*
> □ *feel free to disagree if they have a good reason;*
> □ *ask other people for information and reasons;*
> □ *treat other people's ideas with respect;*
> □ *try to come to an agreement;*
> □ *change their minds if they are persuaded by good reasoning.'*
>
> *Additionally:*
>
> □ *'everyone must look and listen to the person who is talking.'*
>
> **Neil Mercer ('New Perspectives on Spoken English in the Classroom',
> QCA conference, 2002)**

There are clear links to be made not only with drama ground rules but also with those for P4C and circle time. All are based on active listening and collaborative talking and therefore it is not surprising that very similar rules apply. A key difference between the rules above and those of the drama contract (see page 84) are that in drama children are not always actively encouraged to contribute so much as given opportunity. Another difference of course is that, within drama, spoken ideas and thoughts are attributed to the minds of the characters being portrayed rather than the mind of the person voicing them.

Mercer's research (1999 and 2002) suggests that children can be supported to become more able to use language as a tool for solitary and creative thinking.

What is required is:

■ involvement in thoughtful and reasoned dialogue;

■ conversational partners as models of language;

■ practice using language to reason, reflect, enquire and to explain their thinking to others.

Whole-class drama provides a forum that can and usually does meet each and all of the above requirements.

## ■ Pupils' voices on drama and talk

The links between drama, talk, thinking and confidence are to be found through the voices of pupils in Harland's research on the arts (2000).

'I used to be nervous of talking to people... but having drama... because it's something where the teacher has to work a lot with the pupils, whereas the sciences it's teaching, with drama it's not facts, it's what you do, so it's got to be more of a relationship. So that's helped quite a lot because I can now speak to people in authority and teachers and I suppose it has made me more confident in general.'
(Year 11)

'You have to learn to think before speaking.'
(Year 8)

'Drama helps you talk with more people and not be scared to express yourself.'
(Year 7)

'There's a lot of communication involved. If you can't communicate with someone, there's no drama basically and so communication is probably the most important thing in drama.'
(Year 11)

'You can talk and speak your mind and stuff and you can do all sort of things that you wanted to do in drama, even if you are not actually playing yourself, but you can get things out in different ways in drama.'
(Year 9)

'I used to be dead quiet. Now I am dead loud and am not scared to ask teachers things and tell them what I think of things. I never used to, but now [since drama] I tell them if it is not good, or if I don't agree with something.'
(Year 9)

## ■ Drama strategies for sharing thinking out loud

*'Developing thinking requires that children are given the time and opportunity to talk about thinking processes, to make their own thought processes more explicit, thus enabling them to clarify and reflect upon their strategies and gain more self-control.'*

*Carol McGuinness (1999)* ■

Several drama strategies invite participants to share out loud their thinking in role at particular moments within the drama – for example, Thought-tracking (pages 123–124) and Conscience Alley (pages 119–122). This is nothing new in drama. Soliloquies are a well-established device through which characters are able to make public their innermost thoughts. At any point in a drama the teacher may freeze the action and pass by the still participants in turn in order to give them the opportunity to speak aloud their individual character's thoughts.

■ The teacher may gather the class into a circle and place a key character in the middle, inviting the children to enter the space and place themselves in relation to the character in a way that indicates what they think and feel about the character. This can be accompanied by thoughts spoken aloud or by a single utterance to the character. Mismatches between thoughts and utterances may emerge and be explored for motive.

■ At moments when a key character has to make an important decision in a drama the class can be invited to give the conflicting thoughts of the character (see pages 120–121).

■ The class may brainstorm collectively a character's thoughts in a random 'stream of consciousness' style. Some of the character's key thoughts may then be recorded in a thought bubble coming from an outline of the character (see *Resource Sheet 4*).

## ■ Developing a cognitive and affective language for drama

The language and vocabulary used with and by pupils and teachers within drama lessons is important and can shape not only the drama experience itself but the articulation of the experience. The table below offers some 'thinking' and 'feeling' vocabulary that can be used at different stages of the drama process. It links to a task suggested within the Key Stage 3 National Training Materials (DfES, 2002) and is an extension of this task adapted to fit drama.

| Stages | Possible words |
| --- | --- |
| 1. collecting information or ideas or responding to stimulus | respond, imagine, tell, remember, interpret, find, name, suggest, identify |
| 2. generating ideas and questions | explore, question, predict, explain, imagine, create, visualize, suggest, define |
| 3. **making** and devising the drama | invent, imagine, create, visualize, experiment, adapt, suggest, metaphor, structure, select, justify, combine, interrelate, construct, shape, mould, transform, compose, prioritize, explain, express, predict, communicate, interpret, re-interpret, enact, characterize, narrate, reflect |
| 4. refining and presenting or **performing** | reorganize, analyse, combine, adapt, synthesize, justify, demonstrate, rehearse, show, create, present, re-present, enact, re-enact, perform, convey, express, narrate |
| 5. **responding** | reflect, imagine, predict, identify |
| 6. evaluating | compare, contrast, interpret and re-interpret meaning, analyse, judge, summarize, critique, recommend, tell, assess, grade |

*Words in bold are terms considered by the Arts Council to define the stages of drama.*

## ■ Questioning

Teachers' questions within drama, as within any lesson, have a range of functions and purposes and are key to the teaching and development of thinking.

Sometimes a question will be:

■ □ *intended to assess what children know or understand*

'What do you think has been the most important moment so far in our drama?'

'What made you decide to play that character in the way that you did?'

■ □ *linked to finding out more about what the pupils are doing*

■ □ *linked to classroom management*

'Can you be ready to show your freeze-frames in one minute?'

'What might we find when we get to the village?'

■ □ *to stimulate the child's imagination*
Invite children to wonder about a range of possible answers, rather than to seek existing single answers

'Why have you come to this village?'

■ □ *intended to create and find out more about a character*

Asking questions of children who are in role is one method of deepening their engagement with their role. They are required to think a little more deeply about responding appropriately as a character. They also make public their commitment to the drama through their response in role.

Teachers are familiar with the categorizing of questions as either 'open' or 'closed'. Closed questions invite a limited answer and are often linked to recalling information – for example, 'What is the name of this village?', whereas an open question is aimed at eliciting a more discursive and elaborate response – for example, 'What might be happening in this picture?'. The words 'What might?' or 'What could?' give significantly different messages to a child than 'What is?'. The former invite a plurality of ideas and responses whereas the latter suggests that there is a particular answer that the teacher is seeking from the children and that the teacher already knows the answer. There are times when closed questions are necessary and most appropriate and times when open questions are more useful. What needs to be considered is the form and the function of the question in relation to teacher intention and pupil thinking.

The teacher needs to be aware of the range and purposes of questions and then be attentive to the pupil responses so that they can shape the next question in order to promote deeper or broader thought. This is true of questioning both in and out of drama lessons. In drama however the questions can be asked by the teacher as a fictitious character, which can liberate pupils to reply more freely as characters themselves and shift the status of the questioner. For example, instead of the teacher asking the child a question, in a drama it can be the mayor of the village (high status teacher in role) asking the villagers (children in role) a question and the next moment it can be the prisoner (low status teacher in role) asking questions of the same villagers.

## ■ Bloom's taxonomy

In the 1950s Benjamin Bloom researched teachers' questions and linked them to the following linear order of thinking skills.

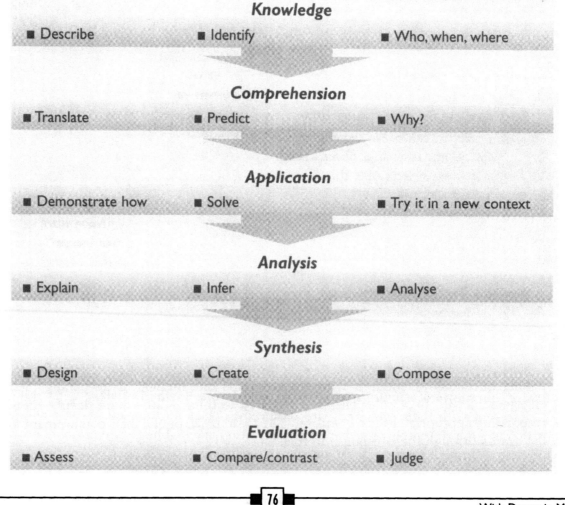

**Knowledge**

■ Describe          ■ Identify          ■ Who, when, where

**Comprehension**

■ Translate          ■ Predict          ■ Why?

**Application**

■ Demonstrate how          ■ Solve          ■ Try it in a new context

**Analysis**

■ Explain          ■ Infer          ■ Analyse

**Synthesis**

■ Design          ■ Create          ■ Compose

**Evaluation**

■ Assess          ■ Compare/contrast          ■ Judge

Most teachers' questions are to do with finding out what children know and understand – Bloom's first two categories, Knowledge and Comprehension. The last four categories (Application, Analysis, Synthesis and Evaluation) are those linked more specifically with higher order thinking skills, which are linked with higher pupil achievement and attainment. Within drama lessons many questions and activities link to the last four categories as process drama is open ended and involves entering a fiction in which most things are unknown and open to being created through negotiation and exploration. It involves creating and devising fictions and performances and evaluating them as participants and observers. The first two categories are more closely aligned to straightforward re-enactments of existing fictions.

Robin Alexander (2000) has carried out research on oracy and pedagogy and has studied the communicative processes in teaching and learning in England, France, India, Russia and the United States. He observed that teachers usually talked more than pupils in lessons but that the quality and purpose of the talk was important and varied considerably in different classrooms and countries. In England he suggests that speaking and listening (within which drama is placed) 'looks like an afterthought'.

Alexander found that different types of questions could elicit very different responses qualitatively, both in terms of length of response and the amount of reflection contained within the response. The most effective interactions were described by Alexander as 'dialogic talk' which was characterized by both pupils and teachers contributing significantly. During these interactions the pupils' own thinking and ideas on an issue or theme were moved forward by the teacher's questioning, which encouraged thoughtful reasoning. Dialogic talk is both possible and effective with groups and whole classes and is highly characteristic of good whole-class drama lessons. Drama also naturally combines action, thought and talk, which, according to Robin Alexander, enables the most effective learning.

## ■ Modelling questioning

When teachers ask questions of pupils, they are modelling different ways of asking questions and can draw attention to, and analyse with the children, the links between the different types of questions and usefulness of the elicited response. They can ask sequences of questions as a character within a drama that enable, support and extend thinking. They can shift characters and ask the same again of the children or ask different questions. An advantage of drama is that it has at its heart what we are now referring to as 'dialogic teaching'.

## ■ Pupils' questioning

> 'Posing very challenging questions is pointless unless we also consider the responses which such questions provoke and how these responses can be built on. To paraphrase Bakhtin: if an answer does not give rise to a new question, then it and the question which provoked it, and the ideas which they contain, are all lost.'
>
> *Robin Alexander (2000)* ■

**PART ONE**

Drama offers structured opportunities for pupils to ask and to practise formulating and asking questions. They are sometimes the questioners and sometimes the respondents in the same drama. Again, certain drama strategies lend themselves directly as a means of scaffolding questions (see also Part Two).

### Hot-seating

Hot-seating enables the class to ask questions of a particular character from within the drama, usually for a limited time (see pages 112–113). The character answering the questions may be played by the teacher, or a child, or even played as a collective role by several people (see page 80). The character usually sits in a chair or 'hot-seat' to be questioned. This activity can be structured so that others may take over as the character being questioned by sitting in the hot-seat that belongs to that character. This encourages active listening and collaborative talk.

Through hot-seating, pupils' questions can be rehearsed, evaluated and refined in the following ways:

- Prior to the 'arrival' of the character in the hot-seat the teacher can invite the children to consider or 'rehearse' in advance what questions they might ask of the character who will soon be hot-seated. What might they ask the character when they arrive?

- Pupils' questions for the character can be written on sentence strips or Post-its and shared for consideration and discussion.

- If the children can only ask one question each, how will they phrase their only question in such a way as to ensure that they gather as much information as possible about the character? This gives time to formulate a question well and consider what is worth asking.

- In groups of about four, with each child having already prepared a question to ask the character, they can then be told that the character will now only answer one question from each group. Together, the group will need to decide and justify which question from among the group to keep and which to discard. This encourages evaluation through sharing of questions and comparing, contrasting and sharing the thinking behind their questions.

The activities above encourage children to consider carefully the value, content and purpose of their own questions before asking them. The drama strategy of Hot-seating enables them to then have immediate and direct feedback once a question is asked from the character. The answers are accepted and feed the emerging drama.

- Questions can be written inside large, empty, individual, group or class question marks as a kind of 'question log' or put on Post-its and stuck around an outline of the character to whom the questions link (see page 116).

- Drama also offers still images and freeze-frames (see page 100) within which the characters can be brought to life and questioned by an audience. This enables questioning of characters at specific key moments to reveal their thoughts, views and standpoints.

## ■ Core questions to review and guide the drama

At different points in a drama there are three core questions that are often asked of the participants in relation to the characters and events at a particular moment in time. (See Resource Sheet 7b.) At this point in the drama:

**1.**
**What DO we know?**
This question invites referential responses and requires recall skills – for example, 'A stranger has arrived in the village. He arrived in a red van.'

**2.**
**What do we THINK we know?**
This requires children to recall, think analytically and infer – for example, 'The stranger arrived alone (as no companion has been seen or mentioned). He is here for a reason but we do not know that reason yet.'

**3.**
**What do we WANT to know?**
This requires curiosity and imagination and leads to further questions – for example, 'Why has the stranger come? What does he want? Is he really alone? Where has he come from? What will he do next? Is he to be trusted?'

These three core questions will give the teacher information about what the children know and can recall, how much they are able to infer from what they know and where the children's imaginations and interests in the drama lie. Asking the above questions gives the teacher information and can create assessment and thinking time in which to decide what strategies to select to scaffold the next part of the drama. Asking children 'What do we want to know?' at different points in a drama gives the teacher a continuous awareness of the children's interests in relation to the drama and whether, as the drama evolves, these interests are shifting. This can then guide the teacher as to where to focus and how to structure the drama next in order to maintain the children's motivation and engagement.

Keeping the drama flowing within the children's areas of interest gives important messages to them. It demonstrates that their opinions, questions and ideas are valid and listened to. It signals that they share the ownership of the drama. They realize that their responses are guiding and influencing the drama and that they are not simply being asked to act out an existing story that the teacher has decided in advance. They get the message that it is worth their carrying on having and sharing their ideas and questions as they are valued and used!

### Hands down

Within drama lessons children are not normally required to put their hands up to ask or answer questions within the drama as the drama strategies give all an opportunity to respond and normally involve turn taking. Raising hands to ask or answer teachers' questions in role is not usually appropriate and indicates that the children are not sufficiently engaged with their role. If the teacher is pretending not to be the teacher then they have no need to put their hands up.

## Clap out

Most drama strategies have built-in processing time in which children can think through their individual or collective responses to questions or formulate their own questions. They also are invited and not pressured to answer or pose questions and can 'clap out' or pass if they do not feel able or comfortable with the situation.

## Shared answers

Through collective role it is possible to elicit group answers to teachers' questions – for example, the teacher asks a group of children a question as if they are one character and anyone in the group may answer as the character being questioned. They need to actively listen to each other in order to ensure that the collective response links together coherently. They may speak in a given order or randomly, according to the way that the teacher feels the activity needs to be set up for any particular group. (The following example is based on *Drama Unit 1*.)

> **Teacher:** Mr Once upon a Time, will you please change your name?
> *(Teacher sets up a closed question which is not particularly demanding.)*
>
> **Child 1:** No, I don't want to. *(Closed response.)*
>
> **Teacher:** Why not? Can you explain?
> *(Teacher increases the challenge and asks for verbal reasoning.)*
>
> **Child 2:** Because it is the name my mother gave me and it belongs to me.
> *(Child gives logical reasons which indicates an affective response.)*
>
> **Child 3:** And I would still think I was Mr Once Upon a Time inside my head, whatever you called me. *(Child gives a logical, cognitive response.)*
>
> **Teacher:** What do you think might happen in the future if you do not agree to change your name? *(Encourages prediction and the linking of cause and effect.)*
>
> **Child 4:** How would you like it if someone said you had to change your name?
> *(Child either does not listen or else chooses to support Child 3 in evading the question or else just wants to respond and redirects the drama through answering a question with a question.)*
>
> **Teacher:** Well it would depend if I thought that there was a good reason for it... and there are good reasons why you should change your name. Can you think what they might be?
> *(Teacher listens, does not reject what the child says but refocuses through another question in order to maintain the focus on encouraging verbal reasoning.)*

The teacher is acting as a lynchpin, listening to what the children say, trying to signal that they are being listened to, while retaining the focus on encouraging them to reason verbally. As the children are all representing the same character they are also having to listen well in order to not repeat themselves or break the flow.

## Speaking object

Sometimes an object can be passed around that empowers whoever is holding it to ask questions of another character (who may be in a hot-seat – see pages 111–113).

# PART TWO

## Structuring the Drama Experience

- **The Drama Contract**

- **Drama Strategies – Choosing and Using**

  *Teacher in Role*

  *Still Image and Freeze-frame*

  *Mantle of the Expert*

  *Hot-seating*

  *Role on the Wall*

  *Conscience Alley*

  *Thought-tracking*

  *Eavesdropping*

  *Rumours*

  *Collective Role*

  *Improvisation*

  *Small Group Playmaking*

  *Forum Theatre*

  *Teacher as Storyteller and Storymaker*

  *Ritual*

  *Other Drama Strategies*

# **T**he **D**rama **C**ontract

Before you embark on drama activities and lessons it is wise to establish some ground rules with the children. Drama in education is a social learning activity that relies on and develops co-operation and a respect for others' viewpoints and contributions. As with any class activity involving groups or a whole class working together, it is necessary to make behavioural and procedural expectations clear at the outset in a purposeful and positive way. In drama we can draw up a drama contract with the children, who will want to know what is expected of them in terms of the operational drama rules and their contributions to the drama. Clear expectations enable participants to feel secure about what it is they are entering into and relaxed enough to contribute.

Good drama teaching and learning is underpinned by generic principles associated with all good teaching and learning. In drama the teacher can make these principles explicit to the class through the drama contract which is agreed with them. The drama contract may link to other class contracts that already exist in relation to behaviour and discipline but it should ideally also be established in its own right. It may be very similar to existing circle time contracts, which are rooted in the principles of socio-drama (see page 42).

(see page 42)

A drama contract benefits from being drawn up with the children rather than just given to them. The more ownership the children have of the contract, the more likely they are to adhere to it. Children know what stops drama from working well and what enables it to work well and be sustained because they understand how dramatic play works. It is worth reminding children that they are skilled at dramatic play as the principles of drama in education (which also involves creating make-believe worlds with others and operating within them) are the same.

Set positively as a contract in the voice of a child a drama contract might include the points on the following page.

**PART TWO**

# The Drama Contract

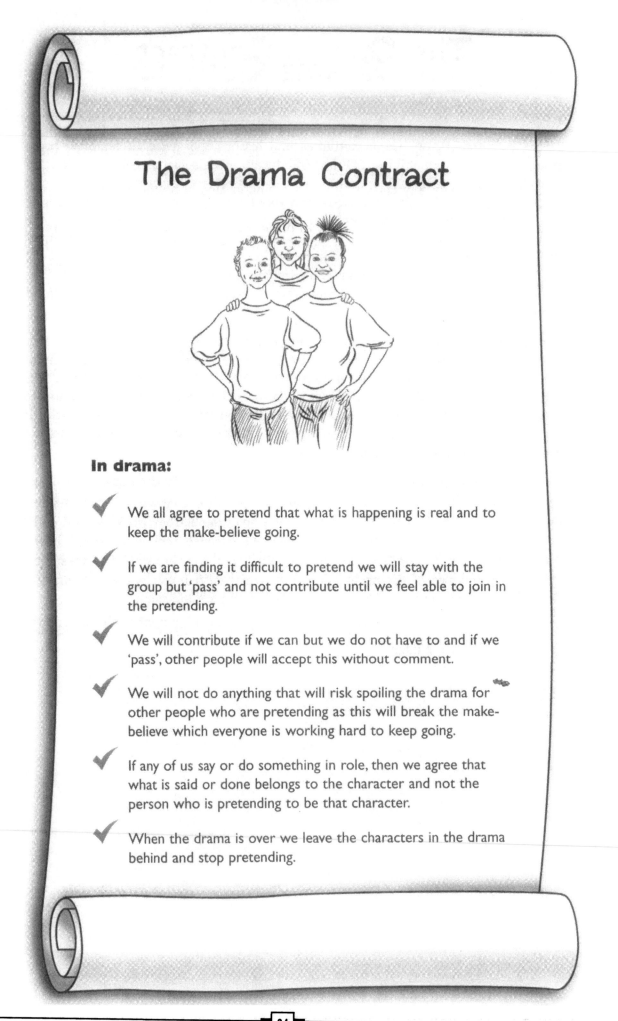

## In drama:

✓ We all agree to pretend that what is happening is real and to keep the make-believe going.

✓ If we are finding it difficult to pretend we will stay with the group but 'pass' and not contribute until we feel able to join in the pretending.

✓ We will contribute if we can but we do not have to and if we 'pass', other people will accept this without comment.

✓ We will not do anything that will risk spoiling the drama for other people who are pretending as this will break the make-believe which everyone is working hard to keep going.

✓ If any of us say or do something in role, then we agree that what is said or done belongs to the character and not the person who is pretending to be that character.

✓ When the drama is over we leave the characters in the drama behind and stop pretending.

**Class drama will not work well if:**

✖ certain individuals are allowed to hog the drama and dominate, thus preventing the inclusion of others;

✖ children feel an unacceptable level of vulnerability and are at risk of being put down, excluded or mocked by others;

✖ the ideas and contributions of any of the children are made unwelcome or ignored by the teacher and/or the class;

✖ the subject matter of the drama itself is not interesting or as relevant to the participants;

✖ the children are not stimulated and have no initial hook into the drama or if they become bored as the drama progresses;

✖ the tasks set by the teacher are too challenging (stressful or confusing) or not challenging enough (boring), in other words they are not well matched to the skills, interests and aptitudes of the participants;

✖ the teacher is using the children as his/her drama puppets and is pushing them into his/her own drama without offering them any ownership or stake in the drama;

✖ the teacher is not listening to or valuing the children's thoughts and ideas and the children are not listening to or valuing each other's contributions;

✖ the teacher communicates a lack of confidence and competence in drama or an embarrassment about working in role;

✖ the teacher him/herself is not committed to the drama and does not engage with and take the drama seriously.

PART **TWO**

# Drama Strategies – Choosing and Using

*'The creative process of the arts involves developing forms of expression which embody the artist's perceptions. This is not a matter of identifying an idea and then finding a form in which to express it. It is through shaping the individual work that the ideas and feelings are given form. Often it is only through developing the dance, image or music that the perception itself is clarified.'*

**NACCCE (1999)** ■

*'Drama in schools and youth theatres only occurs when students experience the content and the form together as one and when the art of theatre is felt and understood within the context of the work being explored.'*

**David Booth in the foreword to Jonothan Neelands (1990)** ■

Drama as an art form has an associated methodology that brings with it an infinitely adaptable set of scaffolding tools called drama strategies or conventions. These support children to participate and think together and to create their own dramas as well as to explore and understand existing dramas and stories.

Each drama strategy can be seen as an active and often interactive, thinking frame, which simultaneously makes cognitive, affective and aesthetic demands on the pupils. When teachers are aware of what type of thinking they wish to foster and know how different strategies work, they can become increasingly skilled at selecting and adapting the most effective and engaging strategies for supporting and developing thinking and learning. Different types and levels of individual, group and whole-class thinking can be specifically practised, developed and expressed.

Drama in education is a medium through which the children's own thoughts, feelings, emotions and creativity can be communicated and understood through aesthetic forms. It also enables access to the thinking of others. The skilled drama teacher is an empathetic adult, who selects drama strategies to scaffold and support thinking and learning in and through an established art form.

There is a range of well-established drama strategies with which many non-drama teachers are already partly familiar. Many teachers already make use of a few well-known drama strategies, such as Hot-seating and Freeze-frame. Often teachers have become aware of these strategies when they have been used within courses on circle time, PSHE, Philosophy for Children, literacy, management and so on. For example, Mantle of the Expert is increasingly being used in a way isolated from the full drama toolbox by a rising number of teachers of Philosophy for Children. However, a growing awareness of drama strategies by many teachers has kindled an increasing interest in drama itself among non-drama specialist teachers, particularly among those wishing to enliven their teaching.

Often a lack of awareness of the flexibility and potential of drama strategies, and a lack of understanding of drama as a whole, results in strategies being used or misused as single activity ingredients which are not combined in a way that produces a fine drama 'cake'. Used outside the context of drama lessons, 'stand alone' drama strategies provide very effective thinking frames that can be used to develop discrete thinking skills. However, drama strategies are most powerful when used coherently as part of an unfolding, sustained drama and fiction making process that offers ownership to the children.

Drama strategies should be carefully selected according to the teacher's learning intentions and purpose. A heightened awareness of the ways in which different children learn best, the ways in which their brains work most effectively and the different types of thinking that teachers are trying to develop, can all influence the choice and suitability of a strategy.

## ■ Drama strategies as 'brain-friendly' thinking frames

Within the creative drama process there is the opportunity for teachers to focus on enabling their pupils to use, develop and apply a range of thinking skills while working in a multi-intelligent and multisensory way. Drama strategies enable access to a variety of visual, auditory and kinesthetic learning experiences and provide a flexible framework for visual, auditory and kinesthetic modes of expression.

Drama strategies enable:

■ thinking to be internal and/or communicated through shared aesthetic form;

■ characters and events to be devised and developed by individuals, groups and the whole class and then to be held still for investigation and reflection;

■ a consideration of characters' motives in relation to actions and events;

■ pupils to become aware of and consider actions and events from their own viewpoints and those of their devised characters;

■ key moments and events to be actively and interactively revisited, reviewed and reconsidered with reflective hindsight;

■ the thoughts and actions of characters in scenes to be revealed, explored and challenged by participants and/or audience;

■ the disparities between characters' thoughts and utterances and their thoughts and actions to be communicated;

■ conflicting thoughts/feelings of the same character to be opened up for consideration;

■ cause and effect, action and consequence, to be explicitly considered through bringing alive alternative scenarios;

■ visual, auditory and kinesthetic communication and expression of the children's own ideas and collective imaginations, thoughts and understandings;

■ the participants to be at one with the action through role play, in the imagined 'here and now';

■ safe distancing through the adoption of role and form;

■ pupils and teachers to engage simultaneously on a cognitive and affective level at moments of cognitive conflict and shift.

PART TWO

## ■ Selecting strategies

The drama teacher is alongside the pupils as the drama unfolds and is a co-participant in the shared thinking and drama process at key moments. The teacher will sometimes opt in to the drama in role as a fellow participant, organizing and facilitating the drama from within, and will sometimes come out of role, to organize and manage the lesson through introducing strategies as the drama teacher. The drama strategies are the teacher's devices that enable pupil engagement and reflection, holding moments still for feeling, thinking and learning.

Teachers selecting strategies might consider:

■ which character or what event or moment they want the children to focus attention on;

■ the type of thinking skill that they are trying to use and develop;

■ whether the children have been static or moving for some time;

■ whether the drama needs to move forward plot-wise or go deeper –
whether to support a free-flow of ideas for possible development or narrow and deepen the pupils' thinking focus at a particular moment;

■ the drama linked capabilities and prior drama experience of the individuals and different groups of children;

■ the degree of support and structure required for individuals and different groups of pupils to succeed;

■ the overall balance of the lesson's activities in relation to visual, auditory and kinesthetic experience, learning and expression;

■ whether the strategies balance in terms of multisensory experiences;

■ a balance of opportunities to work individually, in groups and as a whole class;

■ their familiarity with the strategy;

■ the sound level of the previous activity;

■ the energy levels required in the previous activity;

■ whether groupings need to be changed;

■ whether the strategy is well matched to the source material;

■ whether the strategy can be differentiated for different groups of pupils;

■ whether the strategy needs to support and enable contrast;

■ whether the pupils need to deepen or lessen engagement at this point in the drama;

■ whether equality of opportunity to participate actively is possible for all pupils within the overall lesson;

■ whether there has been a balance of silence and sound, stillness and movement, tension and release, action and reflection.

Drama teachers develop a keen professional sense as to when they should adapt or completely change strategies, shifting the activity or pace, providing continuity or contrast in order to keep pupils interested, motivated and on task. This is true of good teaching generally but in drama the strategies used to do this are drama strategies requiring engagement with a role and a fiction.

For example:

■ If the pupils are new to working in drama then the teacher might select a very secure and non-threatening drama strategy that gives opportunity for pupils to work individually or alone without speech and without an audience, for example, silent occupational mime in a space of their choice.

■ If the pupils have been standing still for a while (Conscience Alley, for example) then the next strategy might be selected to enable movement (for example, Rumours).

■ If the children have been given a restricted opportunity to speak – for example, Thought-tracking in turn, then the next strategy may be selected to give opportunity for more flowing speech – perhaps Improvisation or Small Group Playmaking.

■ If the last strategy has been one involving group-work, for example group Freeze-frame, then maybe the next one will be selected to encourage and enable individual responses – Improvisation or Thought-tracking perhaps.

■ If the children are working too noisily, then the next strategy might be one that involves calming them down through silence, such as guided visualization (with eyes closed).

■ If children are not working well together or one child needs to be shared out, then the next strategy might require new groups – for example, go from group freeze-frames to different groups for Small Group Playmaking.

■ If the drama needs to stay at the same moment in time then the teacher might use Thought-tracking but if they want to move it forward they might use Small Group Playmaking to find out what happens next.

All the strategies mentioned above are explained later in Part Two.

There are times when drama needs to move forward. Young children left to their own devices in drama tend to enact storylines at speed, with little depth and sustained thought. Teachers gauge when to let the drama move forward and when to hold it still to support the processing of information. Drama strategies enable participants to stay in role at a moment in time and to deconstruct what is happening, analyse and reflect upon it, make meaning of it and move on (or back again) with renewed understanding and new perspectives.

Key moments are 'held still' to:

■ enable moments to be recognized as significant in relation to the bigger picture (the whole drama thus far);

■ to be given visual, auditory and kinesthetic (VAK) form to ensure that they are tagged to aid memory through the language, visual processing and spatial memory centres of the brain;

■ allow them to be analysed, discussed, investigated, developed or reflected upon (in or out of role);

■ enable them to be 'owned' or 'co-owned' by the participants;

■ enable the moment to be presented for interpretation by different audiences;

■ allow time for connection with other moments through sequencing or juxtaposition;

■ enable them to be explored in relation to the thoughts, utterances and motives of characters;

PART TWO

- enable empathy and appreciation of different characters' viewpoints;
- enable the abstraction of multi-layered meaning and inference;
- allow them to be constructed, deconstructed and reconstructed in a multiplicity of ways for a range of purposes;
- enable them to be more easily remembered;
- allow time for personal and shared response and reflection.

## ■ Drama strategies support free-flow or focused thoughts

Through drama strategies, teachers are able to offer varying degrees of freedom and constraint to the participants at different points in the drama process. Both freedom and constraint of thought at appropriate points are essential to the creative process. At times a diverse flow of ideas needs to be stimulated and enabled and at other times the creative process demands narrowly focused thought. Although different strategies might seem to more obviously support and enable free-flow or constrained thought, it is over-simplistic to assume that Improvisation will always support a free-flow of ideas and Thought-tracking will always give a constrained focus. Too much freedom at the wrong point can immobilize thought, and Thought-tracking can give rise to a stream of thoughts.

Teachers need to be sensitive to the pupils' creativity at different stages of the drama process, introducing or adapting the basic strategies to free them up or support them as necessary. Of course teachers get better at this with practice and experience. This inter-reactive sensitivity is of course an aspect of good teaching not just of good drama teaching. Teachers starting out on drama need to do so with a basic understanding of drama strategies, what they are called, how to introduce them to pupils and how the strategies might be adapted to ensure that they promote, use and develop the pupils' creative and critical thinking.

## ■ Name the strategy

Children benefit from knowing and using the language of drama. Even with young children, teachers should name the strategies they are using and help them to build their conceptual map of that strategy in action. If children know the specific names of the different strategies, then they become sufficiently familiar with them and in time they will be able to refer to the strategies within the context of creating and devising their own dramas. Specialist language is empowering and specific subject language enables common conceptual and operational understandings to be developed early. Before the advent of the Literacy Hour, children would have had no idea what was entailed in a 'plenary' but this word now carries a host of associated organizational, procedural and conceptual understandings for most primary schoolchildren.

If children are made aware of what is basically expected organizationally in relation to specific named strategies, this will save a considerable amount of the teacher's 'setting up' time. If the teacher says 'I'd like us to set up a Conscience Alley now so that we can find out what contradictory thoughts might be running through this character's head at this moment', no time needs to be spent on operational instructions about getting into two straight lines facing each other and leaving about a metre between the lines and so on. No instruction is necessary about when each person will have their opportunity to speak. The children will know what carrying out a Conscience Alley involves and can set it up with little, if any, prompting. The teacher may decide to introduce adaptations from time to time but what is basically expected from them will already be clearly understood.

## ■ Link the strategies to what the children already know and understand

Most children's understanding of dramas will come from television and videos. Teachers can use this knowledge to assist in the teaching of drama and to help children understand strategies such as Freeze-frame and techniques such as flashback, slow motion and so on. Children soon understand that strategies are a bit like video buttons. Different strategies enable the drama to be held still, moved slowly forward or backwards, fast forwarded or rewound quickly to the start.

Children can also be led to see themselves in drama as makers of fiction, as film makers and editors of their own dramas. By using different drama strategies as if they were editing tools the soundtrack of their drama scenes can be turned down or edited. Scenes can be re-scripted, re-filmed or replayed. Images can be altered and enhanced.

Drama strategies enable the teacher to ensure that all the children (and the teacher) remain within and can contribute to one, whole-class Big Picture drama. Everyone is enabled through the developing structure of various strategies, to create and contribute to the whole – to the Big Picture of the evolving class drama.

## ■ Play with the strategies

Drama strategies are infinitely adaptable and open to development by teachers. The more experienced and confident teachers become at using them, the more experimental they can feel about playing with them, honing them to suit their own class and their own teaching purposes. It is important as a teacher to be able to feel playful and creative. Reflective and experienced drama teachers can break free from the notion that they must follow drama strategies to the letter. A strategy is after all just that – and strategies evolve. Alert teachers are on a voyage of professional discovery in every lesson and are working on a level that is sensitive to the learners' thinking and understanding.

Experienced and innovative teachers will experiment with and personalize drama strategies, tailoring them according to their sense of what the children need next in order to move their thinking forward. They will notice the differences that any adjustments in the way they set up the selected drama strategies make in relation to what the children are able to offer. They will get a sense of when pupils' thinking is enabled to flow or is constrained by the way an activity has been set up or supported. They may even discuss the selection of the strategy with the children. Good teachers will notice when to shift up a gear and add stepped instructions that extend or link the strategies, thus increasing the challenge – for example: 'In a moment I am going to ask you to re-form that still image you made and this time I want you to speak in turn, out loud, the main thought of your character at this moment in the drama... Now I want you to imagine that your still image appears in a newspaper reporting this moment... Give a caption to your image in a way that will arouse sympathy.'

**PART TWO**

Strategies both encourage and depend on pupil engagement, co-operation and individual and/or shared thinking for their success. They also rely for their success on the teacher being well tuned-into the skills of the pupils in relation to the skills being demanded, and on an interactive and attentive awareness of the level of understanding and direction of thinking.

## ■ Set high expectations

When working with drama strategies make it very clear what your expectations are in relation to the various strategies and keep your expectations of children's attention and contributions challenging but safe. If you are asking for a still image, do not settle for less than the stillest image that the children can make. If a moment demands silence then do not accept sounds. If, after evaluation, the children feel that they can re-engage with, re-enact or replay a scene or moment more meaningfully or powerfully, then offer the opportunity. Drama is an art form, even when it is being used as a teaching and learning methodology, and the learning will be strengthened by attention to the form.

For children to learn through drama effectively they benefit from an understanding of how drama works most effectively. Drama strategies are a key element of this. Keep pupils working to a high standard, where they are aware of their own effort and that of others and the intrinsic reward that success through stretching oneself to the edge of a competence zone can bring. Let them feel how enhanced this experience is when it is a collective effort and success. Help the children to feel and see the difference in quality between drama experiences that are slapdash and half committed and those in which children are fully engaged and trying their hardest to make the experience as engaging and meaningful as possible for themselves and each other. But keep it enjoyable, high challenge and low stress, exciting but not frightening.

## ■ The drama strategies

The following pages set out a range of drama strategies, which can be used in their existing form or adapted to suit the needs of your teaching. They make reference to examples in the Drama Units in Part Three.

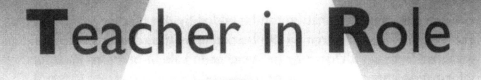

# Teacher in Role

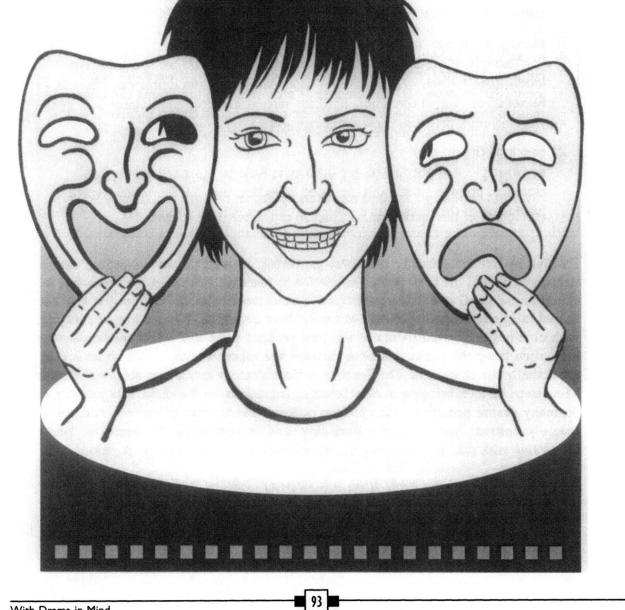

## ■ Through Teacher in Role you can:

■ **start the drama**
For example, the children meet a character (played by the teacher) who gives them information that immediately arouses the children's curiosity, gives rise to questions and opens up the fiction. (*Unit 1, Activity 6*)

■ **deepen the drama**
For example, the teacher in role challenges and questions the pupils as fellow participants within the unfolding drama, helping them to clarify, extend and deepen their thinking and to listen to and reflect upon another character's viewpoint. (*Unit 1, Activity 11*)

■ **develop the drama**
For example, new information can be added by the teacher in role or gathered from the children by the teacher in role in order to elicit further information about a character or event and to move the plot forward. (*Unit 4, Activity 5*)

■ **build, maintain or heighten dramatic tension**
For example, in order to create, stay with and make memorable, moments of significance in the drama. The teacher in role can generate excitement and create suspense. (*Unit 2, Activity 11*)

■ **manage pupil and class behaviour from within the fiction**
For example, 'Mr Once Upon a Time will hear our plans if we speak too loudly.' (*Unit 1, Activity 11*) The teacher as a character in the drama can offer reasons from within the drama itself for silence, full attention, quieter working, adult behaviour, new groupings and so on.

■ **conclude the drama**
For example, it is possible to use Teacher in Role to bring the drama to a close and provide guided and mediated reflection through the solitary voice (soliloquy) of the teacher as a reflective character. (*Unit 1, Activity 19*)

Teacher in Role is possibly the most powerful, interactive and engaging drama strategy of all and the most potent in relation to learning. It enables the teacher to be alongside the pupil as a fellow participant and interactive model and mediator of the shared imagined drama experience at moments of cognition. When adults are playing with children they often naturally slip into pretend roles and when reading stories they often bring the characters alive through the expressive use of voice, as if they are actually the characters. The Teacher in Role strategy formalizes this and takes it a few steps further, bringing in clear learning intentions for the child. It is possible to do many drama activities with children without the teacher going into role but it severely restricts the teacher's flexibility and effectiveness in terms of being interactive with children and shaping experiences at key moments of cognition.

Non-actors need not shy away from this strategy. Teacher in Role does not require the teacher to have significant acting ability. Indeed powerful acting performances by teachers can stun children into not joining in. First and foremost what is required is simply that teachers are willing and able to present a set of attitudes with seriousness and commitment as if they are someone else – to play at make-believe and pretend with their class in a serious way. If a teacher signals embarrassment or a 'we are all messing about together' approach to being in role with children, then the children will follow this lead. Worthwhile and engaging drama is unlikely to result. Conversely, if the teacher is clearly putting real effort into developing a role with integrity, then the children will have a positive role model on which to base their own role play and are likely to support their teacher and thereby the drama process.

Teachers working in role with clear commitment are less likely to have class control problems than those who demonstrate that they feel silly or awkward. An insecure teacher can make some pupils feel uncomfortable and their answer to this may be displacement activity, which throws the drama. However, teachers who can talk to their pupils honestly about any awkward feelings and enlist their support for Teacher in Role are more likely to get pupil support, saying for example' I want to try to be in the drama with you if that is all right with you all. I haven't tried this before and I am going to need your help to make this work. Are you willing to try this with me for a short while and help me?' Far better to try this approach than deny the opportunities and possibilities that Teacher in Role can bring.

The teacher in role presents herself as an imaginary character in the drama but is still in reality the teacher and can shape the drama from within as the character or from outside as the teacher. The teacher in role can be interactive, active or passive at moments of cognition and can choose to stay in role or withdraw from it, whichever is judged to be of greatest benefit to the learner at any moment.

## ■ How do I set up Teacher in Role?

The teacher can take a series of roles throughout a drama for a variety of purposes and can choose to relinquish or share her roles with other participants. If the teacher has signed the role through using a particular object – a hat, for example – then whoever wears the hat can assume the role for a while. The teacher can take the role back as necessary.

Roles need to be selected with care and the overall balance of the teacher's roles considered in terms of their purpose, frequency of duration and status, relative to the role status of the pupils.

Teachers need to ask themselves:

■ What am I trying to achieve with this role; what is its purpose in relation to both the pupils' learning and the drama?

■ What type of role is best matched to my purpose?

■ How will I make it clear to children when I am in or out of role?

■ For how long should I stay in role?

## ■ What am I trying to achieve with this role?

Teachers choose to go into role for different purposes at different points in an evolving drama. They may move in or out of the same role or change roles but must always make it clear to the children when they are in or out of role and who they are pretending to be.

## ■ What type of role is best matched to my purpose?

Roles can be defined in different ways. Most simply they can be seen as either information giving or information gathering.

■ *Information giving*
The teacher in role is giving information as a character, feeding ideas and shaping the direction of the emerging drama from within the role. (*Unit 4, Activity 11*)

■ *Information gathering*
The teacher in role is gathering the ideas of the children and remembering them in order to enable shared thinking. The teacher then welcomes and selects from the pupils' shared ideas, weaving them back into the emerging fiction and giving a clear message to the pupils that their ideas and thoughts are valued and used to shape and inform the drama. (*Unit 5, Activity 7*)

Teachers' roles can also be considered in relation to the relative status that they afford the pupil and teacher. Inexperienced teachers tend to cling to high status roles, for example the King, the Chief and so on. This makes the insecure teacher of drama feel understandably safer about using role without feeling that they are relinquishing class control. High status roles used repeatedly however can set up similar dynamics between pupils and the teacher as the more usual pupil/teacher relationship.

Trying out roles other than high status roles is a necessary and rewarding shift for the teacher of drama. The exploratory and creative possibilities of the drama will be greatly enhanced by varying the status of the teacher's role and thereby shifting the relative status of the pupil's role. Teachers need not feel unsafe about losing control of the class or appearing to do so. They can always come out of role whenever they wish and reassert themselves as the teacher as long as it is kept clear to the class when the teacher is entering or leaving his/her role.

■ *High status: for example, the Mill Owner*
(*Unit 2, Activity 10*)
This is the role of someone in charge. The role carries with it an expectation that the teacher in role will be obeyed. However this type of role can be intimidating and the children may feel restricted in their speech and actions. They may be predominantly obeying and responding to the dominant teacher in role, which may not be particularly demanding or enabling creatively. It is possible to play high status roles in a way that break down stereotypes – for example, the King who is hopeless at his job and reliant on his advisers (who therefore hold the real power).

■ *Mid-status: for example, the intermediary or the messenger from the government*
(*Unit 5, Activity 8*)
This is a useful role that teachers often take. The teacher is in role as the messenger or intermediary acting on behalf of the person in charge, who is not present. This is

a very versatile position to take, enabling the teacher to shift between being either at one with the children or at one with the absent authority. It enables the teacher to withdraw and return back and forth with new messages from their master, the one in authority. It allows the messenger to give or gather information from the children and give or gather information from the absent ruler. It enables the messenger to maintain a safe distance from any hostility to the ruler and to sympathize with the people. It enables the pupils to explain any feelings of hostility to the messenger without the messenger having to respond. It gives a reason for children to communicate messages clearly to a messenger who is only trying to carry accurate messages.

■ *Low status: for example, the person in need of help or the outsider*
Adopting a low status role in relation to children is often very rewarding and encouraging. It often yields very caring responses from them, such as talking or listening to the imprisoned Mr Once Upon a Time usually provokes sympathy and concern in children (*Unit 1, Activity 16*). The children know that the teacher is only pretending to need their help as a character but they feel for the character and are empowered through the drama to support their teacher as the character. The children in role feel needed by the teacher in role and feel that they are important and helpful. They are enabled to engage with the positive feeling of helping another person and this is particularly powerful when this person is the teacher as it is a reversal of the normal situation in which the teacher usually helps them.

■ *Equal status: for example, the teacher and pupils are all villagers together*
(*Unit 1, Activity 8*)
Taking on the same role as the children – all villagers with the same problem to solve for instance – is a levelling experience for both the class and the teacher. It frees the children and teacher up from the status quo, hierarchical, teacher-pupil relationship, enabling the children to treat the teacher in role as an equal partner within the drama. For example, when carrying out a problem-solving activity within the drama, the children's ideas are given the same value and space as the teacher's within the imagined forum.

## ■ How will I make it clear to children when I am in or out of role?

An easy way of presenting Teacher in Role to young children is by asking them if they would like to meet a character from a story that they know and then to tell them that for a little while you will be pretending to be that character (story-person). Check that they understand that you will be pretending before proceeding. You may say that you will only be pretending to be that character when you are sitting in a particular chair or holding a particular object. This is 'signing' the role. It needs to be very clear when you are in or out of role, just as it needs to be very clear when the children themselves are. The teacher's role needs to be 'signed' clearly. To suddenly have your teacher behaving as another person with no warning would be confusing and probably disturbing. Teachers may wish to prepare the children for Teacher in Role by talking with them about it first, explaining who they will be pretending to be and then practising with them for a minute or two. They may stop at intervals to check out with the children that they are comfortable with the teacher being in role. They are usually delighted and intrigued by it. The teacher being actively in role with children also gives a powerful message about the important status being given by the teacher to make-believe play and drama.

## ■ For how long should I stay in role?

Teacher in Role is not an acting trip for the thespian teacher, it is a powerful teaching strategy for all teachers. Having decided on the function of the role or roles that he/she will take, the teacher should then only stay in role for as long as is necessary to achieve the defined purpose of that role. The actual time a teacher is in role may vary considerably from lesson to lesson. The drama-in-education teacher aims to facilitate and offer the majority of the ownership of the drama to the children, to stimulate and invite their thinking and creative ideas. This is not congruent with the teacher in role dominating the drama for long periods and would be unlikely to sustain the interest of the children. They want to take part too! Drama is about the children devising drama with the interactive, in-role support of the teacher as facilitator, mediator and model, not about the children as an audience for a teacher's theatrical performance.

## ■ How can I leave the role?

At the simplest level the teacher can simply state that they are coming out of role. Alternatively or additionally, this can be signalled visually and symbolically by putting down the object associated with the role, for example, the feather that is held by the teacher in role as a Native American Chief (*Unit 5, Activity 4*). The teacher can also move from a physical space that is associated with the role, for example, get up from a particular character's chair.

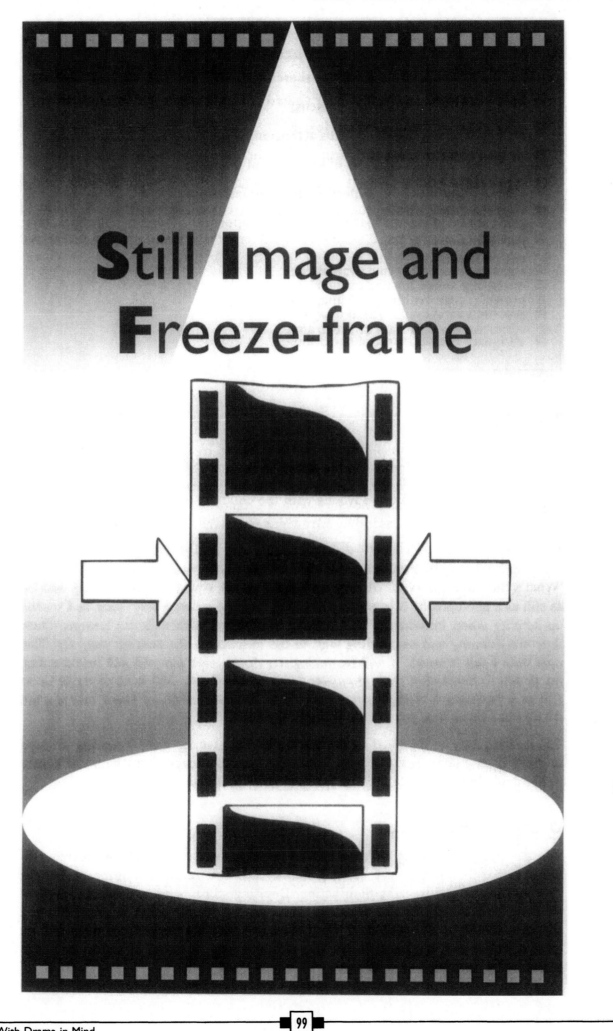

# **S**till **I**mage and **F**reeze-frame

PART TWO

## ■ Through Still Image and Freeze-frame you can:

- ■ hold a dramatic moment still for shared critical analysis and interpretation;

- ■ offer a shared, common visual focus;

- ■ deepen concentration and focus attention;

- ■ support the critical analysis of key moments;

- ■ stop the drama moving superficially at too fast a pace;

- ■ generate curiosity and discussion around important moments and characters within them;

- ■ encourage reflection and evaluation;

- ■ provide a memorable visual image;

- ■ stimulate the next part of the drama.

## ■ Freeze-frame

A freeze-frame is a form of still image that is achieved by simply freezing action. It a strategy that enables a moment in the drama to be held physically still for a purpose. At its simplest, the teacher may simply call 'Freeze!' during the drama or may use a signal of their own, agreed in advance with the children. The children are expected to then keep perfectly still, as if they are a video image that has been suddenly paused.

Young children may find it quite difficult to stay very still initially but they enjoy the challenge and may be practising this skill within games such as the role-play game 'What's the Time Mr Wolf?' It may be helpful to ask young children to 'try and be as still as a photograph'. It is worth practising freezing action a few times as a warm-up activity when introducing this activity to children within drama lessons. Once they are listening and responding well to the instruction the teacher may say 'The next time I call "Freeze!" it will be during our drama and you will not be expecting me to call it. Remember that whenever I call "Freeze!" you will need to try to be as still as a photograph straight away and try to keep very still... I know this is a bit tricky but I think that you can do it if you try hard.'

The freezing may be signalled by the teacher saying nothing, but by moving towards or away from a character or scene. When the teacher moves near, the scene comes to life and when they withdraw, it 'freezes'. *(Unit 2, Activity 6)*

## ■ Still Image/Tableau

There are times when the children will be asked to devise, replicate or create a still image rather than just 'freeze' *(Unit 1, Activity 12)*. This requires a different thought process than simply freezing their action. Devising still images or tableaux involves thinking both creatively and critically. How shall I stand? What impression am I trying to convey to my audience? What are some possible images and what will be most effective and why? and so on. The children may be asked to devise an image individually, in groups or sometimes as a whole class.

**Some activities/exercises for devising still images:**

- A simple warm-up activity might involve the teacher calling out words and the children individually and speedily making a still shape that represents that word – the clown, the winner, sad, excited, and so on.

- Doing the same activity as above but representing the word collectively with a partner or group is more challenging.

- A collective group or class still image can also be formed by the teacher calling a word or phrase and children speedily adding themselves one at a time to create one central image or growing tableau.

- The teacher could add constraints or instructions such as that the people within the image each need to be touching at least one other person or the people within the image should each be looking at another person.

- The children could be asked to devise two contrasting images and move back and forth between them.

The level of challenge can be stepped up as images of varying complexity and purpose are sought and teachers can ask for abstract or symbolic, rather than realistic, images, demanding maybe a more imaginative and creative response.

Devising still images within the context of an evolving drama is more meaningful and multi-layered than the exercises and activities above because there is a contextual reason for devising the image, which gives it meaning and purpose. Within a drama for example, children may be asked to make a still image of themselves as villagers in their homes, about to tell a story (*Unit 1, Activity 2*). This is a way of getting them to engage with their roles in the drama and to engage with a fictional setting and situation. It also focuses the child's attention clearly on the moment to which the image relates. Older pupils may be set a more complex task such as creating a group symbolic still image that represents the Native Americans' fear for the future of their land (*Unit 5, Activity 10*).

## ■ Examples of Still Image/Freeze-frame

### ■ *Image Theatre*

Image Theatre has been developed by Augusto Boal, a Brazilian theatre director, writer and theorist. Boal (1992) believes, like many drama-in-education practitioners, that anyone can act and theatre is not just the domain of theatre professionals.

Image Theatre is a specific form of theatre in which participants make still images that link directly to areas of importance in their own personal lives, feelings, oppressions and experiences (*Unit 3, Activity 2*). These themes are suggested and agreed by the participants – themes such as the family, school, bullying, illness. The group images are sculpted by the audience of 'spect-actors', who treat those within the image as compliant pieces of human clay to be sculpted into a thematic still image produced by consensus. The image is then 'dynamized' (brought alive in various ways) in order to facilitate the making of meanings and to open up what lies behind the image. Image Theatre does not rely on words and therefore is culturally universally accessible, crossing language barriers. It can be linked to therapy. Some Image Theatre techniques are similar to those used in drama in education but the subject matter in drama in

**PART TWO**

schools will normally be safely distanced rather than personalized. However, it needs to be acknowledged that children are bringing their personal experiences and understandings to any drama, as well as their imaginations.

■ *Sequencing images/ Timeline*
Making and presenting a series of still images can enable children to focus on tagging, linking and making sense of a series of key moments in a drama. If the images represent different moments in time, then they can provide a visual timeline (*Unit 4, Activity 8*). When a series of important historical moments in the history of a community are looked at in sequence, cultural heritage starts to emerge and greater cultural understanding results. The series of images as a whole will reveal more than the sum of the parts.

■ *Multiple images*
A single moment in time can be represented by a range of devised images all linked to a particular moment. This enables a single moment to be represented visually in a variety of ways – for example, devising images of the same moment in different places, such as the inside of many different houses in a village just as 'story time' is about to start (*Unit 1, Activity 3*). We might ask older children to represent, through a range of still images, a character's conflicting thoughts or feelings, using symbolic still images or shapes.

When images are looked at as a set, the whole will make greater sense and meaning than the sum of its parts.

■ *Still and Moving Image*
A devised still image in a drama can be activated and brought to life for a few moments (through improvisation) and then frozen again as a freeze-frame image (*Unit 1, Activity 3*). This is a bit like starting with a paused video frame, which is played and then paused again. The moving images in drama (as with videos) can be rewound and replayed at different speeds. The image can also be played or replayed silently or with dubbed sounds or speech.

■ *Thinking aloud in and through the image*
A still image either devised or else arrived at through Freeze-frame can be linked to Thought-tracking, with the characters within the image being asked to speak their thoughts aloud at the exact moment depicted within the image (*Unit 2, Activity 9*).

■ *Speaking aloud in and through the image*
A devised still image or freeze-frame (frozen action) can be developed further by holding the image still while each of the characters within the image is invited to speak aloud what they think their next utterance would be.

■ *Both speaking and thinking aloud through the image*
If characters at a particular 'held' moment are asked to speak aloud a character's next utterance and thought then incongruity of thought and utterance may be revealed. The reasons or motives for this can be considered and discussed with the class – for example, 'Why is it that a character might be thinking one thing yet saying another at this moment? Confusion? Dishonesty? Fear of the sack?'
(*Unit 2, Activity 10*).

■ *Asking questions of characters in the image*

When a moment is held still through either a devised image or a freeze-frame, those studying or 'reading' the image will begin to have their curiosity aroused and will try to interpret and make meaning of the presented image. Linked to Hot-seating, the characters within the image can be questioned by the audience at the exact dramatic moment portrayed and will answer in role. The still image holds the moment still to give time for the revealing of the different characters' motives, thoughts and feelings at a particular moment.

■ *Asking questions of objects within the image*

Still images may contain objects that are empowered to speak, as well as characters – for example, if the children become objects and features within an imagined landscape (*Unit 5, Activity 3*) they can commentate on the action, characters and events almost as inanimate, long-term, eyewitnesses.

■ *Contrasting images*

There may be reason to ask the children to devise and prepare two or more contrasting images for presentation together – for example, a still image that depicts a happy story time before Mr Once Upon a Time arrives, and then a sad one, after Mr Once Upon a Time has been imprisoned (*Unit 1, Activity 13*). Older pupils might be asked to make two contrasting images, one depicting the land of the Native Americans and one representing the same land in the future, in the hands of the settlers (*Unit 5, Activity 10*). They might move from one image to the other to symbolize the change of occupancy, or back and forth between images as in a nightmare. Contrasting images can be devised to depict contrasting attitudes, values, beliefs, emotions and moments in time as well as conflicting thoughts.

Following a Conscience Alley that has made conflicting thoughts explicit verbally, the participants could then be asked to portray the two viewpoints either visually through contrasting still images or visually and kinesthetically through contrasting moving images.

■ *Sculpting images*

Children can make each other into images, for example by using a partner as a piece of human clay and physically 'sculpting' them into a still image. Within dramas, contextual reasons sometimes arise that lend themselves naturally to this activity – for example, within a drama there may be a reason to commemorate someone by making a statue of them for posterity. A person could be moulded into a statue of a character, as a way of commemorating them at the end of a drama (*Unit 5, Activity 14*). One statue could be sculpted collectively by consensus. Statues can be of characters or can be symbolic shapes, using different numbers of people as the human clay.

■ *Forming, melting and reforming images*

'Human clay' can be sculpted, collapsed into a ball, and re-sculpted repeatedly by a sculpting partner but once the human clay knows the shapes their sculptor has made them into, then they can re-form these shapes (without the sculptor) to create a performance sequence of images.

PART **TWO**

■ *Captioning images*

Images once arrived at can be given written or spoken captions either by the makers of the image or by observers who have not been part of the image making process – for example, what caption would Chief Seattle's tribe have placed by his statue, once sculpted? Conversely, a caption can be the starting point for the creation of an image that is made to match the caption (*Unit 5, Activity 14*).

■ *Instructing images*

Images can be physically created through sculpting and moulding people silently as if they are human lumps of clay or alternatively by giving the person verbal instructions and directions as to how they should look and stand. So the statue of a character might be made through giving instructions to the human clay to 'Stand in a proud manner and look directly forward with a raised chin', for example.

■ *Copying images*

In drama, children may be asked to look at an existing image such as an etching, a photograph, a sculpture, a painting or a tapestry, and to use their bodies to make themselves into someone in the picture (or some object in the picture). For example a pupil may portray visually a character they can see in an etching of a Victorian cotton mill (*Unit 2, Activity 4*) or become the whip in the master's hand (*Unit 2, Activity 1*).

■ *Extending and elaborating the image*

Any image, either real, devised or imagined, can become part of an imagined larger or more detailed image. For example, when looking at a photograph or picture book illustration or etching, the children can be asked to make a still image of what lies just out of view, beyond the edges of the picture or else to add something to the existing image (*Unit 2, Activity 7*). These additions might change the meaning of the initial image (*Unit 3, Activity 1*).

■ *Generating still images across art forms*

When there are existing images known to the children that link to the drama then it is possible to ask them to generate additional 'missing' images. For example, a story-drama based on a picture book might use illustrations and pictures from the book to stimulate a drama. During the drama the children may be creating new and additional scenes and plots. The children can then be asked to make themselves into the missing pictures from the storybook that could illustrate the additional scenes. These images could be photographed and stuck in to the actual picture storybook.

Children can be asked to produce or make themselves into object d'art – for example, to become the treasured photograph that a character has is in his wallet, the painting that hangs in the character's home, a tapestry (or wall painting) of a famous historical moment or a commemorative statue (*Unit 5, Activity 14*).

Once children have envisioned, imagined, generated, physically created, observed and analysed still images alone and with others, they are well placed to transform the images into a different 3D form through cross-curricular art and design work and to gain greater understanding of existing representations of art and culture.

■ *Digital/moving imagery and photography/film*

Any still or moving, devised image within a drama can of course be photographed or filmed. The advent of the ubiquitous and handy digital camera and video camera (not to mention some children's mobile phones), adds a new dimension in drama lessons, with still and moving images being recorded during the lesson for further use maybe at future points within the drama. The camera can also of course capture a moment that involves movement and transform it into a still image that can then be used within the drama. Video clips and photographs can be introduced into dramas within the context of the fiction itself – for example, a drama could be stimulated by a photograph of a real person who has supposedly been reported as missing or has lost their memory.

■ *Recording images through drawing*

Sometimes a still image or series of still images from a drama may be recorded as a drawing or series of drawings and form a type of storyboard (*Resource Sheet 10*). Captions and/or thoughts and speech bubbles may be added that link to the image. This supports reflective thought and synthesis.

■ *Presenting images as performance*

When children are making and presenting their still images to others, they should hold the images as still as possible. The teacher sets the standard for the form and an insistence that individuals and groups hold their images very still – 'as still as a photograph' – will set clear expectations and support focus and concentration, physical control and commitment. It will also improve the quality of the image.

When children are showing their images to each other it is worth providing agreed forms through which they do so. It can make the difference between a shoddy and shambling presentation of 'almost still' images with a background of chatter, and a spellbinding theatrical presentation which excites them and which they are justly proud to be part of.

Teachers themselves would be wise to follow the same rules of presentation that they set up with the children. Once a presentation has begun it should be as if the teacher too is at the theatre. There should be respect shown by all for performance and the children should have a clear idea of how important it is to be an active and attentive class audience as well as participant. The theatrical atmosphere will be broken by teachers who move from group to group saying things like, 'Right, that's enough now, stop chattering because we are going to watch this group next. No, stop now because there is no more time to get your bit ready. You should have finished your image by now…' and so on. This is not conducive to spellbinding theatrical presentation.

How still images are put together to form sequences poses a theatrical challenge to be solved. Children can develop their own ways of linking and presenting images for an audience or the teacher might support the process in various ways. A narrative can be used to link images, or captions can be said aloud as links. Holding up written captions can also be a way of moving between images (as in the old silent films) (*Unit 4, Activity 8*).

The following strategies provide a clear structure that teachers may choose to provide to strongly support pupils in presenting a collective series of still images:

■ *Image Carousel or Performance Carousel*
Each group has its image ready to present. The groups are given a performance order. The teacher explains that each group will start off as if they are lumps of clay. At an agreed signal (maybe a word, a sound, background music or a visual signal) the groups will come to life. First Group One will slowly grow into their still image together (possibly counting to five in their heads), hold the image for five silent seconds and will then melt back down into a lump of clay again. Once Group One has completed this 'grow – hold – melt – freeze' sequence, Group Two follows suit. All groups must keep very still and quiet as the others perform. The performance starts with the first group and is not over until every group has had its turn and all children are still again. They are told that they are all part of a bigger performance and they need to pretend that they are on stage throughout, whether or not it is their group's turn to move. This strategy will soon become established and provide a known structure for quality presentation.

The same strategy can be used to link short scenes and short performances and improvisations, not just still images.

■ *Image 'flashes' or 'bites'*
The groups create a series of still images (up to three usually, depending on the age of the children). The group has appointed someone to give the audience instructions as to when they should open or close their eyes. The audience starts off with eyes closed. The performing group quickly gets into its first still image and the designated instructor says 'Open your eyes' to the audience. After just a few seconds, the instructor says 'Close your eyes' to the audience. Once the audience all have their eyes closed, the performing group forms the second still image and the instructor again tells the audience to open their eyes. The process is repeated until the full sequence of images have been seen by the audience. It ends with the audience with eyes closed.

This activity helps focus the audience who see only the still images and not the preparation or transition between them. If the period of time represented by the images is only a few seconds of time within the drama then the effect is of jumping frames of film – for example:

Image 1: She reaches for the phone,
Image 2: She holds the phone to her ear,
Image 3: She puts down the phone and still has her hand on it.

The effect is spoilt if anyone in the still image moves while the audience have their eyes open. This gives a motivating reason linked to drama form for very controlled movement and for giving and following instructions exactly.

# Mantle of the Expert

EXPERT

*'The Mantle of the Expert is essentially an approach to the whole curriculum, and one that resonates with current trends towards active learning and whole language. It is a rare example of truly integrative teaching...'*

Cecily O'Neil in foreword to Dorothy Heathcote and Gavin Bolton (1995) ■

*'I consider that the Mantle of the Expert work becomes deeply social (and sometimes personal) play because students:*

*know that they are contracting into a fiction; they understand the power they have within the fiction; the "spectator" in them must be awakened so that they pervceive and enjoy the world of action and responsibility even as they function in it; and they grow in expertise through the amazing range of conventions that must be harnessed.'*

Dorothy Heathcote (1995) ■

*'A mantle of the expert approach is like a spiral, a continuous path followed by the students through knowledge into theatre and theatre into knowledge on a more and more sophisticated plane as they develop responsibility for their own learning.'*

Gavin Bolton (1995) ■

## ■ Through Mantle of the Expert you can:

- ■ be admitted into the learning community;
- ■ offer shared responsibility to the pupils;
- ■ endow pupils with authority;
- ■ elevate the significance of work tasks;
- ■ model dialogic talk with and for different audiences and purposes;
- ■ provide models of written language for different audiences and purposes;
- ■ enable pupils to participate in and gain understanding of real life challenges;
- ■ enable pupils to experience offering a service to others;
- ■ validate prior learning and enable it to be applied in new contexts;
- ■ provide a shared context for problem solving linked to decision making and accountability;
- ■ provide challenge-based learning with imposed imagined boundaries and constraints.

Mantle of the Expert is a drama teaching strategy and a philosophical approach to learning that was explored, developed and named by the innovative drama educator Dorothy Heathcote in the late 1960s. It has had a significant impact on drama teaching and more recently is being used by some teachers to teach philosophy.

The Mantle of the Expert approach is rooted in drama for learning and involves the teacher placing children in role together as experts in some field and treating them as such with a learning purpose. The children as experts are given important imaginary tasks to do or a significant imaginary service to perform that relies heavily on their having imaginary expertise. The teacher is a facilitator and the children have their usual status raised by being treated respectfully as expert adults with responsibilities. The children gain the pleasurable experience of feeling what it is like to be valued and respected for one's skills, knowledge and expertise and to be given responsibility and relied on by others.

The children will need some prior knowledge in order to take on 'expert' roles such as scientists, doctors, botanists, archaeologists and so on, but their real skills in this area will of course be limited. Clearly no child is a genuine expert in specialist areas and no one involved in the fiction will be expecting them to genuinely carry out real tasks expertly. However, within a make-believe that everyone has contracted into, the participants can all pretend that they are all experts and treat each other as such. As imaginary experts they may find themselves able to, for example, mummify a dead king, sail a ship safely through a fierce storm, trap dangerous animals, discover cures for diseases, solve crimes and mysteries, unravel past cultures, discover and interpret archaeological finds... They may need some basic knowledge or information in order to initially engage with and sustain the role of expert in some field, but if everyone agrees to accept for the sake of the drama that they are experts then they may proceed safely as such without risk of ridicule.

As the drama evolves the children's role as experts will be used for an active learning purpose. They may be motivated to really research their imagined area of expertise in order to sound, behave and feel more convincing as an expert within the drama and they will learn in, through and between the drama sessions.

The community of fellow learners provided by the drama will have all contracted into sustaining the same make-believe, treating each other as competent experts and reaping the 'feel-good' factor of doing so as well as learning and experiencing success at carrying out tasks linked to the drama.

## ■ An example of Mantle of the Expert

The class may already be studying or have studied a period in local history and have acquired some knowledge of previous inhabitants of the area such as Vikings or Anglo-Saxons. They may have visited the local museum and seen displays of artefacts or researched using the internet, or gathered information through books or videos. The teacher may give some key factual information or research tasks that will be relevant to the series of drama lessons before they start.

Expert archaeologists are invited by a local farmer to study photographs (real or imaginary) of objects that have recently been dug up in his nearby fields. He will not take them to the site. The farmer (teacher in role) wants the views of the archaeologists. What might these objects be? Is this a significant find? Has there been anything else like it discovered in the locality previously? The experts will convincingly or tentatively offer information and their opinion based on what in reality may be very limited knowledge. They will sound like experts. The farmer will be very interested and grateful for any information or advice. Should the farmer alert the press? Will his site now be more valuable? Can he profit from the finds? Will they pay him to be allowed to dig? If he finds anything valuable, will it belong to him? He will not take them to the site. They will just have to trust him.

- The experts can use real or imagined photographs as primary source material and can research previous archaeological finds in the area, possibly using the internet (maybe even by visiting or revisiting the local museum), knowing that they will return to talk with the farmer at a future date when they have found out more.

- The farmer (teacher in role) wants to sell his story to the local press and they will probably advise the farmer not to. They will need to persuade him against this through reasoned argument. If they take the unlikely line that the farmer should sell the story then he can ask their advice as to how and what he should say. They will not want hoards of curious people arriving on the land.

- The farmer writes to the archaeologists saying that he has received a good cash offer on the land from an anonymous property developer. He genuinely needs the cash and is inclined to sell. The archaeologists draft a formal reply together. The response and content of the reply will be up to them but they are likely to consider whether the mystery offer is genuine. Who might his anonymous person be? Has the farmer really received an offer at all? Is someone who knows the real value of the find and significance of it trying to buy the site? Is the farmer trying to con them into coming up with an offer for the land somehow?

- The archaeologists will have met together. They may have now discovered that the finds are very significant and the site is likely to yield many more artefacts. The teacher may have joined them in role as a fellow archaeologist able to offer information too if necessary. They persuade the farmer to take them to the site and take part in an imaginary dig. They will have found out or been told in advance how archaeologists proceed with a dig – that is, divide the area into grids, use spades then trowels and then brush away the soil, label each object, measure and record where exactly it was found, and so on.

- The farmer needs to be persuaded through reasoned argument not to sell quickly to the anonymous buyer (who is demanding a quick sale).

- Once the finds have been recovered they are taken to the museum and together the experts will try to piece together what information they have. What do these objects tell them about the people who once lived on this site? New photographs may have been added now of more recent finds.

- The museum curator (teacher in role) wants an exhibition of the finds set up in a way that helps the visiting public imagine and understand what life was once like on this local site. Using the photos as if they were the real objects, the children as experts will now decide how to display them and will be asked to write a short paragraph alongside each object. They may be asked to collate a catalogue of the exhibition, give make-believe press interviews to radio and TV or to prepare a press statement. They may be asked to prepare a guided tour around which they can take others.

# Hot-Seating

## ■ Through Hot-seating you can:

- **help participants to engage with, discover and understand the thoughts, motives and actions of a particular character at a specific point in the drama;**

- **give participants a shared visual and aural focus;**

- **help develop an understanding of a character and character development;**

- **give a range of contextual opportunities and purpose for practising questioning and interviewing skills.**

Hot-seating is a well-established drama strategy, of which many teachers have some knowledge. At its most basic it involves having the opportunity to talk with a character for a short while and ask them questions. The character usually sits in a particular chair that is referred to as the 'hot-seat'. However, a chair does not have to be used and it is possible to freeze action and ask a character to step out of a scene and be available for questioning. The questioners ask questions as themselves and are not in role. The character being questioned answers in role.

## ■ How do I set up, sustain and develop Hot-seating?

■ First find out what the children already know about Hot-seating. You may find that they have experienced hot-seating already in some way and have preconceived ideas about what it might involve.

■ Then ask the children if there is anyone in the drama that they would like to meet. You can gather their ideas of characters that they would like to talk with and question and ask them to justify their choice. You could restrict the number of characters that will be available for hot-seating and agree to bring on the character or characters that they offer the strongest reasons for wanting to meet.

■ You could offer the children the opportunity to invent and talk to other imaginary characters who are close to the person they want to find out about instead of talking to the character him/herself. For example if we want to know more about a character, we can bring in and hot-seat a friend or relation of that character. In A Victorian Cotton Mill (*Unit 2*) for example, instead of hot-seating the victim of the mill accident, we could talk to his mother or to the doctor that treated him (neither of whom were present) or to a character who was present.

■ The children could hot-seat an object that can become empowered to speak, such as a storybook that is never fully read anymore because Mr Once Upon a Time (*Unit 1*) keeps interrupting on the opening page.

■ Place a chair somewhere prominent and explain that while you are sitting in that chair you will be pretending to be the character being hot-seated. Explain that once you leave the chair you will cease to represent that character. Check that the children understand. You could have a brief practice to make sure.

■ You may decide that the character in the hot-seat will carry an object to make it clear visually who they are. For example, Mr Once Upon a Time might hold his van keys or wear a hat. Chief Seattle (*Unit 5*) could hold a feather.

■ If several characters are being hot-seated in turn or you want to make it particularly clear to young children or reinforce the reading of the character's name, then you might decide that the character will wear a sign, badge or label with their name on. You could have a prominent name sign hung on the character's chair.

■ Before bringing in the character, ask the class to consider in advance what questions they might ask the character when he/she sits in the hot-seat. This gives opportunity for formulating and considering questions in advance, allowing preparation and thinking time as well as time for refining or rehearsing their questions. It avoids an embarrassing silence or conversely a torrent of shallow questions. These intended questions may be remembered or recorded (see *Resource Sheet 6*).

■ Limit the number of questions that children can ask the character in the hot-seat. You could say that the character in the hot-seat will answer only one question from each child or group. With guidance, this helps improve the quality of questioning.

■ You can put a time limit on how long the character will be in the hot-seat. It is often better to leave the questioners still curious and wanting to know more from the character than carry on too long with hot-seating the character and lose the children's attention and interest.

■ You might invite others to come and sit in the hot-seat and take over being the hot-seated character. This enables several children to have the opportunity to speak as and for the character. It links to the notion of a collective role or voice and requires good, active listening to ensure consistency.

PART TWO

# Role on the Wall

## ■ Through Role on the Wall you can:

> ■ encourage shared, reflective and critical thinking about a character within the drama at a point in time or at several points in time;
>
> ■ provide a visual focus for the recording of a character's thoughts, feelings, attributes and so forth, at particular points in the drama;
>
> ■ give opportunity for consideration of a character's development through analysing a series of roles on the wall based on the same character at different points in the drama;
>
> ■ establish a record that can be revisited and possibly amended as the drama develops and we learn more about a character;
>
> ■ act as a focus and support for group or whole-class discussion about characters and their characteristics.

## ■ What is Role on the Wall?

Role on the Wall is a simple and visual way of gathering together, centralizing and recording what the drama participants think or feel about a character in the drama. The teacher can simply draw a big outline of a head or body and display it centrally on the wall (or on the floor with the children gathered around). The outline can be as simple as a stick-man or a pre-prepared accurate representation of the character's head or body outline (*Resource Sheet 8a*). This outline, which represents the 'role' or character, might have the character's name written on it and there may be several running simultaneously for different characters.

## ■ What do I do with the Role on the Wall?

Outside, along and within the outline is space in which the children can write what is important and what they wish to record about the character. The teacher can act as the scribe, recording what young children want to say about the character at any particular point in the drama and keeping it displayed as a record. This is particularly useful with young children who may have a flow of ideas about the character but can be held back by their early writing skills and slow speed of recording.

Older children might write on the Role on the Wall themselves in turn or record what they wish to contribute on Post-it notes, which they then are invited to stick on to the Role on the Wall. They could be asked to justify and explain their contribution, for example, 'I have written that Mr Once Upon a Time is selfish. I think this because he keeps interrupting and spoiling stories.' (*Unit 1, Activity 18*)

Post-it notes are a very flexible tool when working with Role on the Wall. Individual or group comments and information about the character can be gathered around a large outline on Post-its, they can of course be removed if necessary at some future point. If the children change their minds about a character during the course of the drama, previous comments and observations about the character can be reconsidered and, if necessary, removed or put to the edge of the paper as a reminder of discarded comments, for example, 'I think Mr Once Upon a Time is not selfish. This is because I know from listening to his thoughts in the thought-tracking, that he was just trying to be helpful.'

■ The teacher may invite a range of open responses about the character from the children by asking questions such as 'What do you think about this character?' Alternatively the teacher may narrow and define the focus by asking, for example, 'What might this character be feeling at this particular point in the drama?' 'What do we think are the positive characteristics of this character?' 'What do we think we know about this character?'

■ The teacher can create a thinking frame around the Role on the Wall. There could be columns around the head or body outline with the headings 'What we know', 'What we think we know' and 'What we want to know about this character' (*Resource Sheet 8b*). The children can place their responses in the most appropriate column. Other frames might be 'Positive characteristics', 'Negative characteristics' and 'Interesting characteristics' (*Resource Sheet 8c*) which link to Edward de Bono's thinking categories. Another frame might have the three headings: 'Thoughts', 'Feelings', 'Actions' (*Resource Sheet 8d*).

■ The children could also place their comments and observations at the part of the body outline that is most appropriate, for example, 'Chief Seattle hears the voices of his forefathers', could be placed near the ears of the outline; 'He loves the land', could be placed near his heart.

■ Role on the Wall is most often done as a whole-class or group activity but a booklet with a series of individual Role on the Wall outlines on A4 can act as a child's individual record of responses to a character throughout a series of drama lessons. The child fills in the booklet from time to time over several lessons and has an ongoing record of a character's development and their own changing perceptions about the character.

## ■ Bringing Role on the Wall to life through positioning

A living and more kinesthetic extension of Role on the Wall can be created in the following way. A person places themselves as a named character in a central space. In turn the children enter and place themselves physically in relation to that character, indicating what their response to that character is by the way they place themselves and the position they take up. For example one child might stand close to Mr Once Upon a Time and say, 'I think that he is upset because... and I want to take care of him.' Another child might turn their back on Mr Once Upon a Time and say, 'I think he is a nuisance and I just want him to go away.'

PART TWO

Conscience Alley

## ■ Through Conscience Alley you can:

■ hold still a key moment at which an important decision is about to be made by a character in the drama;

■ help children to consider and give voice to alternative views and standpoints;

■ offer the framework of a balanced argument;

■ make public the pros and cons of a particular course of action and its possible effect;

■ give a structured opportunity to practise persuasive speech;

■ enable the whole class to 'get inside the head of' a key character at an important moment and empathize;

■ facilitate and open up the process of decision making;

■ enable the children to have a sense of shared ownership and influence over character's decisions that will affect the direction of the drama.

## ■ What is Conscience Alley?

Conscience Alley is sometimes referred to as 'Decision Alley' or as a 'Thought Tunnel'. When there is a key moment for a character in a drama, at which a decision has to be made, this strategy is a way of holding the moment still and involving the whole class, giving every individual the opportunity to influence the character as they make that decision. At its simplest the class members become voices in the head of the character, or his conscience speaking to him out loud.

## ■ How do I set up Conscience Alley?

This is usually set up with the children standing in two straight lines about a metre apart and facing each other (rather like a 'long set' in country dancing).

Make sure that the children realize the decision that the character is wrestling with and then make it clear exactly what they are being asked to do and when. For example:

'Mr Once Upon a Time is deciding whether or not he is prepared to change his name. He is having difficulty making up his mind. There are voices in his head and in a minute you are going to have the chance to be those voices. In a moment Mr Once Upon a Time [probably the teacher in role] will walk between the lines in which you are standing. He will stand close to every person in turn. If you are standing in this line (to his left) then, when he is closest to you, you will have the opportunity to say out loud to him why he should change his name. Make sure that you give him a good reason. If you are standing in the opposite line (to his right), then when he is standing closest to you, it will be your chance to give him a good reason why he should not change his name.' (*Unit 1, Activity 16*)

- You may wish to point out that there is no compulsion to contribute and children can 'pass', signalling this by clapping their hands when it is their turn. Mr Once Upon a Time will then pass them by and move on to the next person.

- You can tell the children which viewpoint they are going to take – in other words, in which line they will stand and which line of action they will justify.

- You can let the children decide their own viewpoint and stand in the most appropriate line.

- You can ask the children to stand on the side that holds the opposite viewpoint to the one they really hold, thus challenging them to come up with a good reason that supports the opposite viewpoint to that which they really think.

- You can let children repeat what someone else has said if they want to speak and join in but cannot think of an idea of their own or if they hear their idea spoken by someone else first.

The two facing lines can be made to represent something within the setting of the drama – for example, the lines can become the walls of the prison cell in which the character is walking back and forth or they could be the bank of a river along which the character is canoeing. It is also possible to extend the lines so that each person has more than one opportunity to persuade the character and give more than one reason out loud. This can be done by the child breaking away from the initial line after they have had their turn and going to stand at the other end of the line (again this is a bit like a country dancing move). The character will pass by again for as many times as the child breaks away and rejoins the line. It is also possible that the character can simply pass up and down the original line more than once to give multiple opportunities.

It can be motivating if the teacher (who is probably representing the character) says, 'I have not made up my mind. I do not yet know what I am going to do. It will depend on what you say to me. Whichever line gives me the best reasons will be the one who's advice I will follow. You will know when I have made my decision because I will join that line.'

Children's thoughts and ideas can be recorded on *Resource Sheets 5a* and *5b*.

## ■ What can I expect to hear?

What transpires and is shared is persuasive speech, logical reasoning and justifications for alternative courses of action. There can also emerge an open consideration of cause and effect, for example, 'You should change your name because then you won't have a reason to keep interrupting the people's stories and annoying them.' Or alternatively, 'No, you shouldn't change your name because you will still think that you are Mr Once Upon a Time inside your head anyway, whatever anyone calls you.' Conscience Alley can be used outside a drama lesson at other times when the teacher wants to structure an opportunity for the class to influence a decision maker and consider together aloud the pros and cons of courses of action.

PART TWO

The conflicting thoughts and reasons arising can be developed into:

■ *Writing*
The reasons given for and against a course of action could be recorded in straightforward headed columns. This could be organized for the whole class if the children write their reasons and justifications on Post-its and then they are centralized. The columns of reasons that result can then be regarded as a writing frame for persuasive writing supporting a viewpoint or for producing a written, balanced argument, giving both sides.

■ *Speaking*
The jotted reasons can become a prompt sheet for the character to speak their reasoning out loud (as a type of soliloquy), vocalizing the thinking for and against a particular course of action. The teacher could model this, using the pupils' Post-it contributions.

Recording the conscience can also be carried out in small groups or individually, possibly using *Resource Sheet 5a*.

■ *Moving image/Soundscape*
With older pupils, conflicting thoughts can be used as the basis of a piece of abstract movement. If the character's conflicting thoughts were represented in a dream, what would that look like? How might the thoughts look as a still image? How might they look as a moving image? As a still or moving image with sound...or words?

# Thought-tracking

PART TWO

## ■ Through Thought-tracking you can:

- ■ help children to hold a moment still and engage more deeply with the thoughts and reactions of the character they are portraying at that moment;

- ■ enable and model active listening to the thoughts of others;

- ■ give opportunity for pupils to reflect on any disparity between the inner thoughts of their character and their public speech and actions as that character at a given moment;

- ■ give opportunity for pupils to reflect on any disparity between the inner thoughts, speech and actions of other characters in the drama at a given moment.

## ■ What is Thought-tracking and how does it work?

Thought-tracking is an activity that is now familiar to many teachers. At its simplest it involves the teacher freezing the action in a drama and then tapping the shoulders of children in role, signalling their opportunity to speak aloud their in-role thoughts at this moment. The contributed thoughts are usually just a sentence or two and therefore the teacher can move fairly quickly among the whole class, gathering a range of in-role thoughts that are voiced aloud and made public. In recent years teachers have tended to move away from the physical tapping of shoulders and the signal might be just that when the teacher is standing nearest to a particular child it is their opportunity to speak their character's thoughts aloud.

## ■ Examples of Thought-tracking

- ■ This activity links usually to Still Image or Freeze-frame. Either the action is frozen at a moment in time and the thoughts of the characters in the scene heard or else a still image is devised and then their thoughts heard. Less often, their thoughts are heard with a moving image, as if it is some form of soliloquy.

- ■ Sometimes the still image is held and the thoughts heard, followed by the next real utterance of the character (or vice versa). This can reveal that a character is thinking one thing but saying another for some reason that might be explored.

- ■ Sometimes a scene can be played silently or a still image presented to others and the audience can be invited to actively attach themselves to particular characters within the scene and speak their thoughts for them. This is an extension of Thought-tracking, requiring a significant level of attention and empathy. It involves tracking the thoughts of other characters and, because of this, has close links with Conscience Alley.

- ■ Thought-tracking of one character can be a shared activity, with a group all having opportunity to speak in turn as the thoughts of the same character (see Collective Voice).

*Resource Sheet 5c* can be used to support this strategy.

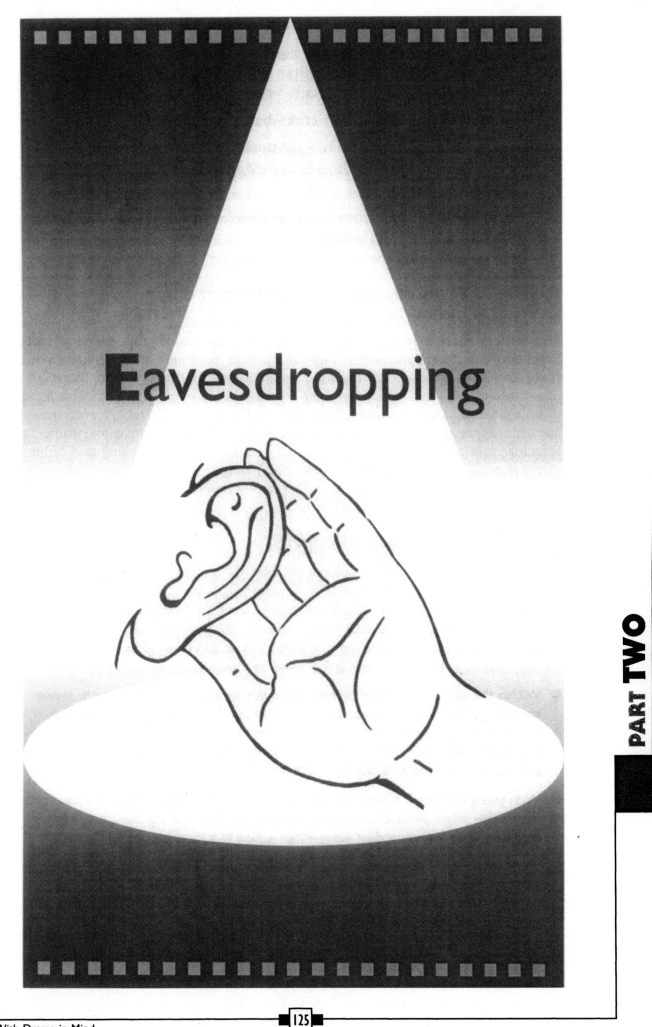

# Eavesdropping

PART TWO

## ■ Through Eavesdropping you can:

- ■ give opportunity for everyone to listen into each other's scenes that contribute to the emerging collective whole-class drama;

- ■ give creative ownership of parts of the drama to individuals and groups;

- ■ enable individuals and groups to consider how their own contributions and scenes fit alongside others and relate to other scenes within the collective and emerging fiction;

- ■ give an opportunity for characters to move from public speech and action to more private speech and action.

## ■ What is Eavesdropping in the context of drama?

This strategy enables you to set up and listen to conversations that are supposedly happening in different places simultaneously within the drama or conversations that could have been heard at different times in the drama. In drama we can listen in to conversations even though we were not actually within earshot. We can also listen in on conversations that might take place in the future. Those who are overheard have the opportunity to contribute to the shared drama. An example would be listening in to telephone conversations and finding out what is being said behind closed doors (*Unit 1, Activity 10*). Eavesdropping might enable us to hear a character reveal thoughts and feelings to a friend or family member that they would not be able to reveal easily elsewhere in the drama.

## ■ How do I set up Eavesdropping?

The teacher may simply tell the children that she will be moving between groups and when she is standing close to a group their scene will come alive for as long as she is nearby listening. The groups should not interact with the teacher. When she moves away the scene freezes and the next group scene the teacher stands near will then come alive. The groups should wait their turn with stillness and quiet so that they can hear the conversations. This makes the action seem like a sequence of scenes in a play.

- ■ Within the drama there may be 'real' reasons that could give rise to a character eavesdropping on other characters – for example, Mr Once Upon a Time (who has exceptional hearing powers) can hear people talking about him inside their houses. The teacher in role as Mr Once Upon a Time might move between groups listening to people talking about him.

- ■ With young children it is helpful to attach a signal to the eavesdropping, for example, the teacher might pretend to turn the sound up or down on a group, using a big imaginary volume knob and/or exaggerated action of a hand cupped to the ear.

- ■ With older pupils the teacher may not need to signal or move between groups at all. He might simply tell them that they will now be doing Eavesdropping. If the pupils are familiar with the strategy they can start and stop their own scenes in sequence and remain still during each others'.

*Resource Sheet 2a* could be used to record anything significant that has been overheard at particular points in the drama.

# **R**umours

**PART TWO**

## ■ Through Rumours you can:

> ■ quickly create a high level of class interaction in role;
>
> ■ rapidly generate a lot of information and potential plot material;
>
> ■ raise the energy level of the class;
>
> ■ encourage children to listen to each other and to embellish and build on each others' ideas;
>
> ■ encourage reflection on the nature, purpose and unreliability of rumours.

Like Eavesdropping, Rumours opens up a level of dialogic intimacy and conspiracy. It enables the quick generation of lots of information that can be selected from as the drama progresses. It is also a fun activity that gets the children to mix together and move closer physically, thus helping to break down barriers and the group to gel.

## ■ How do I set up Rumours?

■ The participants usually have space and time constraints within which to spread and gather rumours. The children are asked to make up and listen to each others' rumours about a character or maybe an event. They move about quickly in gossipy fashion, listening to and gathering rumours. As they do so they may amend their own rumour, add to it or change it completely.

■ Afterwards the teacher may gather some of the rumours through class discussion, thus sharing them openly. They might consider which rumours could be true and which are clearly implausible?

■ The teacher can add information or direction through contributing specific rumours. For example, when gossiping about the arrival of the stranger (*Mr Once Upon a Time*) the teacher could say 'Have you seen the hearing aid he is wearing?' The teacher knows that Mr Once Upon a Time has a hearing aid as it says so in the storybook but the children do not know this yet. The teacher is using a 'rumour' to feed information into the drama (*Unit 1, Activity 8*).

■ A rumour probability line can be created by asking the children to each place their rumour along an imaginary line. One end of the line is labelled 'Possibly true' and the other end is labelled 'Cannot possibly be true'. The children decide how likely it is that their rumour could be true and then place themselves at an appropriate place on the line, relative to placement of other people's rumours. This can lead to their justifying their line position to their neighbours (see *Resource Sheet 2b*).

■ It can be poignant for the character that the rumours are about to speak their thoughts. This can give an insight into the feelings of the victims of rumour. It can be done through Teacher in Role (see pages 93–98) or maybe through Collective Voice (see page 130).

*Resource Sheet 2a* could be used to record rumours heard.

# Collective Role

With Drama in Mind

## ■ Through Collective Role you can:

■ give a contextual reason for active listening to ensure continuity of role;

■ offer shared ownership of key roles;

■ join in as a fellow contributor to the role;

■ choose to model the role and its associated speech register;

■ ensure that everyone stays involved in the same shared fiction.

If there are some children who are allocated key roles in class dramas this can be over-demanding or over-empowering for them and demotivating for others with lesser roles. Key roles do not have to be played by only one person throughout a drama. The Collective Role or Collective Voice strategy can be used to enable a group to all speak as a character in the drama at particular points. This does not mean that the group speaks simultaneously but that any person can take a turn to seamlessly speak as the shared character. One person speaks, closely followed by another, carrying the speech on with attention to consistency of role.

## ■ How do I set up Collective Role?

■ Collective Role may take place with the children seated in a circle and taking turns to speak, 'clapping out' or passing if they do not wish to contribute.

■ Those who are representing the one character might be asked to place themselves physically close together or even to interconnect themselves. This physical unity can support a feeling of psychological unity in the participants.

■ The teacher may introduce the rule that anyone may speak as the character in any order but that no person may make two consecutive contributions.

■ The teacher may invite any pupil to speak as the character without organizing turn-taking. This requires the group to be sensitive to each other so that no one person dominates, everyone has opportunity to contribute and no one talks at the same time as someone else.

■ An object that supposedly belongs to or symbolically links to the character can become a 'speaking object' and whoever is holding the object speaks as the character – for example, a feather could be passed around and whoever holds it speaks as the Native American Chief (*Unit 5, Activity 4*).

■ The class can be divided into two groups and two collective roles can have a dialogue, with each character's voice being provided by a different group. This actively involves the whole class in a dialogue – for example, the class can together question a collective bully (*Unit 3, Activity 14*).

■ The class can be divided into two groups and the thoughts and speech of a character can be heard. One group speaks collectively as the character's thoughts (collective Thought-tracking) and the other as the character's spoken utterances. The thoughts and utterances can be heard separately or else there can be interplay between thoughts and speech. This is a very challenging activity but gives opportunity for conscious and subconscious shared interplay.

# Improvisation

With Drama in Mind

## ■ Through Improvisation you can:

- ■ enable the pupils to free-flow sections of the drama for a while;

- ■ focus pupil attention on a situation or event;

- ■ give a sense of individual and shared ownership of the content of the drama;

- ■ give opportunity for the teacher to gain a sense of and assess a range of competencies – for example, the pupil's ability to speak and listen, to sustain a convincing role in co-operation with others and maintain a make-believe verbally;

- ■ open up new areas within the drama or else explore existing areas in greater depth and from different viewpoints;

- ■ move the drama plot forward or find out more about aspects of the drama so far;

- ■ explore a range of possible outcomes and effects of an action or event in the drama;

- ■ provide the raw material for developing into scripts and reworking for performance.

Improvisation is possibly where drama in education is closest to dramatic play. Improvisation is playful and underpins drama. It involves the children spontaneously making up scenes within the drama, offering unrehearsed speech and action as the drama unfolds live. Improvisation might be set up for individuals, pairs, groups or for the whole class.

For some teachers improvisation is the area of greatest concern when doing class drama. This tends to be because the teacher has had experience of its being set up too loosely, without sufficiently clear and shared purpose and it has become no more than class dramatic free play without much commitment, focus or depth. Badly managed, it can become an excuse for children to mess around rather than dramatic play with purpose. Well managed, it is dynamic, engaging and creative.

Improvisation is most powerful and productive when the children care about the drama and feel that their character has a stake in the scene that is about to be improvised. Improvisation can be highly engaging because the children know that what will emerge is as yet unknown.

## ■ How do I set up Improvisation?

The children need to know three things in order to improvise, just as they do in order to play successful make-believe games.

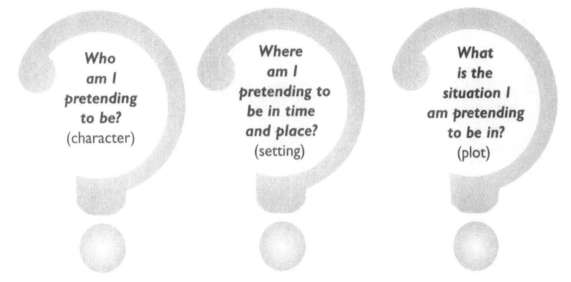

**Who am I pretending to be?** (character)

**Where am I pretending to be in time and place?** (setting)

**What is the situation I am pretending to be in?** (plot)

Once the children know the answer to these questions then they are in a position to improvise with others in the same imagined fiction.

■ Make sure that the improvisation has a definite starting point and, with young children, a definite finishing point and that it does not go on for too long. Agree a signal with them for starting and stopping the improvisation, such as 'Freeze!' or a gong or a raised arm in the air that means 'Please finish, I am waiting to move on'.

With older pupils it is worth playing with improvisation. You can let them decide when to stop improvising and at other times you can challenge them to stay in role in the scene, past the point when they would like to withdraw. Discuss whether it was productive to carry on for longer. Did it lead to deeper thoughts and contributions or did it degenerate and lose focus? Which way do they prefer and why?

■ Improvised scenes can be replayed in different ways with different outcomes. What happens if a character in the scene does not speak for a while when the scene is played again? What happens if we replay the scene but decide to play the character differently, so that the character reveals more or less of him/herself? What happens if we bring another character into the scene? What happens if we have the same characters and we play the scene again but with different information available to the characters?

■ Improvising in front of your classmates as an audience can up the stakes and change the experience for participants. It can lead to greater effort or it can raise anxiety levels in a way that hampers the process. A good compromise can be to facilitate the replay as performance of scenes that have been improvised already. This might or might not involve rehearsal time. This effectively then becomes playmaking.

**PART TWO**

# Small Group Playmaking

### ■ Through Small Group Playmaking you can:

> ■ give opportunity for groups to create scenes that contribute to and give shared ownership of the whole-class Big Picture drama;
>
> ■ give purpose to the refining of scenes for an audience, which may have been originally improvised;
>
> ■ enable all pupils to have a more significant level of input into the group play than may be possible in the whole-class drama;
>
> ■ give opportunity for pupils to direct each other with an audience in mind;
>
> ■ give a contextual reason for scripting.

Young children enjoy making up plays that usually consist of a few short scenes and tell a story. Within the whole-class drama lesson, Small Group Playmaking is formalized and managed by the teacher, who asks the children to prepare a short scene or two that they can show to each other. This playmaking activity could happen as a drama activity in its own right but it can equally be very effective when used as a narrative strategy within evolving whole-class dramas. Prepared scenes based around a given character, theme or moment in the class drama can illuminate and add to the shared fiction (*Unit 3, Activity 15*). The teacher should set the parameters to ensure that the scenes will fit together as a whole and not be so disparate that the unity of the whole-class drama is lost rather than enriched.

### ■ How do I set up Small Group Playmaking?

Guide children away from a long series of scenes that lack clarity and will be too taxing on the attention span of the intended audience. Left to their own devices this is usually the outcome with less experienced drama participants. As pupils become more experienced at devising, performing and responding to drama they realize that a great deal can be conveyed with just a single word or image.

■ Set time limits for preparation and the length of the short play. You may restrict the number of scenes. Make clear what the focus and purpose of the playmaking is – for example, 'We want to find out in your short plays about something important that has happened in the history of these people. Your play will have only three short scenes and will not last longer than five minutes. You will need to rehearse the play at least once.'

■ As the short plays are intended for an audience, the children need to be audience conscious from the start. 'What will be the first and last thing that the audience see and hear? Think about where you want your audience to be placed when you perform your play. What will the view be like for members of the audience in different positions?'

■ The groupings for pupils working together are important. You may select groupings or let pupils select their own, or make them random in some way. Ring the changes so pupils do not always work in the same groups.

# Forum Theatre

■ **Through Forum Theatre you can:**

■ develop an interactive dialogue and stimulate debate between the audience and actors as 'spect-actors';

■ empower the audience to take action that will empower the oppressed characters within a scene or short play;

■ give structure and focus for critical and reflective analysis;

■ enable audiences to observe, analyse and influence actors' actions and responses within scenes and to consider alternative outcomes;

■ make links between cause and effect;

■ give transferable skills and confidence to children that enable them to problem solve and assert themselves in various ways in order to alter oppressive situations in which they find themselves;

■ help children to know and understand their own strengths and weaknesses and those of their antagonists.

Forum Theatre is one of Augusto Boal's types of interactive theatre. It breaks away from the idea of a passive audience and encourages interaction, dialogue and interchange between actors and audience. Together they address and try to resolve issues that are negatively affecting the characters. This is a highly structured and stylized, shared, problem-solving activity. It distances and deals collectively with real life problems through moving in and out of role. It can be used to look at difficult issues safely through manipulating a fiction together. Issues might include peer pressure, drug abuse, tolerance, conflict resolution, bullying (*Unit 3, Activity 13*) and so on.

## ■ How do I set up Forum Theatre?

■ Ask a group to prepare a scene (from improvisation) for enactment in front of the rest of the class. The scene will be linked to some sort of oppression such as bullying and the situation within the scene should be left unresolved.

■ Invite the audience to watch the scene once, straight through without interruption.

■ Now replay the scene but tell the class that this time, anyone in the audience may stand up and shout 'Stop!', and give advice at that point to the oppressed character (the protagonist), about how to behave or respond differently to the oppressor (antagonist). The scene is then replayed or carried on, following the advice given. 'Stop!' may be shouted more than once if it is felt to be necessary.

■ Alternatively the audience 'spect-actor' who stops the action may ask to take the place of the oppressed character and play it differently for others to observe and comment on. The scene may end up being replayed several times in different ways and hopefully there will be a resolution.

■ Dialogue managed between the actors in role and the audience is a central feature of this type of theatre and essential in order to extrapolate the learning.
A facilitator, known as 'The Joker' (usually the teacher) manages the process and the interchanges. Intervention is usually rewarded by applause.

# Teacher as Storyteller and Storymaker

## ■ Through Teacher as Storyteller/maker you can:

■ **Provide a background narrative for valuing, acknowledging and commenting on the pupils' own actions**
– for example, children miming jobs of mill workers could be accompanied by a teacher narrative saying, 'It was late in the day at the cotton mill. Some of the children had been working for almost 12 hours...' (*Unit 2, Activity 5*). This builds atmosphere, helps establish a shared setting and supports engagement with role.

■ **Model different language registers/conventions and extend vocabulary**
– for example, as the Mayor, the teacher can use formal speech to address the townsfolk when asking for plans to solve the problem of Mr Once Upon a Time, 'My good townsfolk, as you are all aware I am the Mayor of this town and I am afraid that I have to ask for your assistance...'(*Unit 1, Activity 14*)

■ **Move the drama on in time and provide narrative links**
– for example, 'At last the moment had arrived for them to leave the land of their forefathers...'(*Unit 5*)

■ **Retell events from the drama as a narrative to guide reflection and to focus the pupils' attention** – for example, 'That night, as they slept, they remembered the voices of their ancestors...'

■ **Build tension**
– for example, '...and they dreamed about what might happen the next day...'

■ **Manage behaviour from within the drama**
– for example, 'The huntsmen were skilled hunters, they moved in silence across the ground...' This narrative signals that the children need to move very quietly without directly asking them to be quiet as they work.

■ **Conclude the drama**
– for example, 'And so it was, that the people left the land that they loved.'

The teacher can act as a storymaker or storyteller at different points in the drama for different purposes. The pupils are in the position of being a knowing rather than naive audience for the teacher's narrative because they are engaged in the drama to which the narrative links. Therefore the narrative has a strengthened personal relevance.

## ■ How do I set up a Teacher as Storyteller/maker?

You need the full attention of the children. This may be acquired by:

■ simply asking for their attention before you start the narrative;

■ using a strategy or signal that gains their full attention first, such as, if the children are asked to 'freeze' their action at some point, then while they are still and silent the teacher can move into storymaking or storytelling;

■ gathering the children around you before starting the narrative;

■ leaving a seated class circle and rejoining it as the storyteller or storymaker;

■ defining a particular chair as the storyteller's chair or using an object such as a stick or a staff to denote that you are storytelling.

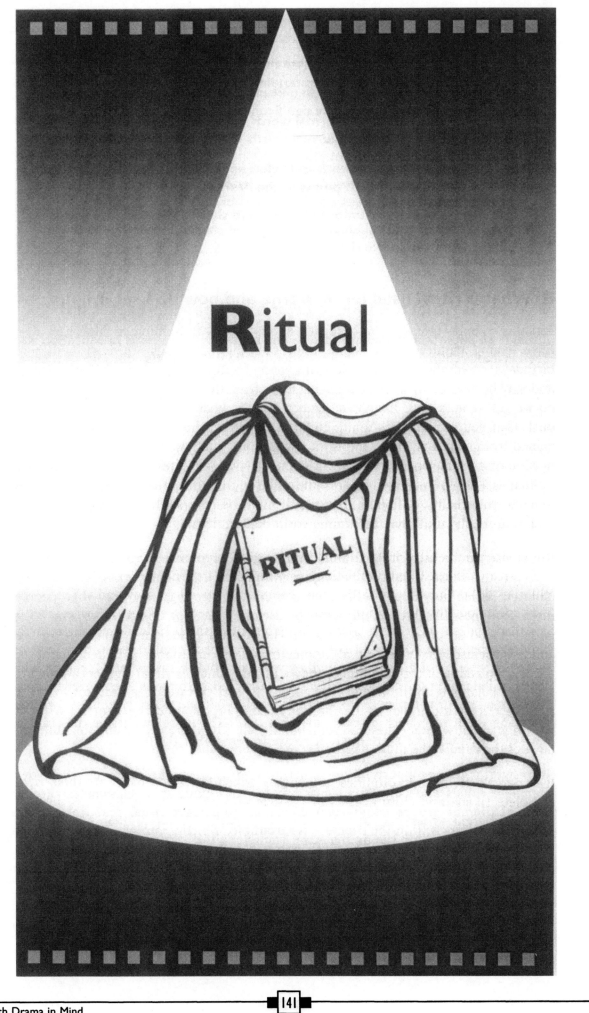

# **R**itual

PART TWO

With Drama in Mind

### ■ Through ritual you can:

■ help pupils to develop an understanding of cultural symbolism;

■ facilitate reflective thinking at significant moments in the drama;

■ imbue stylized actions and formal words with great significance and meaning linked to the drama;

■ offer a very secure framework and reference point that can be repeated or returned to at different points in the drama;

■ give a sense of cultural unity, belonging and shared ownership to the participants within the ritual.

### ■ What is ritual used for in drama and how do I set it up?

Ritual is an important element of theatre and is used within drama in education also. Even young children have some understanding of rituals, through bedtimes, birthdays, assemblies and so forth. With young children, rituals may be very simple and may be devised by the teacher using ideas from the children – for example, 'How do we get to Storyland? I can't remember exactly what I have to do with this story dust. Can you remember?' Young children will soon draw on their understanding gained from story and films and offer suggestions, such as 'You sprinkle it on your head and say some special words.' Teachers of young children sometimes introduce a ritual as a way of making it clear to the children that they are entering a drama and moving from reality to fiction. The ritual might be reversed to transfer back from fiction to reality and leave the drama world behind them.

Ritual also can be used in the drama itself to give importance to particular moments or to create a sense of cultural belonging within the fiction – for example, when the children decide how to call a fictitious community meeting, how and when people may speak (possibly through the symbolic use of a 'speaking object'), how a meeting is called and so on (*Unit 4, Activity 5*). The ideas should ideally come from the children themselves. Once a ritual for meetings has been established, then whenever there is a meeting of the community they will carry out this ritual and feel a growing sense of belonging to the imagined community and culture. It is best not to make rituals too long or complex as the children need to be able to carry them out without worrying about whether they can remember it all. The more ownership the children have of the rituals, the more likely they are to remember them.

It is worth giving opportunities sometimes to children to make up their own complete rituals and cultural rites of passage and guide their classmates through them. Different groups could each create an important ritual that links to the imagined culture within the drama – for example, a birth, coming of age, marriage, death, the change of seasons, a full moon. As they create fictitious rituals and ceremonies together, children pool together those rituals that are familiar to them and gain a greater understanding of them in the process.

# **O**ther **D**rama **S**trategies

## ■ Visualization

This is not a drama strategy as much as a technique that can be used effectively within drama to help children to imagine the setting within which the drama takes place or to imagine what a character or a scene looks like (*Unit 1, Activity 1*). The children close their eyes and are given language laden with visual reference and imagery. They try to visualize in their mind's eyes what is being described. Sometimes they are invited to add their own detail to the visualization out loud verbally and share it or else visualize further privately.

Following a visualization young children can be asked to sketch or paint what they have seen in their minds' eye using either imaginary or real drawing and painting tools.

## ■ Paired Storytelling/Storymaking

Asking children to tell each other the drama as a story at different points, either as storytellers or as characters within the drama, helps consolidation and reflection (*Unit 5, Activity 6*). It also means that, if the teacher wants them to write the drama in story form, then it has been rehearsed verbally first. This supports the writing. However, linking drama too frequently with 'writing afterwards' can be counterproductive unless the writing arises for a purpose that links directly and feeds back into the drama.

## ■ Eyewitness

This encourages active watching and listening. Children are asked to witness scenes as onlookers who will then be asked about what they have seen by someone who was supposedly not present. They may be asked about what they have seen by a particular character in the drama or else just by the teacher as an interested person. Sometimes what the eyewitness can see of a scene may be deliberately restricted – for example, by asking them to look at it through a tube while covering one eye or by looking through fingers that are making a peephole (*Unit 1, Activity 5*). This means that parts of scenes are seen but parts are missed and other people may be able to add missed details.

## ■ Occupational Mime

This is perhaps self-explanatory. The children are asked to imagine that they have particular occupations or jobs that are relevant to the drama – for example, when pretending to be Native Americans they might mime hunting or skinning buffalo, making a canoe or cooking on a fire. It is a useful way of helping children to engage with their roles in a non-threatening way but should not be used for long periods of time unless there is a particular purpose. Setting up scenes in which children are miming occupations gives a familiar reference point that can be re-created at different points in the drama and used. For example, the children return to miming

**PART TWO**

their familiar everyday tasks on a different day in the drama but a stranger (Teacher in Role) arrives in the scene and starts asking questions.

If teachers are returning to a drama that they started in a previous lesson then returning to a piece of occupational mime can be a quick way of getting back into the drama and re-engaging with roles.

## ■ Speaking Objects

Strange as this may sound, this really works! The children are invited to become objects in a scene. The objects that they become can have the opportunity to speak and maybe to comment on characters they have seen or know well, or events which they have witnessed. For example, when doing a drama about Mr Once upon a Time with children (*Unit 1*) we set up Mrs Slush's room at story time. One child entered the circle and said he was the roaring fire. Another child curled up in front of it and said she was the cat. A child entered and said he was Mrs Slush's favourite storybook… and so on. The objects can be questioned by other children who stay out of the scene – for example, a child may ask: 'Storybook. Which is Mrs Slush's favourite story?' or 'Cat. Do you always stay in at story time?' Teachers can remain alert to the cross-curricular opportunities that are thrown up by the objects the children decide to become – for example, painting the reflection in the mirror, listing the contents of the wastepaper basket, writing the favourite story in the book…

The idea of Speaking Objects links well to the way that young children perceive objects as being alive. It also supports children to understand personification.

## ■ Meetings

Meetings within dramas are a good way of bringing the class together in role for a shared and particular purpose. In class drama, teachers need to give opportunity for individual, group and whole-class working in role. The meeting can be a forum for the latter. The children may bring to the meeting information and news that has arisen through their group-work. The meeting weaves it all back into one drama. Meetings may be formal – for example, the Mayor wishes to speak to the townsfolk or Chief Seattle wishes to address his people (*Unit 5*) or they may be more informal, such as the townsfolk gathering together in the street for a good gossip and moan about Mr Once Upon a Time interrupting their stories (*Unit 1*).

Formal or informal meetings give children the opportunity to practise different types of speech register for different purposes and audiences. They also give opportunity for considering and practising citizenship.

## ■ Soundtracks/Sound Collages/Voice Collages/Soundscapes

Creating soundtracks, sound collages and/or voice collages/soundscapes is a means of focusing on giving and receiving an auditory experience linked to the drama. Sound collages are very flexible. They gather sounds in a sound mix. They are different from sound tracks, which are linear and realistic. A sound collage plays with sound in an experiential and experimental way. Sound collages can involve sounds, voice and words or just sounds alone. They can be spontaneous or rehearsed and performed. The children can work in groups or as a whole class to bring together sounds on a theme or setting or linked to a particular moment or character. The sounds might be juxtaposed, repeated, have variation in pace and volume and so on. They may be made by voices and bodies, instruments, objects. The sound collage may involve using single words or fragments of speech from the drama. They can be used live or recorded as background to scenes or images to which they link.

Children could be asked to make the sounds in Mrs Slush's room (*Unit 1*). We might hear a cat miaow, the rain on the window, the scraping of a chair, the words 'Once Upon a Time', the crackling fire (made by screwing up paper). They might do this as it could really have sounded or else they might orchestrate the sounds of the room.

Sound collages or landscapes of sound (soundscapes) are often prepared by groups and presented to the rest of the class, who close their eyes to focus solely on the auditory stimuli. The performance can be presented by surrounding the listening children with the sound.

Linear soundtracks can be presented to each other to stimulate the imagination of the listener to fill in the unknown gaps and make a story in the mind. Sound collages and soundscapes are more abstract and atmospheric rather than literal and try to capture the essence of something rather than present a linear and realistic series of sound effects.

## ■ Sensory Tour

This involves one child leading another (who has his/her eyes closed) around the room and helping the led child to imagine that they are elsewhere. The leader offers descriptions of the place that the 'blind' child is supposedly passing through and also seeks out convincing multisensory experiences to add to the illusion. For example, the 'blind' child's hand might be led to touch a curtain and he/she may be told that it is the Mayor's gown that is being touched.

## ■ Reading Images Through Senses

This involves thinking and responding in a multisensory way to an image (*Unit 4, Activity 2*). When looking at an etching of a Victorian Cotton Mill for example, we can imagine ourselves stepping inside the picture and consider what the mutisensory experience of that might be. In role, children can be asked to talk about the sounds and smells as well as the sights, and to say what they are touching within that picture and what it feels like. For example, ' I can smell the oil of the machines and their sound is deafening. The thread is cutting into my hands, which are sore and tired. I can see a small boy climbing out from under the loom.' Sharing these virtual multi-sensory responses makes the setting vivid and 'real' and supports engagement with the fictitious setting.

# PART THREE

# **D**rama **U**nits

## ■ How to use these drama units

The following units of work are intended to exemplify a developmental and cross-curricular approach to the use of drama as a creative teaching and learning medium as outlined earlier in this book. The units are intended to support rather than constrain the teacher. It is hoped that teachers using these unit plans will listen to and observe the children attentively during the drama and use their contributions and ideas to weave into and shape the drama itself, rather than always work in a linear and prescriptive way through the activities. It is intended that, as teachers grow in confidence, they will be increasingly creative, playful and risk-taking in their drama lessons and will want to make these units their own, selecting from them and adapting them as necessary, depending on the children and their responses. The units may be considered to be most successful when they have been discarded altogether and give way to teachers developing their own drama plans with understanding of the medium and how and when to use the strategies effectively.

There is no time allocation specified for each unit of work or for the activities within them as this would be over-prescriptive and restrictive. Teachers will need to judge for themselves when an activity needs longer or has gone on long enough by gauging the level of the children's ongoing engagement. A unit of work will span several lessons or more, depending on the amount of time given to various activities and to the integration of the teacher's and pupils' own material and ideas. Teachers may decide to skip some activities or substitute others. They will need to be sensitive to the children's needs and emotions throughout and be guided by this more than any pre-existing unit plan.

Although the following units are linked to national curriculum Key Stages, teachers should remember that Key Stages are man-made divisions. In practice any of these units can be used with any Key Stage; any activity can be adapted by the sensitive teacher and made accessible to any age group. The units are open to being simplified for younger pupils or being made more challenging for use with Key Stage 4 and beyond.

All the drama strategies suggested in the units are fully explained within Part Two of this book.

## ■ The Drama Units

### Unit 1 (Key Stage 1) – Mr Once Upon a Time

This uses a picture book story as a stimulus. However it would be possible to develop the drama if necessary without having access to the book itself. It explores how best to deal with a stranger who arrives in town and persistently and naively interrupts the locals' storytelling.

### Unit 2 (Key Stage 2) – The Victorian Cotton Mill

This unit focuses on bringing alive a child-focused history topic, through the primary use of a visual image and a short piece of historical text. The unit explores the working conditions and exploitation of child mill workers and the power and influence of the mill owners. It also explores the notion of evidence and reform.

### Unit 3 (Key Stages 2 / 3) – Bullying

Bullying is a real issue in all schools, although often hidden. This unit demonstrates how to set up and focus on a fictitious bullying scene and how to engage safely with the different participants within it. It exemplifies ways of deconstructing situations and enabling individual and shared reflection, and tries to help participants recognize ways that they can be empowered to bring about positive changes.

### Unit 4 (Key Stages 2 / 3) – Building an Imaginary Culture and Community

Communities are central to many dramas and this unit demonstrates how to gradually set up an imaginary culture and community with a class. The imagined community can then become a forum for safely exploring issues of concern to real communities, past and present. How cultures identify and sustain themselves becomes increasingly apparent throughout.

### Unit 5 (Key Stages 2 / 3) – Chief Seattle's Speech

This unit explores the main themes of conservation and colonization, using as source material a famous speech reputedly given by Chief Seattle to the US government in 1854. The drama places a strong emphasis on the importance of cultural and spiritual heritage and the connections between Native Americans and the land.

# Mr Once Upon a Time

## KEY STAGE 1 (YEAR 1/2)

**This unit uses as its focus a picture book entitled *Mr Once Upon a Time* by Remy Simard and Pierre Pratt (Annick Press Ltd, 1998). Access to the picture book is desirable but not essential as the story outline is provided below.**

Do *not* read the story to the children before you start. You can read small parts of the story as a lead in to the activities but if the children know the story they may recall and then re-enact the existing story rather than use it as a frame to imagine and create their own story-drama.

## Universal themes

- Fear and rejection of outsiders.
- The human need to belong to a place and people.
- The importance to cultures of oral storytelling.
- Crime, punishment and justice.

## ■ Story outline

*Every evening, in a faraway rainy village, the villagers enjoy storytelling in their homes. One day a strange man in a red van arrives and irritates the villagers by interrupting their stories. It turns out that his name is Mr Once Upon a Time and he is answering his name when the villagers tell stories starting with this phrase. Eventually the situation becomes intolerable to the villagers. The people complain to the police, who trick him into a cell and lock him up without trial. The villagers' storytelling can now*

*continue but it is spoilt as they keep thinking of Mr Once Upon a Time in prison. Because of this they cannot enjoy their storytelling any more. The Mayor calls a meeting and says they must release their prisoner. The villagers are trying to think of other ways to solve their problem when the youngest child in the village suggests that they get him to change his name. Mr Once Upon a Time becomes Mr The End and never arrives in homes again until stories are finished.*

| | Drama strategy | Purpose | Grouping | Teacher guidance and possible cross-curricular links |
|---|---|---|---|---|
| 1 | Visualization | ■ Initial engagement with role, setting and plot<br><br>■ To create an internal visual key image<br><br>■ To stimulate an imagined multisensory response | Individual and then whole class | Read the first page and show the picture of the people storytelling in their lit windows. Ask the children to close their eyes and imagine that they are inside one of the houses at story time. Ask them to think about what they hear… see… smell. You could give them opportunity to say or record aloud some of these thoughts. (Resource Sheet 1)<br><br>*ICT link (digital imagery and computer aided design)*<br>*Digital photos of the window scenes could be taken and superimposed on house images.* |
| 2 | Still Image | ■ To physically engage with a role<br><br>■ To set up paired interaction in role | Pairs | Ask the children to get into a space in pairs. They are going to pretend to be villagers. Ask them to make themselves into a still picture of a storytelling scene as seen through a window. They can base it on the one in the book or create their own. |
| 3 | Paired Storytelling<br><br>Still Image/ Freeze-frame | ■ To create the setting<br><br>■ To begin to link image, action, thought and speech in relation to role<br><br>■ To encourage paired interaction in role<br><br>■ To rehearse a successful story opening | Pairs | Explain to the children that they will re-form the still image from Activity 2 and, at a signal from you, they will bring the scene to life. One person will tell the other the opening sentence of a story of their own creation. They will tell only the opening sentence to their partner before freezing the action again and leaving their partner wanting more of the story.<br><br>Give them a moment or two to think about their opening sentence before reforming the still image. Let each partner have a turn as storyteller.<br><br>*Literacy link*<br>*Write the many opening sentences on paper sentence strips to be made available to the class.* |

| | | | |
|---|---|---|---|
| 4 | **Eavesdropping** | ■ To enable every person to share their story opening verbally<br><br>■ To ritualize active listening<br><br>■ To stimulate imaginations through offering modelled, imaginative story openings | Pairs and whole class | Ask the pairs to reform their still images once more. Tell them that you will pass by each still image in turn as if you are passing by each village window and eavesdropping at story time. As you pass by each person in turn, they will come to life and speak their story opening aloud for all to hear.<br><br>They will freeze again after giving their opening. |
| 5 | **Eyewitness**<br><br>**Thought-tracking** | ■ To engage with an imaginary key character and moment<br><br>■ To support clarification of in-role thoughts about another character<br><br>■ To enable sharing of thoughts about an event and character | Individual and then whole class (in circle facing outwards) | Ask each child to make a peephole with their thumb and a finger. Ask them to imagine that they are looking through a crack in their curtains as the stranger arrives and gets out of his van. Strangers rarely visit this village. What are they thinking as he arrives? Around the circle give each child in turn the opportunity to speak aloud what they are thinking as they look at the stranger. |

**PART THREE**

| | Drama strategy | Purpose | Grouping | Teacher guidance and possible cross-curricular links |
|---|---|---|---|---|
| 6 | Improvisation<br><br>Small Group Playmaking<br><br>Teacher in Role | ■ To deepen engagement with role and situation<br><br>■ To practically explore and develop the plot<br><br>■ To encourage empathy<br><br>■ To encourage individual and group problem solving<br><br>■ To encourage dialogic talk | One group and class audience | Tell the children that the centre of the circle is an acting space and represents the house of Mrs Slush as she is about to tell her evening story. Invite a few children to place themselves in the acting space as Mrs Slush and her children.<br><br>The child who is to play Mrs Slush is asked to tell the children a story that begins 'Once upon a time'. They may improvise getting ready for the story first – for example, stoking the fire or letting the cat out. Every time Mrs Slush starts the story, the teacher in role as Mr Once Upon a Time will surprise the class by knocking on the door and interrupting them. The teacher is aiming to innocently frustrate and irritate the Sludges into interacting and responding with the teacher in role. |
| 7 | Still Image<br><br>Performance Carousel<br><br>Improvised Small Group Playmaking<br><br>Hot-seating | ■ To offer pupils ownership through creative extension of storyline<br><br>■ To synthesize a scene into one sentence<br><br>■ To present a series of visual images or short scenes that stimulate meaning making and questioning<br><br>■ To elicit information of interest to the children | Groups of four and then whole class | Ask the children to make a group still picture showing a village scene with an incident involving the character of Mr Once Upon a Time. Ask them to caption the scene.<br><br>Set up a presentation of each still image in turn (possibly through Performance Carousel). You may wish to bring it alive for a minute or two.<br><br>Invite the audience to question any of the characters in the scenes. |

| | | | |
|---|---|---|---|
| | **Teacher as Storyteller** | ■ To provide a narrative model | | The teacher could appear to read from the storybook and ad-lib the imagined text for the newly created additional scenes, in the style of the author. |
| **8** | **Rumours** **Teacher in Role** | ■ To encourage information giving and gathering ■ To create collective fiction at speed ■ To break down physical distance between the class members ■ To develop and model reasoning | Whole class | The villagers would have become increasingly frustrated and annoyed with Mr Once Upon a Time. Ask the children to think of one thing that they want to say about him to their fellow villagers. Ask them to gather together into one big class group and when the teacher shouts 'Rumours!' everyone (including the teacher) will have a short time to rush around gathering and spreading whispered rumours about Mr Once Upon a Time. You can add information you know to be true – for example, he has a hearing aid. Afterwards you could gather the rumours together with the class and consider the nature and purpose of rumours. **Maths link** *What is the probability of different rumours being true? Which of them could possibly or not possibly be true? Why? (Some of these could be recorded on Resource Sheet 2a)* **PSHE link** *Why are rumours started and spread? How do they make rumour-monger and victim feel? How might we respond in positive ways to hearing rumours?* |

**PART THREE**

| | Drama strategy | Purpose | Grouping | Teacher guidance and possible cross-curricular links |
|---|---|---|---|---|
| 9 | **Eavesdropping (telephone conversation)** | ■ To support in-role dialogue<br><br>■ To give opportunity for using formal and occupational speech | Pairs (seated back to back) | Tell the children to decide in their pairs who is to be Mrs Slush and who will be a policeman. Ask them to improvise a telephone conversation between the two characters. Mrs Slush is officially complaining to the police about Mr Once Upon a Time interrupting her stories.<br><br>**Literacy link**<br>*You may decide that the policeman will record details, prepare a statement or that Mrs Slush will need to fill in an incident form.* |
| 10 | **Eavesdropping** | ■ To give every child the opportunity to be heard performing<br><br>■ To gather and share ideas on the same moment and theme | Pairs and whole class | Tell the children that you will pass by each of them in turn and whoever you are standing nearest to has the opportunity to speak aloud a sentence or two from the telephone conversation they improvised in Activity 9.<br><br>**Literacy link**<br>*The shared ideas can form the basis of a letter of complaint* |
| 11 | **Improvisation**<br><br>**Teacher in Role** | ■ To encourage group problem solving in role<br><br>■ To encourage planning, questioning and challenging in role<br><br>■ To encourage the analysis of courses of action | Small groups and then whole class | Ask the children in role, to agree group plans that might solve the problem of Mr Once Upon a Time and his interruptions. You could gather their ideas in role as the Mayor and invite inter-group questioning.<br><br>You could ask for a positive, negative and interesting aspect of each group's plan (Resource Sheet 3) |

| | | | |
|---|---|---|---|
| 12 | | Whole class circle (standing) | The class circle represents the boundaries of the prison cell and each child represents one of the prison bars. |
| | Thought-tracking | ■ To encourage empathy<br>■ To tag a thought and visual image<br>■ To share thoughts and feelings about a key moment | The children in turn have opportunity to speak aloud the thoughts of the imprisoned Mr Once Upon a Time, who is represented by the teacher seated in the centre. |
| | Teacher in Role | ■ To provide a model of thinking aloud and give access to the teacher in role thoughts | The teacher in role can speak aloud Mr Once Upon a Time's thoughts either at the beginning, if support and modelling is required, or at the end to bring the soliloquy to a close.<br><br>*Literacy link*<br>■ *Thoughts could be recorded (Resource Sheet 4).*<br>■ *Allow Mr Once Upon a Time to write one letter or card from prison or allow him one phone call (possibly taped), to an imaginary recipient of his choice.* |
| 13 | Still Image<br><br>Eavesdropping | ■ To re-play a previous activity in a different context (Activity 4) and consider the effect on performance<br>■ To hold still an affective moment for reflective thinking | Group, individual and whole class | Ask the children to return to their earlier storytelling still images. This time when you pass by each child they will have opportunity to tell their story opening as before (or changed) but this time without their hearts in it. Every time they start to tell a story they will be thinking of the poor, imprisoned Mr Once Upon a Time alone and sad in his cell. |

**PART THREE**

| | Drama strategy | Purpose | Grouping | Teacher guidance and possible cross-curricular links |
|---|---|---|---|---|
| 14 | Improvisation<br><br>Teacher in Role | ■ To encourage whole-class problem solving<br><br>■ To consider together the pros and cons of a variety of possible courses of action<br><br>■ To give opportunity for the teacher to model formal speech | Whole class | The teacher in role as the Mayor calls a meeting to inform the villagers that they cannot keep Mr Once Upon a Time imprisoned without trial. The Mayor asks the villagers what they want him to do with the prisoner. You could use a very formal speech register as a model – for example, 'My good townsfolk. As you are all aware I am the Mayor of this town and I am afraid that I have to ask for your assistance with a rather delicate matter...' |
| | Conscience Alley | ■ To share openly the pros and cons of a suggested course of action | | When a course of action is being considered – such as whether to throw Mr Once Upon a Time out of town – the teacher can ask the children to form two lines facing each other. The teacher passes between the lines. One line of children gives reasons *for* and the other line gives reasons *against* any action being considered.<br><br>*Literacy link*<br>*The pros and cons can be recorded and form a writing frame for a spoken, balanced argument or a persuasive letter to the Mayor or local newspaper (Resource Sheets 5a and b)* |
| 15 | Improvisation<br><br>Teacher in Role | ■ To encourage reasoned discussion and justification | Groups | What alternative name could the children offer Mr Once Upon a Time? In groups, ask the children to work in role and come up with a new name for him. They should be able to explain the reason for the group's choice of name when asked by the Mayor (teacher in role). |

| | | | | |
|---|---|---|---|---|
| 16 | **Conscience Alley**<br><br>**Teacher in Role** | ▪ To consider pros and cons of a course of action<br><br>▪ To consider the importance of one's name in relation to self | Whole class | How will the children persuade Mr Once Upon a Time to adopt a new name? With the children in two lines you pass slowly up the middle in role as Mr Once Upon a Time. As you pass through, the children in one line will, in turn, give you a reason each why you should change your name – for example, 'It will show the villagers that you are really trying to get on with them.' The children in the other line will each give you a reason why you should not change your name – such as, 'Your mother gave your name to you.' |
| 17 | **Collective Voice**<br><br>**Teacher in Role** | ▪ To encourage private and shared reflection about the drama and the issues within it<br><br>▪ To give opportunity for shared ownership of the missing details of the story-drama | Whole class | Tell the children that many years have passed. You will pretend to be a child and they are all pretending together to be one grandparent. This is the first time that the grandchild (teacher in role) will have heard about the events long ago relating to Mr Once Upon a Time.<br><br>The teacher as child will ask questions about the past, trying to ensure that the questions are not merely asking for recall of factual information. The class will have opportunity in turn to answer the questions as the grandparent.<br><br>▪ Where had Mr Once Upon a Time come from?<br>▪ What was the worst thing that he did?<br>▪ What did you feel when he was put in prison?<br>▪ What happened after he was let out of prison?<br>▪ Where is he now? |
| 18 | **Role on the Wall** | ▪ To gather and categorize information about a character at the end of the drama | | Following Activity 17 the children could record what they know, think they know and still want to know about Mr Once Upon a Time (Resource Sheet 8b). |

**PART THREE**

| | Drama strategy | Purpose | Grouping | Teacher guidance and possible cross-curricular links |
|---|---|---|---|---|
| 19 | Teacher as Storyteller | ■ To model narrative storytelling<br><br>■ To bring the drama to a satisfactory close based on their ideas and thereby retaining their ownership of the fiction | Whole class | Using what you have heard from the children during Activity 17, bring the drama to a close by telling their grandmother's version of the story back to them as a third person narrative – for example, 'After Mr Once Upon a Time was set free the villagers felt happier. Soon people started to treat him more kindly…' |

# ■ Some possible follow-up cross-curricular activities

Now read the storybook to the children if you wish. Draw from the children the similarities and differences between the published story and their story-drama.

They could:

- Tell and then write their own version of events (in the style of the author).
- Paint missing pictures to add to the storybook (in the style of the artist).
- Script or re-script a short piece of key dialogue from the story-drama.
- Make a pictorial map of the village and label it.
- Write a newspaper report on the release of Mr Once Upon a Time.

# The Victorian Cotton Mill

## KEY STAGE 2

This unit uses as its focus a Victorian etching entitled *Love Conquers Fear* (Manchester Public Libraries Service), which can be found on Resource Sheet 7a).

There are many available etchings and photographs that relate to child labour in Victorian times. There are also a range of texts and documents readily available through school libraries, educational publishers and library and museum services. The children can search via the internet for additional authentic images and text that may be linked into the drama. Dr Barnardo's has a range of powerful Victorian photographs that can be purchased and used educationally.

## Some background information

■ Cotton mills relied on women and children as cheap labour.

■ Children were paid a few pennies a week.

■ Children as young as six years old worked with dangerous machinery for up to 12 hours a day.

■ Meal breaks were infrequent and short.

■ Machines were cleaned on Sundays by children.

■ Children who worked too slowly or fell asleep were given the strap.

■ Sometimes sleeping children fell into machines and were killed.

■ Machines were unguarded and injuries such as crushed hands, tangled hair and scalping were common.

■ In 1850 there were 331,000 cotton mill workers and 15,000 were under 14 years old.

■ By 1868 some children were 'short-timers' who worked up to 30 hours a week and had at least 15 hours of schooling.

## Universal themes

■ Exploitation
■ Child labour
■ Power and corruption
■ Industrialization
■ Wealth and poverty
■ Health and safety at work

## PART THREE

| Drama strategy | Purpose | Grouping | Teacher guidance and possible cross-curricular links |
|---|---|---|---|
| **Reading images through the senses** | ■ To encourage focused multisensory engagement with, and access to, the image<br><br>■ To move towards engagement with role, 'as if' they are within the picture | Four groups | Divide the class into four groups.<br><br>Ask **Group A** to look at the picture with a focus on the sounds that would be heard if the picture came alive.<br><br>Ask **Group B** to focus on what they would smell if the picture came alive.<br><br>Ask **Group C** to focus on what sources of movement there are in the picture and what those movements would look like if the picture came alive.<br><br>Ask **Group D** to focus on what people are touching in the picture and what it might feel like. (It would be possible to have another group that focuses on 'taste' but this may be a little limited within this picture.) |
| **Soundscape** | ■ To encourage aural and kinesthetic engagement with the image and setting for the drama | | Ask **Group A** to use their bodies as instruments (and/or use actual instruments) to make a sound collage or soundtrack that can be repeated, to go with the picture. |
| **Devising performance** | ■ To encourage group interaction which integrates visual, aural and kinesthetic activities<br><br>■ To share and record imagined experience visually, aurally and kinesthetically | | *Music link*<br>■ *This could be developed into a group composition, which could be recorded in some way and then used to link with the movement (Group C) or as a background for the verse written by Group B describing the smells or the tactile experiences (Group D). This could be presented to an audience.*<br><br>**Group B** – Ask this group to work together to describe the smells as if they are in the picture (present tense). |

| Activity | Aims | Description |
|---|---|---|
| Literacy activity (possibly leading to performance poetry) | ■ To record and share imagined experience in words <br> ■ To use visual image as a stimulus for the written and spoken word | **Literacy link** <br> *These descriptions can be written down on sentence strips – for example 'I can smell stale sweat filling the air.' Each person in the group can write one sentence on a paper strip and then negotiate the order of the sentences to create a collective description, a piece of 'shared writing' about the smells. This could be performed in some way.* |
| Movement/ devising dance | ■ To use visual image as a stimulus for movement <br> ■ To share and record imagined experience kinesthetically <br> ■ To link aural and kinesthetic thought and experience | **Group C** – Ask the members of this group to each focus on a different movement from within the picture, such as the crawling boy or the tapping of the master's crop. They should use their bodies to exaggerate and repeat the selected movement in slow motion. The body can become the moving object itself – the body moves as if it is the master's whip, for example. <br><br> The individual group members' movements can then be linked to each other and a group movement sequence created. Sound could be added, such as the cracking sound of the whip as it moves. <br><br> **Dance opportunity** <br> *This could be rehearsed and put with machinery sounds, music or the sound collage created by Group A.* |
| Literacy activity (possibly leading to performance poetry) | ■ To encourage an imagined tactile response to the image | **Group D** – Ask this group to list the tactile experiences within the picture – for example, bare hands and feet on wood, forearms on cotton strands, the leather crop in the fingers, the inside of a jacket pocket, the warm hand on a shoulder, the warm air of a whisper, and so on. |

**PART THREE**

| Drama strategy | Purpose | Grouping | Teacher guidance and possible cross-curricular links |
|---|---|---|---|
| **Sensory Tour** | ■ To encourage empathy<br><br>■ To encourage close working in partnership with the focus on the quality of the partner's experience | | **Art and Design link**<br>*Group D could then prepare a tactile experience based on this image either for each other or another group to experience. Ask the children to gather materials that represent those in the picture – a ball of wool for the thread, a stick for the whip, some cotton wool for the flax, for example.*<br><br>Ask the children to place the objects around the room and then to lead a partner on a conducted tour of the cotton mill in the picture. The person being led has their eyes closed. The person leading tries to build their partner's belief that they are in the cotton mill, inviting them to touch the placed objects and building up the tour. For example, 'You are now touching the master's whip… he has hurt a good many children in this mill with it… touch it here… feel the handle…' and so on. |
| 2 **Reading the Image** | ■ To encourage a free-flow and sharing of ideas<br><br>■ To encourage speculation | Whole class | Ask the children to simply talk about the picture with you. You could have a free discussion or else you could ask questions.<br><br>■ What *might* be going on in this picture?<br>■ Which part of the picture interests them most and why?<br>■ In turn, complete the sentence, 'I wonder …' For example, 'I wonder what the boy is whispering.'<br>■ What words would they use to describe the facial expressions (or the poses) of the characters?<br><br>You could use *Resource Sheet 7b* to focus in on, and maybe record, what they know, think they know and want to know when they look at this picture. |

| # | Activity | Objectives | Grouping | Description |
|---|---|---|---|---|
| 3 | Group discussion in preparation for a drama activity | ■ To encourage the children to look in detail at the picture with a specific focus<br>■ To encourage a supported and shared interpretation of an image | Groups of four | Photocopy the picture (Resource Sheet 7a) and ask the children in groups of about four to circle or label areas of potential danger within the picture – the boy under the working loom or the whip for instance.<br><br>You could discuss the relative levels of danger. Which are potentially lethal? What are the likely potential injuries? |
| 4 | Tableau (Still Image) | ■ To locate a drama space<br>■ To enable children to engage with an imagined role and setting | Whole-class circle | Tell the children that the centre of the circle represents the mill room in the picture. You may wish to locate the imaginary windows and loom for them.<br><br>Invite up to ten children in turn to look carefully at the picture and then to come to the centre of the circle and place themselves within the drama space as one of the characters. As they enter they simply explain who they are and then hold a still position – for example, 'I am the man with his hands in his pockets, listening to the factory owner', or 'I am the woman leaning across the loom.' The remaining children are audience. |
| 5 | Improvisation | ■ To give opportunity for verbal and active engagement with role<br>■ To create the atmosphere and setting for the drama | Whole class | Explain that the scene will come to life, just for a minute or two, and that those in the scene will have the opportunity to improvise for a while. The scene that they depict should portray just an ordinary day in the factory. They should speak and behave as their character in the picture. There will probably be several people talking at once, as this is improvisation not performance. |
|  | Teacher as Storyteller | ■ To establish a clear start to the improvisation |  | You may wish to guide the children into the improvisation using a teacher narrative – for example, 'It was a typical day in the mill. The air was hot and dusty and the sound of the machines was deafening....' (click fingers to signal the start of the improvisation). |

PART THREE

| | Drama strategy | Purpose | Grouping | Teacher guidance and possible cross-curricular links |
|---|---|---|---|---|
| | **Pupil as Narrative Storyteller** | ■ To set the scene for the improvisation<br><br>■ This encourages active audience engagement, participation and comment | Whole class | You could ask the audience children to narrate aloud to themselves what they are witnessing, as if they are the commentators on the improvisation – for example 'The master looks annoyed and he is tapping his whip on his hand. The man he is talking to looks worried…' |
| 6 | **Tableau (Still Image)**<br><br>**Eavesdropping**<br><br>**Freeze-frame** | ■ To bring a still image to life in a controlled and focused way<br><br>■ To return to an established moment as a shared and clear starting point<br><br>■ To give opportunity for making public contributions to the drama as a whole<br><br>■ To maintain focus on specific characters and parts of the scene | | Explain to the children that you want to find out with them what is happening in different parts of the scene that they have just improvised. Ask them to re-create the tableau (Activity 4) and explain that when you are standing near different characters and groups of characters, they will come to life and be heard. When you move away from them they will freeze back into a tableau. This can be a repeat of their original improvisation or they may improvise anew.<br><br>There are likely to be ideas that have been shared through the improvisations that can be used and woven into the evolving drama. |

## ■ Accident at the mill

For the next part of the drama you could let the children decide on their own mill accident based on the dangers they have already considered, or else you could use an authentic, documented accident, such as the one on the right. Whichever you choose, the same drama strategies can be used.

### ICT opportunity

*The children could use the internet to research real mill accidents and select from them as the basis of a re-enactment within the following drama.*

'When I went to the spinning mill I was about seven. The whole was strange to me. The dust, the hissing and roaring, the bad language. One boy sat down to rest. In moments he was fast asleep. The master happened to pass. Without warning he gave the boy a violent slap, which stunned him. Half asleep he ran to the machine and in five minutes his left hand got tangled with the machinery. Two of his fingers were crushed to a jelly.'

*Child mill worker*

| | Drama strategy | Purpose | Grouping | Teacher guidance and possible cross-curricular links |
|---|---|---|---|---|
| 7 | Tableau (Still Image) | ■ To actively engage all pupils in a key moment within the drama<br><br>■ To offer shared ownership and individual stakes in the evolving fiction | Whole class | Ask the children to re-create the original tableau from Activity 4. Invite the children who have been audience to add themselves to the tableau as additional characters. Entering one or two at a time, they should offer a statement about themselves as they enter, so that everyone hears who they are – for instance, 'I am a young boy and I am sweeping the floor', or 'I am the daughter of the woman at the loom. I am nine years old and I do the same job as my mother.' |
| | Improvisation Freeze-frame | ■ To integrate the whole class into the opening scene and define its start and finish | | Bring the scene alive and let it run for a couple of minutes before calling 'Freeze!' and holding it for a few seconds. |

**PART THREE**

| | Drama strategy | Purpose | Grouping | Teacher guidance and possible cross-curricular links |
|---|---|---|---|---|
| | **Preparation for re-enactment** | ■ To introduce the next scene's basic content | | Ask the children to sit down where they are and listen. Explain that in a moment there will be an accident in the mill. Read aloud the account of it (see previous page). Negotiate who will represent the main characters. If the example above is used then you will need to decide who is the boy and who is the master. Explain that there will be no real physical violence and that the slap should be mimed (possibly in slow motion). |
| 8 | **Freeze-frame** **Teacher as Storyteller** | ■ To re-establish a particular moment in the drama ■ To set the scene and provide atmosphere ■ To offer a model of narrative | Whole class | Explain that in a moment the children will re-create the freeze-frame from Activity 7 and that you will narrate the scene opening – for example, 'It was late in the day at the cotton mill. Some of the children had been working for almost 12 hours…' |
| | **Improvisation** **Freeze-frame** | ■ To bring the account of the accident to life through re-enactment ■ To hold still a key moment in the drama and ensure a united end to the scene. | | Following the teacher narration click your fingers as a signal for the improvisation. They should build up to the accident. The participants should freeze again a few moments after the accident. |
| | **Forum Theatre** | ■ To offer opportunity for evaluation, direction and substitution by 'spect-actors' | | Withdraw a group of up to four children to watch the scene as directors. After they have seen it once through they may make suggestions to the actors for an improved re-play or exchange places with a character for the changed re-enactment. |

With Drama in Mind

**PART THREE**

|   |   | Objectives | Grouping | Activity |
|---|---|---|---|---|
|   | **Freeze-frame** | ■ To hold a key moment still in preparation for Thought-tracking |   | Finish with a freeze-frame. |
| 9 | **Thought-tracking** | ■ To reveal the inner thoughts of the eyewitnesses and others present at a key moment | Whole class | Explain that you will pass by each still person in turn and as you pass by, they have opportunity to speak aloud the inner thoughts of their character at the moment after the accident has happened. |
| 10 | **Teacher in Role** | ■ To introduce a moral dilemma<br><br>■ To discover the pupils' responses (in role) to injustice, coercion and intimidation<br><br>■ To highlight contextual tensions about voicing the truth<br><br>■ To raise children's awareness that literacy can be abused as power over the illiterate | Whole class | Explain that you will be in role as the mill owner for a while. Explain that the accident is going to be investigated by a factory inspector whose arrival is imminent and that you will be talking with the children to find out what they are going to say to him. You want them to make it clear that you are a good employer, very safety conscious and that the boy who had the accident was a simpleton. Anyone who says a word against you will be fired. How you play the role is up to you but initial subtlety rather than immediate intimidation may be most productive.<br><br>*Literacy link*<br>*You could ask the class to write witness statements. You could scribe these on the pretext that the mill workers were mainly illiterate. This is an opportunity for you to scribe publicly and inaccurately in favour of the mill owner and ask the class to sign it as the truth. Remind them that they can't read or write.*<br><br>Using Resource Sheet 8a you could gather the children's thoughts about the mill owner at this time. |
|   | **Role on the Wall** |   |   |   |

| | Drama strategy | Purpose | Grouping | Teacher guidance and possible cross-curricular links |
|---|---|---|---|---|
| 11 | Teacher in Role | ■ To give opportunity for the pupils to 'spill the beans' or 'keep mum' retrospectively<br><br>■ To help build up a collective account of the accident<br><br>■ To challenge the children in role to adopt a particular standpoint<br><br>■ To demonstrate an awareness of how we adapt our speech for different audiences<br><br>■ To give opportunity for extended responses<br><br>■ To offer an opportunity for alternative means of communication<br><br>■ To encourage the visioning of ideals | Whole class | Explain that you now enter in role as the visiting factory inspector who is investigating the accident. The class will return to their factory work and you will pass among them asking questions of them. The mill owner is not present as you talk with them. How you play this role is likely to affect the pupils' responses. You could play it in different ways and discuss whether this results in any changes in response. You could play it as:<br><br>■ a sympathetic reformer, such as Lord Shaftesbury;<br>■ an impartial official gathering evidence;<br>■ someone who is clearly colluding with the mill owner.<br><br>Questions might include:<br>■ What exactly did you see?<br>■ What can you tell me about the boy who had the accident?<br>■ How would you describe your employer?<br>■ How might the accident have been prevented?<br>■ Do you feel able to speak with me freely or is anything preventing you from doing so?<br>■ Are there any changes you think should be made as a result of this accident?<br><br>*Literacy link*<br>*You could give the class the opportunity to write an anonymous note to the factory inspector (which could fall into the hands of the mill owner).*<br><br>An additional challenge might be to find a way of letting the factory inspector know the truth without writing it in words and without telling him verbally! |

| | | | | |
|---|---|---|---|---|
| 12 | Image Theatre | Groups of four | ■ To encourage a consideration of comparisons<br>■ To develop an understanding of symbolism | Ask the groups to create and rehearse two still images and to find a way of moving slowly and clearly, back and forth between them. The first image should portray the 'reality' of their life as mill workers and the second image should portray an 'ideal' image of how working in the mill could be in the 'ideal' future. The two images may be symbolic or emotional representations or could simply be contrasting scenes.<br><br>You may decide that sound or speech can be added by the participants or you may provide suitable background music. |
| 13 | Performance Carousel | Same groups as above | ■ To give opportunity for the sharing of group performances within a theatrical framework | Each group in turn now has the opportunity to present their two images. Each group performance should link seamlessly and without interruption to the one before and after it. |

## ■ Some possible follow-up cross-curricular activities

### Art and Design

The internet is a good way to view Victorian etchings. The mill accident could be the subject for an etching design.

### English

Consider how the accident was recorded in writing:

■ in the mill owner's newspaper
■ by the factory inspector
■ by the doctor
■ by a factory reformer
■ by the child's teacher (imagining that he had one)
■ in a transcription of what the victim said.

### History

This drama could open up an investigation into factory reforms and the lives of famous reformers. It also opens up further investigation into other forms of child labour in the past.

### Citizenship and PSHE

This drama can link to investigating the laws that protect children from exploitation by employers, historically and now. Comparisons can be made between the level of protection that children have in different parts of the world today (possibly linked to Geography).

PART THREE

# Bullying

## KEY STAGES 2 / 3

Bullying is deliberate, conscious, wilful and hostile behaviour that is carried out repeatedly with the knowledge that it is harmful. It is not necessarily linked to anger. Bullying is a form of oppression that can take various forms:

■ **Verbal** – e.g., name calling;

■ **Physical** – e.g., tripping people up, kicking, punching;

■ **Exclusion** – e.g., deliberately excluding someone from a game;

■ **Extortion** – e.g., taking someone's possessions or money, probably in a threatening way.

It is likely that some bullying happens in any school. By its nature it is usually hidden from view and therefore teachers are unlikely to be fully aware of the extent of it. It is a serious problem for many children (even leading to suicides) and most children will have been distressed by experiencing or witnessing bullying at some time.

The techniques that Boal uses in his Theatre of the Oppressed (TO) can be used or adapted within schools to help open up the issue of bullying and try to enable all participants to empathize and to see alternative ways of behaving or responding.

Dealing with bullying through drama may touch upon sensitivities for many children. Teachers are not drama therapists. It is important that the drama work remains fictitious and is based around archetypes, not known individuals. The children must not be allowed to replicate real current situations or use classmates' names. Nor should the teacher slip from fiction to reality and start to talk

## ● Universal themes

■ Oppression
■ Non-verbal communication
■ Conflict resolution
■ The power of unity
■ Protection of the weak/survival of the fittest
■ Inclusion and exclusion

about real class incidents within the drama. It is also important that the children are clear that the behaviour exhibited in the drama is the focus and that any behaviour within the drama is detached through role play from the real child.

Drama can be used to:

■ bring the issue of bullying into an open forum for discussion;

■ understand the victim's perspective and empathize with their feelings;

■ give children opportunity to express their feelings and experiences of bullying;

■ try to understand why children bully and how they might stop;

■ consider strategies for dealing more effectively with bullies, including alternative responses to them.

| | Drama strategy | Purpose | Grouping | Teacher guidance and possible cross-curricular links |
|---|---|---|---|---|
| 1 | Tableau/Still Image | ■ To introduce the theme of bullying, visually and symbolically<br><br>■ To encourage pupils to consciously analyse and respond to each others' body language | Whole-class circle | Explain that you want someone to come into the centre of the circle and, by their physical appearance alone, appear powerful.<br><br>Invite another child to enter the circle. They need to communicate with their bodies that they are more powerful than the child who is already positioned in the circle. There should be no bodily contact between the participants.<br><br>A third child then enters and has to appear more powerful than the second and so on. This activity should be carried out in silence and can be restarted several times with different groups of children.<br><br>Discuss this warm-up activity with the class afterwards. Which images seemed to communicate greatest power and why? What body signals do we associate with power? Are they all aggressive signals? Which body signals do we associate with lack of power? |
| 2 | Tableau/Still Image<br><br>Teacher in Role<br><br>Image Theatre | ■ To encourage children to 'read' body language<br><br>■ To encourage empathy with the victim, visually and symbolically | Whole-class circle | Invite a child to go into the centre of the circle alone and strike a still pose as 'a bully'. Explain that you will now enter the circle and place yourself as 'a victim'.<br><br>Give opportunity for a few children in turn to join you in the centre and add themselves to the still image as supporters of the victim. Challenge them to find a non-confrontational way of supporting you that does not signal aggression towards the bully. |

| | | | | |
|---|---|---|---|---|
| | | ■ To encourage pupils to consciously analyse and respond to each others' body language<br>■ To give opportunity for the modelling of assertive, positional support | | |
| **3** | **Class discussion in preparation for drama activity** | ■ To share ideas and gather definitions of bullying<br>■ To raise children's awareness of what can constitute bullying | Whole class | Ask the children what different types of bullying there are, avoiding mentioning identifiable examples based on their experiences. You might wish to categorize any examples within the four basic types (see page 173).<br><br>List the types of bullying on long paper strips using a thick felt-tip pen. Examples should include not just physical bullying but also name calling, excluding children from play, extortion and so on. You may wish to offer a definition of bullying. |
| **4** | **Still Image** | ■ To enable all pupils to engage with role and theme<br>■ To devise a collective image as an initial stimulus for improvisation | Groups of four | Give each group one of the paper strips with a type of bullying written on it.<br><br>Ask each group to make a still image that conveys the type of bullying written on their paper strip. Two people in the group will be the bullies (one bully and one bully supporter) and the other two will be the victim and the victim supporter. Encourage them to listen to each others' ideas and try ideas out before selecting. |

**PART THREE**

| | Drama strategy | Purpose | Grouping | Teacher guidance and possible cross-curricular links |
|---|---|---|---|---|
| 5 | Improvisation | ■ To support sustained engagement with role<br>■ To develop plot<br>■ To encourage verbal communication of make-believe<br>■ To give opportunity for moving image as a contrast to static image<br>■ To break down moments of bullying into steps | Same groups as above | Explain that in a moment the groups will bring their still image of 'Bully and Victim' to life for no longer than a minute. They can use speech but no physical contact between bullies and victims. You will signal the start and end of the short improvisation and if they need to finish earlier then they should 'freeze' and wait still and silently for the other groups to finish.<br><br>Ask the children to particularly focus on exploring the early moments that are leading towards bullying.<br><br>*Health and safety*<br>*Ask the children to avoid fight scenes. If any fighting is portrayed, it needs to be stylized in slow motion with no actual physical contact between pupils. It also needs to be clearly in role.* |
| 6 | Captions | ■ To synthesize an image in words | | Ask each group to make up a one sentence caption to accompany their image. |
| 7 | Performance Carousel | ■ To give each group the opportunity to present their scene<br>■ To provide a shared reference point and experience<br>■ To allow the groups to watch each others' scenes and see how each scene fits within the whole | Whole-class collectively in groups | Ask the groups to all get into their group still image positions again. In turn each group's image will come alive again. The group enactments will each commence with each group in turn saying their caption. While one group performs, the other groups should remain frozen but attentive to each other.<br><br>This will result in a continuous sequence of group's images coming to life and freezing again. Each will last for about a minute There should be no interim movement or chatter between scenes. This is intended to produce a seamless whole-class performance. |

| | Technique | Objectives | Organisation | Description |
|---|---|---|---|---|
| 8 | Still Image | ■ To offer a shared focus for whole-class discussion and analysis | Whole-class circle (seated) | Select one group's scene and ask that group to re-create their opening still image in the centre of the class circle. |
| 9 | Thought-tracking | ■ To give opportunity for sharing a diversity of in-role thoughts<br>■ To encourage empathy and highlight that there are a range of undisclosed responses in bullying situations | As above | Ask each character in the scene to speak aloud an 'in-role' thought at the moment portrayed by the image. Remind the children that within the group there is a bully, bully supporter, victim and victim supporter. |
| 10 | Forum Theatre | ■ To raise pupils' awareness of ways in which victims can empower themselves<br>■ To offer an opportunity for shared analysis<br>■ To help pupils reflect on the group dynamics of bully and victim and ways that the dynamics can be altered | As above | Ask the group to re-play their short scene. Ask the audience to focus on the victim. Is there anything that the victim says or does that could help them to not be a victim? Is there any advice that they could offer the victim (for example, eye-contact, movement, gesture, assertive but non-confrontational comment or action, perhaps). In other words, is there any way that the victim could behave differently and cease to be a victim? |
| | Improvisation | ■ To offer the possibility of alternative victim responses and behaviours leading to alternative outcomes | | Replay the scene (possibly allowing it to be extended through improvisation) with the victim following the advice received from the audience (or alternatively, allow one of the audience to be a substitute victim who will respond differently.) |

PART THREE

| | Drama strategy | Purpose | Grouping | Teacher guidance and possible cross-curricular links |
|---|---|---|---|---|
| 11 | Conscience Alley | ■ To offer shared ownership of the victim's thoughts<br><br>■ To bring out into the open constructive strategies and collective advice that can support victim to change their victim signals and behaviour | Whole class | You could create a Conscience Alley to represent the conflicting voices inside the victim's head. The class creates two lines facing each other and the victim passes up the middle, listening. As he passes each person, one line gives him good advice about how to assert him/herself positively. The other line gives poor advice, which would result in the person remaining a victim. |
| 12 | Preparation for Hot-seating | ■ To check that the person/people about to be hot-seated are consenting<br><br>■ To consider which aspects of a bully's psyche they would like to better understand | Whole class then pairs/group | Ask the child who was playing the bully in the central scene if they are prepared to be hot-seated as a bully by the audience and, if not, ask for a volunteer (or collective group of volunteers) to be a substitute for the bully.<br><br>Before hot-seating the bully (or collective bully), ask the children, in pairs or small groups, to consider key questions that they would like to ask the bully – for example, 'Have you been bullied yourself?' 'What do you think people think about you?' 'Why have you picked on this person?' 'What would make you stop?' and so on. |
| 13 | Collective Voice or Collective Role Hot-seating | ■ To help pupils understand what might motivate or demotivate a bully | Seated main character and audience seated (facing him/her) | Open up the questioning of the bully (or collective bully). Make sure that the questioners realize that they have a limited amount of time to question the bully and should do so clearly and dispassionately. The bully will answer their questions honestly. |

| | | | |
|---|---|---|---|
| | **Forum Theatre** | ■ To demystify bullies and personalize them more<br><br>■ To focus on effective questioning<br><br>■ To encourage evaluative and constructive, interactive feedback on the validity of each others' performances | Discuss afterwards whether the bully was convincing. The role can be replayed differently by the same actor or by others taking the role, following feedback. |
| 14 | **Collective Voice/ Conscience Alley (derivative)** | ■ To give the opportunity for resolution<br><br>■ To encourage real bullies who are listening to make links with their own actions and consider the possibility of changing behaviour<br><br>■ To enable all pupils to consider the possibility that bullies can be helped to change their behaviour | Class circle (standing)<br><br>The bully (or collective bully) stands in the middle of the class circle. The class members have the opportunity to move across the circle past the bully and say something private and constructive to him/her as they pass. What they say is intended to encourage him/her to reflect on and change his/her behaviour towards the victim – for example, 'You want to change really don't you?' 'You would like yourself more if you stopped bullying,'<br><br>It might be more empowering for participants to use a vacant chair and pretend that the bully is sitting in it rather than talk to a real person. |

**PART THREE**

| 15 | Drama strategy | Purpose | Grouping | Teacher guidance and possible cross-curricular links |
|----|----------------|---------|----------|------------------------------------------------------|
|    | Improvisation leading to **Small Group Playmaking** | ■ To improvise and then rehearse conflict resolution<br><br>■ To practise group problem solving | Whole class in groups | Ask the class to get back into their performance groups and make their original still images again (Activity 4). This time, when they bring the scenes to life, the challenge is to improvise a way out of the bullying situation that they enacted earlier and diffuse the situation in a way that is, ideally, satisfactory for the bully, bully supporter, victim and victim supporter. |
|    | Performance | ■ To role-play ways of successfully dealing with potential bullying situations<br><br>■ To make explicit and name successful strategies for diffusing and dealing with potential bullying situations | | If any group considers that they have satisfactorily diffused the potential bullying situation in their re-play, then offer them the opportunity to perform their scene as a model and celebrate their success.<br><br>Performances should be applauded and the effective strategies abstracted and made explicit (by the teacher if necessary.) |

# Some possible follow-up cross-curricular activities

This might be an opportune moment to make sure that the pupils are all aware of the contents of the school's anti-bullying policy. They may have opportunity to contribute the pupils' voice to its review, possibly through a School Council.

## PSHE

Make four Roles on the Wall (*Resource Sheet 8a*) and place them around the room. Label them as:

- Bully
- Bully supporter
- Victim
- Victim supporter

Sub-divide in two the space around each Role on the Wall, sub-heading the spaces, 'Words' and 'Actions'. Invite the children to write words and actions that each character could say and do to help resolve conflict. These could be written on Post-its and stuck on as the children move between the different Roles on the Wall, reading each others' ideas and adding their own.

## Literacy

The thoughts inside the victim's head and the thoughts inside the bully's head could form two contrasting verses for a poem. This could be a piece of shared writing based on the thoughts that were gathered in the drama.

## Literacy/Art and Design

The small group plays could either be scripted or made into storyboards (*Resource Sheet 10*).

**PART THREE**

# Creating an Imaginary Culture and Community

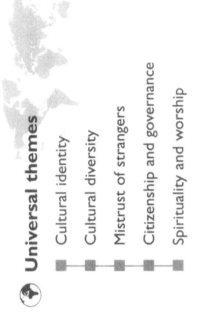

## KEY STAGES 2/3

In drama we can imagine that we are any people, at any time and in any place. **This enables classes to create entirely fictitious worlds from the past, present or future or to try to pretend to be in real past times, using historical knowledge, artefacts and images as a stimulus and support within the drama.**

This unit offers a range of strategies for creating an imagined community. Like any community it can be strengthened through imagined adversity – external and internal threats, which can be presented, played out and possibly resolved through drama. The more engaged the children are with their imaginary community and the more they understand about the way it functions, what its members believe and what their individual place is within it, then the more potential there is for using that community as a powerful forum for the collective exploration of citizenship and other aspects of the humanities. Once a viable, make-believe community has been established, it can be used to explore and deal effectively with issues and problems in role that can then be linked outside the drama to issues in the real lives of the children. It can also be used as a means of gaining transferable social, moral, spiritual and cultural understanding.

## Universal themes

- Cultural identity
- Cultural diversity
- Mistrust of strangers
- Citizenship and governance
- Spirituality and worship

## ■ In what ways do cultures identify themselves and convey their beliefs?

If we consider the ways that cultures distinguish themselves, through language, customs and costume for example, and the legacies of past cultures – art, music, writings, documents, stories, sculptures, artefacts, burial sites, rituals, festivals, ceremonies and so on – then this gives us a starting point for the building blocks of creating new, imagined cultures.

## PART THREE

| | Drama strategy | Purpose | Grouping | Teacher guidance and possible cross-curricular links |
|---|---|---|---|---|
| 1 | **Working in role (map-making)** | ■ To give shared ownership to the place where the drama will be set<br><br>■ To encourage engagement with an imagined setting and role<br><br>■ To consider the effect of humankind upon the environment | Whole-class circle | **Focus:  Where do we live?  What does it look like?**<br><br>Put a large sheet of paper in the centre of the circle. Invite the children, one or two at a time, to enter the circle and draw on the paper, which will become a class pictorial map. As each child draws a natural or man-made feature on the map, they say what they are drawing, as if they live in this place, adding some local knowledge – for example, 'This is the river that runs through the village. We swim here in the summer'; or 'This is my house. I was born here.' You may wish to define the time or place in some way for your own purpose – 'This is a place long ago and there are no cars here. They haven't been invented yet'; or 'This place is very remote island.'<br><br>The activity can be carried out in two stages: first the natural environment can be mapped and then the man-made environment can be added. If, for cross-curricular reasons, the drama is to be located in a real geographical place (e.g. the rainforest, an African village, the South Pole), then this activity could be carried out after showing photographs of a real environment. |
| 2 | **Visualization** | ■ To heighten pupil engagement through evoking imagined multi-sensory experience | Whole-class circle | Ask the children to close their eyes and imagine that they are in the environment that is depicted by their map. Ask them to silently think what they can see in their mind's eye. Then invite anyone to say aloud what they can see, and describe it. They may refer to things that are on the map or mention things they can see that are not on the map, as long as it fits. |
| | Ritual | ■ To engender a sense of unity and belonging through sharing a repeated sentence opening | | Each contributor should start their sentence with, 'I can see…'. For example, 'I can see a fast-flowing river sparkling in the sunlight.' |

With Drama in Mind

| Reading Images Through Senses | ■ To tag imagined setting mulitsensorily | | Move on to what can be heard, smelled, touched, tasted and so on. You can join in with them and model the change to different senses. For example, 'I can hear the sound of children laughing in the forest.' 'I can smell fish cooking on the open fire.' |
| | | | |
| | ■ To create a visual representation of what has been collectively imagined | | Following this virtual, multisensory activity, give the children opportunity to add to the class pictorial map new things that have been mentioned. |
| | | | ***Geography link*** <br> *You may wish to use this map as the basis of further work in Geography. For example, add a scale and key, redraw it non-pictorially using conventional map symbols, place it within the context of a larger imagined map. Look at real maps and consider where in the real world your imagined place could be.* |
| | | | ***Drama/Art and Design link*** <br> *Ask the children to face outwards in a circle and imagine that they are standing at the highest point in their imagined land and looking outwards in different directions. Ask them to say, in turn around the circle, what they can see in their mind's eye and then ask them to draw or paint it. When placed all around a room, a 360° view of the imagined setting will be created.* |

PART **THREE**

| | Drama strategy | Purpose | Grouping | Teacher guidance and possible cross-curricular links |
|---|---|---|---|---|
| 3 | Occupational Mime | ■ To support engagement with the role and setting<br><br>■ To further develop verbally a shared conceptual framework of the imagined place | Whole class | **Focus: What do we do in this place?**<br>Ask the children what sort of everyday tasks would need to be carried out in this place on an ordinary day – for example, gathering wood, fishing, sweeping houses and so on. |
| | Still Image | ■ To further develop visually a shared conceptual framework of the imagined place | | Ask the children to get into a space and make a still picture of themselves carrying out an everyday task in this village. When you click your fingers, they will come to life and carry out the jobs for a short while. They can interrelate in role if they wish. |
| | Teacher as Storyteller | ■ To further integrate, support and reinforce the emerging, collective fiction<br><br>■ To give a shared sense of belonging | | Tell the scene – for example, 'It was early in the morning and the villagers were up early, carrying out their everyday tasks. Some were sweeping...' Click your fingers at the end of your narrative for the scene to come alive for a couple of minutes. |
| 4 | Ritual | ■ Give opportunity for everyone to contribute to the emerging, collective culture | Whole-class circle | **Focus: What sort of people are we?**<br>Going around the circle, each child has opportunity to say aloud and complete the following sentence: 'We are the sort of people who...' For example, 'We are the sort of people who work hard.' 'We are the sort of people who don't like strangers.' |

| | | | |
|---|---|---|---|
| **5** | **Speaking Object** | ■ To raise pupils' awareness that an object can be imbued with culturally symbolic significance | You could pass an object, such as a stone, stick or shell, around the circle to signal whose turn it is to speak. The object can be passed straight on if the receiver does not wish to speak. Invite, but do not insist on, contributions. |
| | **Teacher in Role (shadowy role)** | ■ To gather collectively agreed information on the way that the imagined community or society is structured and organized | **Focus: How do we organize ourselves as a people?** Tell the children that you will be asking them some questions about their community and that you would like them to answer you in role as knowledgeable community members. You will be in 'shadowy role' – a neutral questioner who is gathering information and has a temporary role (no one in particular in the drama). They are the experts on their community.<br><br>Whole class |
| | **Mantle of the Expert** | ■ To empower the children by bestowing great imagined knowledge on them<br><br>■ To focus pupils' attention on generically significant aspects of communities and cultures | In role, through direct questioning, elicit key information about the people and their past and the way that the community is structured in terms of hierarchy and decision making. This could take place formally at a meeting of the community which you attend as a visitor, or you could just talk more informally to the participants. It may be helpful to ask some of the following questions. Make sure that you ask the first two:<br>■ How are decisions made in your community? (*Citizenship link*)<br>■ How are meetings of this community called? (*Citizenship link*)<br>■ Does your community live in fear of anything now or has it in the past? (*Social, Moral, Spiritual and Cultural link*)<br>■ Do the people here have any particular shared beliefs and special places associated with these beliefs? (*RE and/or SMSC link*)<br>■ Are there places of cultural importance and significance to your people? Where are they and how are they looked after? Who is able to enter? How and when? (*RE and/or SMSC link*) |

**PART THREE**

| | Drama strategy | Purpose | Grouping | Teacher guidance and possible cross-curricular links |
|---|---|---|---|---|
| 6 | | | | ■ Are there objects of cultural importance and significance to your people? If so where are they kept and how are they looked after? Who sees them/handles them and when? (RE and/or SMSC link) <br><br> ■ How are messages, warnings, and news passed between people in this community? (Media studies and communication link) <br><br> ■ What is the attitude of your community to strangers? (SMSC link) |
| | Still Image <br><br> Captions | ■ To encourage collaborative discussion, decision making and co-operation <br><br> ■ To encourage them to consider what events might be of significance to cultures <br><br> ■ To offer shared ownership of the imagined culture and fiction | Groups of about four | **Focus: What is significant in the history of our people?** <br> Ask the group to decide on an important moment or event in the history of this community. Then ask them to represent this moment or event as a still image and to give it a caption. |
| | Performance Carousel | ■ To build knowledge of a shared, imagined history | | Explain that each group in turn will move silently into their still image, hold it still for five seconds, then call aloud the accompanying caption, holding it still for a further five silent seconds before melting the image to the ground in slow motion. The next group will then move seamlessly into re-creating their image and so on until every group has had a turn. The sequence of imagined historical images should flow without interruption, like a wave. |

With Drama in Mind

| # | Activity | Objectives | Grouping | Notes |
|---|----------|-----------|----------|-------|
| 7 | Improvised Small Group Playmaking | ■ To bring alive and share episodes from the history of these people | | You could ask the children to bring the still images to life for a few moments and improvise the historical scene or event being portrayed. |
| 8 | Hot-seating | ■ To give opportunity for clarification<br><br>■ To engage the whole class with each others' contributions to the collective fiction | The same groups of four | Each scene in turn can be held still and the characters questioned in more detail by the audience about what is being portrayed. They should answer in role. |
| 9 | Performance Carousel (Timeline) linked through Teacher as Storyteller | ■ To give a chronological understanding of the imagined history of the culture or community<br><br>■ To enable the teacher to acknowledge, use and link the pupils' contributions cohesively | The same groups of four | You may wish to replay the scenes from the previous activity in a chronological sequence negotiated and agreed with the children.<br><br>You can use the children's captions (Activity 6) as prompts for you to create a narrative, linking together the scenes as episodes in the history of this people, or else hold up the captions themselves as the scene introduction and link (as in the old silent films). |

PART THREE

| | Drama strategy | Purpose | Grouping | Teacher guidance and possible cross-curricular links |
|---|---|---|---|---|
| | **Working in Role (Occupational Mime)** | ■ To re-establish a previous activity to support re-engagement with role | Whole class | As in Activity 3. Ask the children to mime carrying out everyday jobs. |
| | **Teacher in Role** | ■ To sign that the teacher will be in role | | Tell them that in a moment you will enter as a visitor and that a class improvisation will follow. |
| 10 | Improvisation | ■ To introduce a problem to be solved (in role) | Whole class | Enter the community and move among the people, interacting and responding to them.<br><br>Tell them that you wish to speak to the person or persons who are in charge of the community. You have a very important matter to discuss formally with their leaders. (The way that you make this request and the responses should be governed by the earlier questions put to the community in Activity 5: How are decisions made here? How are meetings called?). |
| 11 | Meeting | ■ To stimulate a structured, community meeting which follows collectively agreed and understood procedures<br><br>■ To give a sense of unity and community belonging<br><br>■ To stimulate collective problem solving within a shared fiction | Whole class | Encourage the class to follow any community signals, rituals or structures that they created earlier (Activity 5) in order to set up a convincing community meeting. The children are collective decision maker/s (or their agreed representatives) and you are a visitor to be formally heard.<br><br>Having established and entered their meeting as a visitor who wishes to speak to the decision makers, the role you take and the choice of problem that you introduce to this community and thereby to the drama could include:<br>■ I have left a very sick child at the boundary of this village. The last village turned us away. Can I stay here with my child until he/she is well enough to travel on? |

| | |
|---|---|
| | ■ You have a rare and precious plant that I am told is the only medicine that can cure my sick child. I realize this plant is precious to you and is in short supply. Will you sell me/give me some? I am poor and this is my only child. |
| | ■ I would like to trade with you. I am interested in selecting and purchasing an object from one of your sacred places. You can name your price. |
| ■ To give a forum for placing the fictitious community under threat in some way<br><br>■ To encourage class discussion in role<br><br>■ To encourage higher order thinking (including problem solving) together, about complex issues<br><br>■ To actively think through complex issues presented fictitiously that have real life parallels | ■ I am a journalist. Would it be possible to live among your community for a few weeks and make a TV programme/publish an article about your people. My viewers/readers would be interested. You can name your price and have censorship/editorial rights. |
| | ■ I am a well-known archaeologist who would like to negotiate the right to dig on your land. I can help you learn more about your forefathers. Anything found will belong to your people. You may agree to my borrowing and exhibiting some of the artefacts that I expect to find. You can draw up a contract with me. |
| | ■ I have come to warn you! There are people heading this way who intend to take your village by force. They are more powerful than you. |
| | ■ I have fled my own community/country because my life is at risk from a cruel dictator if I stay. Please can I come and live within your community. |

PART THREE

## ■ Tailoring the activities

The activities in this unit are deliberately broad and generic as they are intended to provide a flexible drama structure that will support teachers in developing a range of possible community based dramas, possibly set at different points in history and/or in a range of either real or imagined places. The community based dramas can be tailored to fit into cross-curricular humanity themes, for example:

■ The community could be set up to be an industrial Victorian working community and the visitor could be introducing news of the spinning jenny.

■ It could be a Saxon community that receives news from the visitor that they are about to be invaded by Vikings.

■ A seventeenth century rural community could be being asked to accommodate a young orphan who may be a plague victim.

■ A fictitious refugee could be seeking asylum from a real or imagined tyranny.

■ A rainforest community could be asked by the Western world for a rare plant.

Having defined a specific problem to be considered and solved within the drama by the pretend community, teachers will need then to select appropriately from the range of drama strategies available (see Part Two), according to their purpose and intended outcome. For example:

*Still Image* – Later, a new still image could be added to the sequence from Activity 6 as a way of recording this further event/problem in the history of the community.

*Conscience Alley* – This could be used next as a way of considering the pros and cons of any of the courses of action that the community is being asked to decide on in Activity 11.

*Thought-tracking* – Each person in the community could be invited to speak aloud their thought in relation to what the visitor is asking of them at this point in the drama.

*Role on the Wall* – This could be used as a way of reflecting on what is known at this point in time about the visitor and what needs still to be discovered.

*Small Group Playmaking* – This could be used as a way of playing out what might happen if a particular decision is taken and a certain course of action is followed.

*Rumours* – The visitor might withdraw for a while and have to come back for his/her answer. Rumours could abound as soon as he withdraws.

*Teacher as Storyteller/Storymaker* – This can be used to relate as a story what happened when the visitor came (and left). It might be used to pull the drama together and jump everyone forward in time, to what happened next. 'At last the visitor was given his answer and left the meeting…. …When he had gone the people… …Weeks passed, until one day…'

# ■ Some possible cross-curricular activities

These can arise naturally or be engineered to arise 'naturally' from within the drama. Cross-curricular activities can also be carried out between drama lessons or after the chapter has concluded.

## Writing in role

Maybe the visitor has to put his/her request in writing or the community records the minutes of the meeting in some way.

Reasons for writing documents may arise from the drama – for example, lay-off notices to workers, a contract between the archaeologist and the community, a bill of sale, a passport, a newspaper report.

This episode in the life of this community could be important enough to record in a sacred book that tells of its history.

## Storytelling

This episode in the life of these people could become a story passed on from generation to generation, from the old to the young. Ask the children to tell the story of what happened when the visitor came, to someone who has not heard it (or pretends not to have). Record the storytelling on tape or video.

## Scriptwriting

The small group plays or scenes that have been created within the drama could be scripted afterwards. The scripted scenes could be given to another class for turning into a short performance, which could then be watched and evaluated by the scriptwriters. There would be a genuine need for producing a clear script and directions and the scriptwriters could receive actor feedback on their scripts.

## Art and Design

Maybe a sculpture, carving, stained-glass window or wall painting could be designed and/or made, that commemorates this chapter in the history of the community.

## Dance

Maybe there is a festival or ceremony that involves a dance that portrays/commemorates this moment in the history of the community – for example, the day the plague came or the invasion by Vikings. This could be stylized. The created dance could be taught to another class and its significance explained.

## Music

Perhaps musicians composed music to depict this episode in the history of the community and it is recorded for posterity in some way. Possibly it is played on particular occasions.

A ballad could be created that tells the story of the visitor and what followed.

## Geography and History

Maybe the internet (or library) could be used to research and gather information and images that can be used in the drama – for example, finding out about rainforest plants for healing, researching the symptoms of the plague, and so on.

The drama could be shared via a school website using text and image and pupils' voices (in and out of role).

## Media/ICT

The drama could be turned into a film.

**PART THREE**

# Chief Seattle's Speech
## (1854)

**KEY STAGES 2 / 5**

This speech is believed to have been spoken by Chief Seattle in 1854. He was a peaceful Native American leader of the Suquamish tribe who reputedly delivered this speech to the American government in Washington D.C. when they wanted to purchase the land inhabited by his people. The speech and the only existing photograph of Chief Seattle are on *Resource Sheets 11 and 12.*

## Universal themes

- Conservation
- Environmental sustainability
- Cultural unity and diversity
- Spiritual beliefs
- Religion
- Colonization
- Threatened culture and heritage
- Rites of passage
- Naturalism
- Surrender

Native American music could be used to provide an atmospheric background at times during the lesson and to aurally tag meaningful moments to support engagement and future recall.

## PART THREE

| | Drama strategy | Purpose | Grouping | Teacher guidance and possible cross-curricular links |
|---|---|---|---|---|
| 1 | **Visualization** | ■ To support engagement with the speech through its visual images | Whole class | Ask the class to close their eyes as you read the poem aloud to them. Suggest that they might find that they have a picture or pictures in their minds as they listen. |
| 2 | **Literacy task in preparation for a drama activity** | ■ To help the children to engage with the landscape | Groups of about four | Ask each group to go through the speech and underline words that are connected to different senses, for example:<br><br>**Group 1** – Sight<br>**Group 2** – Sound<br>**Group 3** – Taste<br>**Group 4** – Touch<br>**Group 5** – Smell.<br><br>The 'Sight' groups could be subdivided to record what can be seen moving and what is seen that is static. |
| | **Working in Role** | ■ To support engagement with role<br>■ To imagine multisensory experience linked to fictional landscape | Class circle | Tell the children that you want them to imagine that they are in the Native American landscape with you. Invite them to say, in turn, what they can see, hear, taste, smell, touch, as if they are there. They may add descriptive detail. Anyone contributing should start their sentence with, 'I can see...' or 'I can hear...' and so on. You model this first, for example, 'I can see the river flowing past, glittering in the sunlight.' This activity can be done around the circle with eyes closed to aid visualization.<br><br>*Literacy link*<br>*Write the sentences on paper sentence strips. The sentences can then be rearranged through class or group consensus to create a piece of shared writing.* |

| | | Objectives | Grouping | Description |
|---|---|---|---|---|
| 3 | **Still Image (class Tableau)** | ■ To engage physically with the imagined landscape<br>■ To create a physical landscape in 3D | Whole class | The Native Americans believed that they were as one with the natural objects and the elements. Invite the children to physically become an object or part of the landscape. In turn they have opportunity to enter the drama space and to say aloud what they are representing. |
| | **Speaking Objects** | ■ To encourage elaboration and description | | The children can add information or description, for example, 'I am a craggy rock. From where I stand, I can see for miles,' or 'I am the river. I move the canoes along and I am full of fish.' Join in. You can model by entering first if necessary. |
| 4 | **Teacher in Role**<br><br>**Still Image** | ■ To enable every person to share their story opening verbally<br>■ To ritualize active listening<br>■ To stimulate imaginations through offering modelled, imaginative story openings | Whole class | Ask the class to re-form their still landscape images once more. Tell them that you will pass through the landscape in role as Chief Seattle. You could sign this by carrying a feather as the Chief. Ask, 'If the Chief could hear the voices of his forefathers as he passed through the landscape, what might the voices have said as the Chief is about to hand over his people's land to the government?'<br><br>As you pass by as Chief Seattle, each participant has opportunity to speak to you as if they are an ancestral voice. You could pass through the landscape twice, the first time listening and the second time listening and responding. |
| | **Speaking Objects** | | | |
| | **Voice Collage Improvisation**<br><br>**Performance** | ■ To reinforce the voices associated with a key moment<br>■ To represent a character's memory, thoughts and state of mind through the use of sound | Groups or whole class | Ask the children to recall what they said to the Chief. Ask them to imagine the ancestral voices carrying on flowing and echoing in and out of the Chief's mind. What might this sound like? There might be repetition, changes of pace, silent moments, changes of rhythm and volume, voices speaking singly or together or over each other. This activity could be improvised and then maybe refined, rehearsed and performed. |

**PART THREE**

| Drama strategy | Purpose | Grouping | Teacher guidance and possible cross-curricular links |
|---|---|---|---|
| Movement | ■ To develop a verbal, visual and kinesthetic experience linked to the analysis of verbs in a text | Whole class | **ICT link** *Tape the sound collage. The recording could then be used as the background for movement sequences created using movements referred to or inferred within the speech.* |
| **5** Brainstorm | ■ To share ideas in order to stimulate thinking  ■ To consider moments of cultural significance | Whole class | *'Each ghostly reflection in the clear waters of the lake tells of memories in the lives of our people'* Ask the children to suggest what these memories could be – for example, a successful buffalo hunt, the death of a Chief, enemies attacking, and so on. Accept all possible suggestions positively. |
| Still Image Movement Freeze-frame | ■ To engage with key cultural moments and tag them visually and kinesthetically | | Now ask the children in groups of four to negotiate, agree and make a still image of a reflection in the lake that depicts an important moment in the history of these people. In turn the still images will be made, held still and then brought alive silently or with sound, for a few moments before being frozen. |
| Performance Carousel | ■ To provide a reflective record of a key moment | | You could use a Performance Carousel to present these performance pieces.  **ICT/Literacy link** *Use a digital camera to record the still images. These could be used to stimulate linked creative writing later.* |

| | | | |
|---|---|---|---|
| 6 | **Mantle of the Expert**<br><br>**Storytelling** | ■ To encourage speaking and listening with partners (questioning, explaining, describing, reporting)<br><br>■ To deepen engagement with role and culture<br><br>■ To support the creation of a shared fiction | Pairs | Ask the children to get into pairs with someone whom they have not yet worked with. One person will pretend to be an elder and the other a child. The elder will tell the child about an important moment in the history of their people, orally passing on important cultural information. The child will listen and may question the elder to elicit more information about the history of the tribe. |
| 7 | **Ritual**<br><br>**Teacher in Role**<br><br>**Speaking Object** | ■ To deepen personal engagement with a shared, imagined culture<br><br>■ To commit publicly to belonging to the same fictitious community<br><br>■ To model or to gather information<br><br>■ To give equal opportunity to speak and be listened to | Whole-class circle | In turn the children have opportunity to complete the sentence, 'We are the sort of people who...' You may decide to be a fellow Native American and join in, possibly starting in order to provide a model – for example, 'We are the sort of people who teach our children well.' You could take the role of a visitor who wants to know about the people. Passing an object around the circle to signal whose turn it is to speak would add to the sense of ritual – maybe a 'speaking' stone, a feather or a stick (if you do not have a peace pipe!).<br><br>*Art and Design link*<br>*Design and make an artefact that belongs to the tribe and has significance – perhaps the object that a speaker holds which empowers him to speak.* |

**PART THREE**

| | Drama strategy | Purpose | Grouping | Teacher guidance and possible cross-curricular links |
|---|---|---|---|---|
| 8 | Teacher in Role<br><br>Meeting | ■ To challenge and threaten the community and an existing culture<br><br>■ To stimulate reasoned argument in response to a community problem<br><br>■ To encourage verbal rather than physical emotional responses | Whole class | Tell the children that you will take the role of an important messenger from the American government. Gather them to meet you and tell them officially that they will have to give over their land to the government or else be wiped out. They will be given places on a reservation. Be a messenger of the government and a go-between (an intermediary between the Native Americans and the government).<br><br>Avoid stirring up a confrontation and do not allow physical contact. You are only the messenger. If confrontation arises, freeze the action and ask the children to replay the scene a different and calmer way, encouraging reasoned argument. What are the key points that they want you to convey on their behalf to the government? You are aiming in role to gather important and heartfelt messages and reasoned arguments from the Native Americans to take back to the government. You can be slightly sympathetic but you have a job to do. |
| 9 | Rumours<br>(under the guise of 'Whispers') | ■ To communicate and gather perceptions and feelings<br><br>■ To build tension and control in a stylized way | Whole class | The government official has left. What do the people say among themselves now that they know that they will have to leave their homeland? What are their fears?<br><br>Ask the class to stealthily and silently move around as if stalking or hunting. Whenever you give the signal, 'Whispers', they whisper a worry to the nearest person, for example, 'We will not belong in any other place,' 'Maybe this is a trick,' and so on. |
| 10 | Image Theatre | ■ To encourage discussion focused on prediction and contrast | Groups of about four | Ask the children to create two still images, the first will represent life as it is now and the other as they fear it will be in the future. The images may be literal or symbolic. 'Real' present and future scenes can be |

| | | Objectives | Grouping | Description |
|---|---|---|---|---|
| 11 | **Movement** | ■ To encourage individual and group reflection<br>■ To tag learning visually, aurally and kinesthetically<br>■ To give a reason for synthesis | Groups of about four | depicted, or alternatively you could ask the children to make more abstract images that represent aspects and feelings about the present and future.<br><br>Once the groups have devised two contrasting still images ask them to find a way of moving in a controlled way, back and forth between the images slowly and repeatedly. They may do this silently or you might invite them to add sound or speech. Alternatively, you could use Native American music as a soundtrack for the movement cycle. |
| | **Performance Carousel** | ■ To link group performances to form a whole-class performance | | Let the children practise before presenting their group's images in turn, possibly through Performance Carousel. |
| 12 | **Small Group Playmaking** | ■ To develop practically an understanding of symbolic acts, objects and representations | Groups of about four | It is the moment when the tribe are leaving their homeland. This means that they will be leaving the remains and voices of their ancestors behind. Is there any way that those departing could leave something of themselves behind on or in the land, for posterity? Gather suggestions from the children and then ask them to share further ideas in groups before preparing a short group scene or presentation (no more than a couple of minutes presenting their ideas). Examples could include the burial of a precious personal object, construction of a totem pole, marking the land in some way, perhaps with a rock carving. Again, Performance Carousel could be used. |
| | **Performance Carousel** | | | |

**PART THREE**

| | Drama strategy | Purpose | Grouping | Teacher guidance and possible cross-curricular links |
|---|---|---|---|---|
| 13 | Tableau/Still Image | ■ To encourage reflection<br>■ To consider how images portray messages through media | Whole class | ■ One at a time the children have opportunity to place themselves in a whole-class, whole tribe, imaginary photograph taken on the day that they left their homeland. Tell the class that the photograph is for a newspaper and will become very important historically. How do they want to portray the tribe for posterity? |
| 14 | Sculpting Images | ■ To encourage reflection at the end of the drama through a considered portrayal of the main character | Pairs | ■ There is only one known photograph of Chief Seattle (*Resource Sheet 12*). Ask the children in pairs to take turns to sculpt each other into a statue of Chief Seattle that would portray him as he might wish to have been remembered.<br><br>■ A statue park can be created with half the class looking at each others' statues before themselves becoming the next statues. |
| | Captioning | ■ To synthesize a visual image in words | | *Literacy to drama link*<br>*Ask each child to write a caption on a big piece of paper, to go with the statue they have sculpted. Then spread the captions around the room and ask the children to go and stand by a caption other than their own and make* |
| | Still Image | ■ To synthesize words in a visual image | | *themselves into a still image to go with that caption.* |

# ■ Some possible follow-up cross-curricular activities

## Literacy/ICT/History
There are several internet sites that give different accounts of Chief Seattle's speech and question its authenticity. Gathering and contrasting different versions of the speech could be interesting.

## Art and Design/Design and Technology
Planning and making totem poles and headdresses that use representational symbols and images.

## ICT
Only one photograph of Chief Seattle exists. Create other imaginary photos of him using a digital camera to record them. Searching the internet will lead to various sites that link to Chief Seattle and the history of his people.

# PART FOUR

■ **Photocopiable resource sheets**

# ■ Using the Resource Sheets

The following photocopiable resource sheets are mainly generic. They can be used or adapted to suit the needs of teachers and their own dramas or used with the drama units in Part Three. Some of the Resource Sheets are unit specific but most can be used more generally as thinking frames or methods of recording thoughts, feelings and actions. Many may also be useful in lessons other than drama. Some of the strategies in Part Two have more than one Resource Sheet linked to them and teachers will need to decide which one is most appropriate to their needs.

*Resource Sheet 1* can be used to record multisensory aspects or imagined multisensory responses to images or text.

*Resource Sheet 2a* can be used to record significant things heard within a scene.

*Resource Sheet 2b* enables what has been heard within a drama to be considered in relation to accuracy. It encourages children to think critically and analytically about what they have heard within the fiction.

*Resource Sheet 3* is a thinking frame based on Edward de Bono's work. It encourages children to categorize their thinking about a course of action in terms of its negative, positive and interesting aspects, possibly prior to decision making.

*Resource Sheet 4* can be used to record the thoughts of a character at a particular moment in the drama. Several might be completed at a key moment to record a range of thoughts of various characters. Alternatively, a collection of these sheets can be used to track a character's thoughts over time to consider character development.

*Resource Sheet 5a* can be used to record the group's collective utterances and advice to a character. It has two lines of thought, where pros and cons of courses of action can be listed. It is again a type of thinking frame that could be used to record ideas to help construct a persuasive argument. It also lists the thinking that has influenced the decision of a character at a key moment. The sheet encourages the justification of decisions.

*Resource Sheet 5b* is another visual way of recording the case for and against a course of action. It can be used at a moment of indecision for a character, encouraging the weighing up of pros and cons. Again, this sheet encourages the justification of decisions.

*Resource Sheet 5c* is for recording the collective thoughts of a character. It enables several children to complete one thought bubble each to contribute to the overall thinking of the character. Alternatively, it could be used to record two lines of thoughts – the pros and cons that a character is considering. It could also be used by talking partners, to record their combined thinking about characters and events.

*Resource Sheet 6* can be used to record and refine questions before they are asked of characters in hot seats. It could also simply be used to record questions about the drama that have been raised in the participant's mind. Recording questions before asking them enables questioning to be reflected on and if necessary improved. It also means that questions can be gathered by the teacher for the character to answer, either at the time or later.

**Resource Sheet 7** is the visual stimulus central to Unit 2, 'The Victorian Cotton Mill'.

**Resource Sheet 7b** is a thinking frame that enables pupils to consider and categorize what they 'know' at different points in a drama. It also encourages children to consider and record what they would like to know. This develops curiosity and lets the teacher know what are the main areas of interest to the children at any point. The differentiation between what is 'known' and what is 'thought to be known' in columns one and two encourages inference to be separated out from 'fact'.

**Resource Sheet 8a** enables children to record whatever they wish to about a particular character at a particular point in the drama, or else just to record characteristics and general impressions. Children may have a set of these sheets, with one for each main character.

**Resource Sheet 8b** encourages and supports categorization of thoughts about characters, enabling facts to be recorded, inference to be considered and curiosity to be raised. It could be used prior to hot-seating a character, who might be able to clarify what children think may be true or want to know about them.

**Resource Sheet 8c** encourages categorized thinking about characters. It uses an Edward de Bono thinking frame and is adapted for use in drama, supporting children to consider characteristics and categorize them as negative, positive or interesting.

**Resource Sheet 8d** can be used to separate out a character's thoughts, feelings and actions (which of course are inter-linked). It is interesting to consider them separately and then possibly re-link them with flow arrows to examine the inter-connections.

**Resource Sheet 9** links particularly to Boal's Image Theatre, in which reality and ideal are considered through making them into images and considering the steps people would need to take to move from one to the other. This sheet helps children to record their drama-created images and record their ideas as to steps that might lead to change.

**Resource Sheet 10** is a basic storyboard and can be used to reflect upon, synthesize and record the drama in key images. It can be a means of recording images that have been previously arrived at through Freeze-frame. The added captioning encourages synthesis – summing up a whole image using a single phrase or sentence.

**Resource Sheet 11** is is a transcript of Chief Seattle's speech to the American government in 1854, upon which Unit 5 is based. There are alternative versions of this speech available through internet searches and debate as to which one is authentic.

**Resource Sheet 12** This is the only known photograph of Chief Seattle (from whom Seattle got its name). An internet search can reveal other images and photographs of his people plus further information on the history of the Suquamish tribe.

**Resource Sheet 13** This empty statue plinth has space for a commemorative statue and an inscription on the plaque. It can be used to reflect on the ways that key characters from the drama might be remembered for posterity. This activity encourages reflection and synthesis. How would this person want to be remembered? How do we want them to be remembered? These images may have been already made in the drama by people standing as if they are the statue. The still images could be revisited and recorded through drawing.

| | |
|---|---|
| **I can taste...** | |
| **I can feel and touch...** | |
| **I can smell...** | |
| **I can hear...** | |
| **I can see...** | |

Rumours about _____

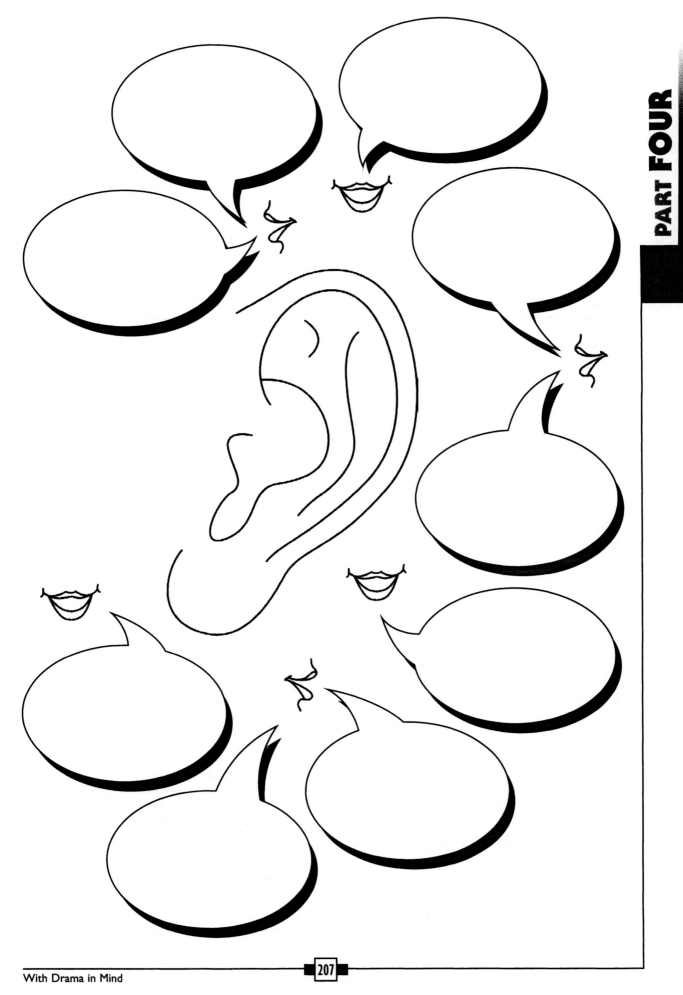

**PART FOUR**

With Drama in Mind

## How likely is this rumour to be true?

The rumour is:

Definitely not true    Definitely true

| 0 | 1 | 2 | 3 | 4 | 5 | 6 | 7 | 8 | 9 | 10 |

The reason I think this is because:

---

The rumour is:

Definitely not true    Definitely true

| 0 | 1 | 2 | 3 | 4 | 5 | 6 | 7 | 8 | 9 | 10 |

The reason I think this is because:

---

The rumour is:

Definitely not true    Definitely true

| 0 | 1 | 2 | 3 | 4 | 5 | 6 | 7 | 8 | 9 | 10 |

The reason I think this is because:

With Drama in Mind

PART FOUR

The plan is:

| What is positive about this plan? | What is negative about this plan? | What is interesting about this plan? |
|---|---|---|
| | | |

Based on an Edward de Bono CORT thinking skills strategy.

Permission granted by The McQuaig Group Inc., 2004

Name of character ----------------------------------------------------------------------

The moment is ----------------------------------------------------------------------

This character's thoughts:

With Drama in Mind

_____ is trying to decide

whether or not to _____

**PROS**

**CONS**

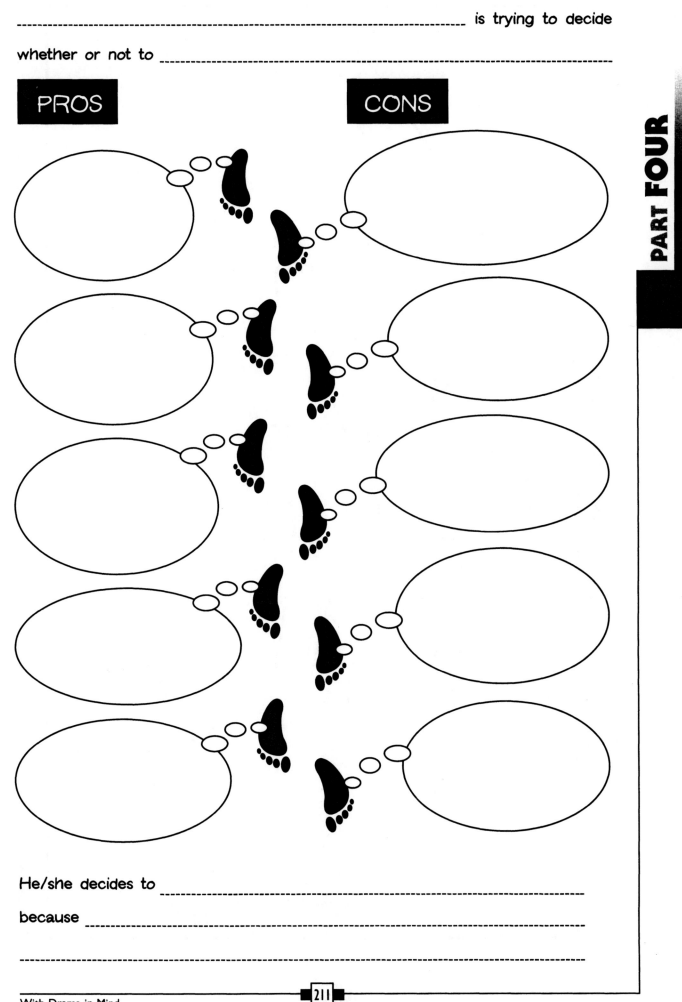

**PART FOUR**

He/she decides to _____

because _____

_____

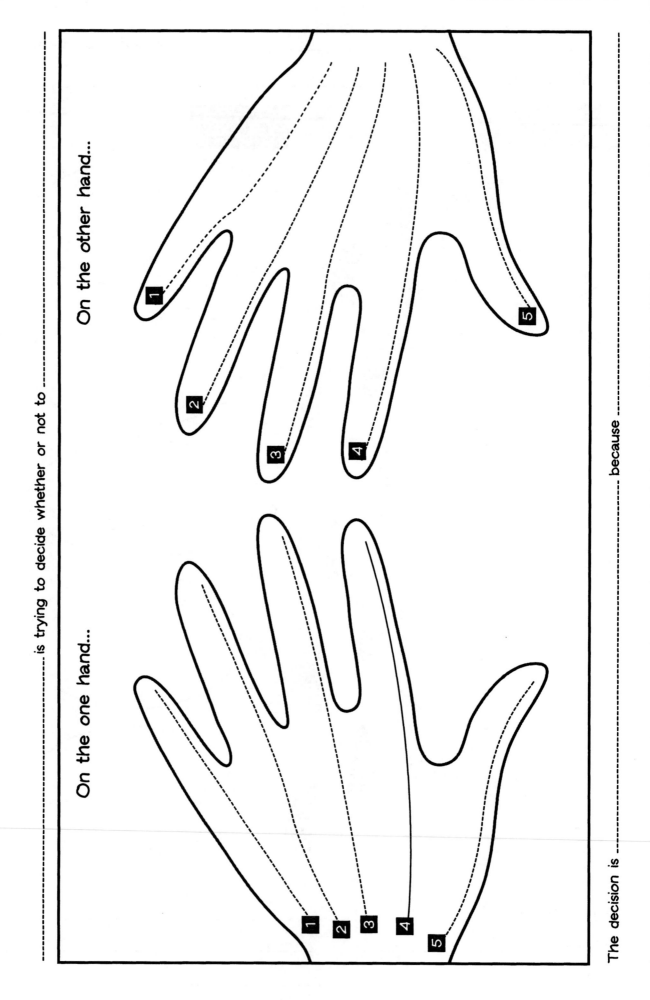

On the other hand...

On the one hand...

................................ is trying to decide whether or not to ................................

The decision is ................................................................ because ................................

The moment is_____

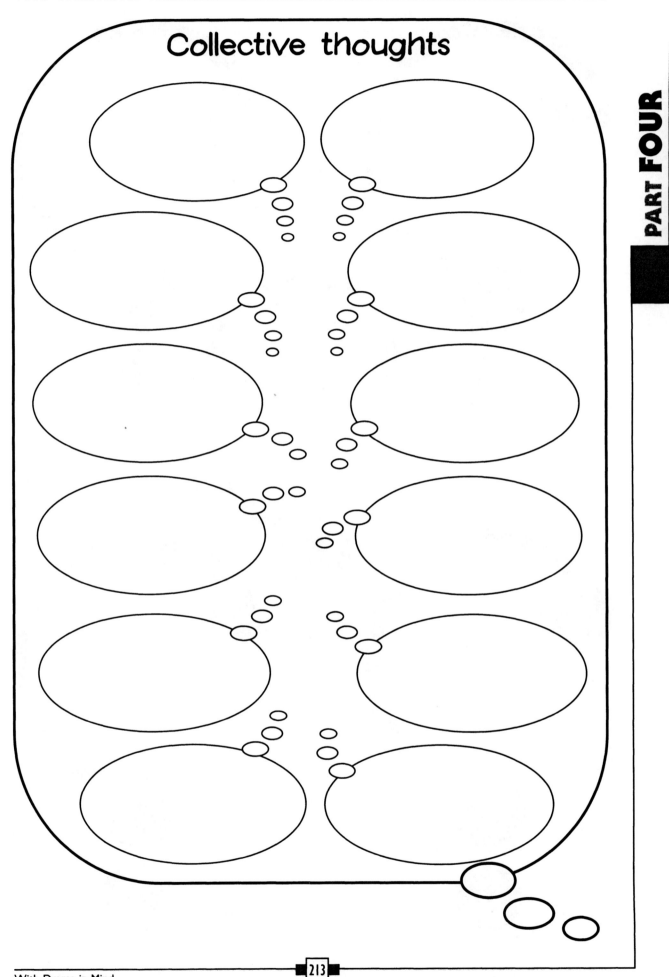

Collective thoughts

PART FOUR

# Questions I would like to ask

With Drama in Mind

*Love Conquers Fear* (Manchester Central Library)

| What I know... | What I think I know... | What I want to know... |
| --- | --- | --- |

Thoughts/feelings/observations about this character:

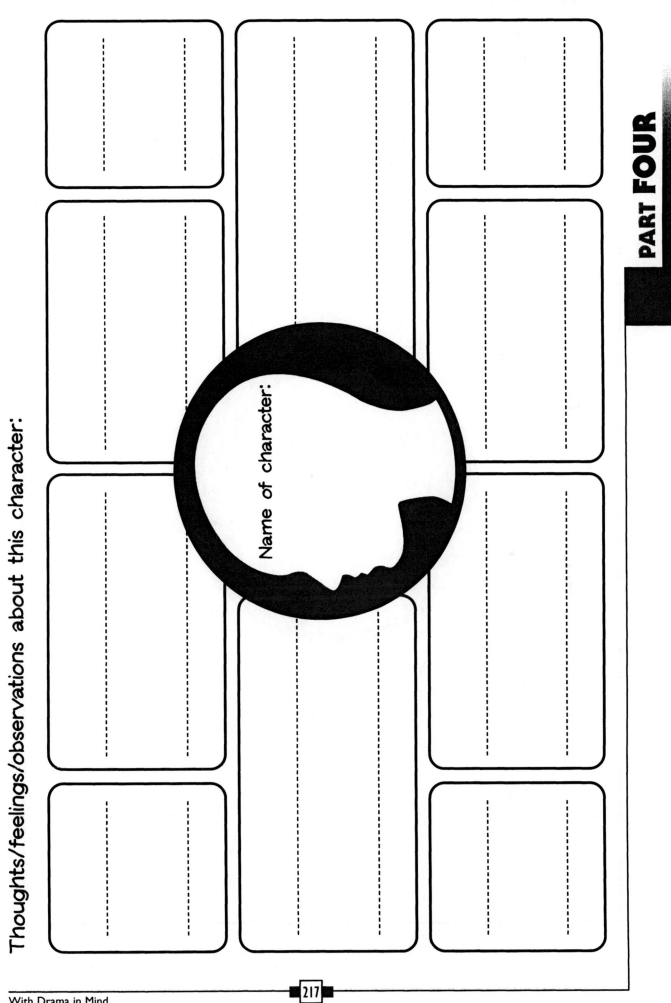

Name of character:

PART FOUR

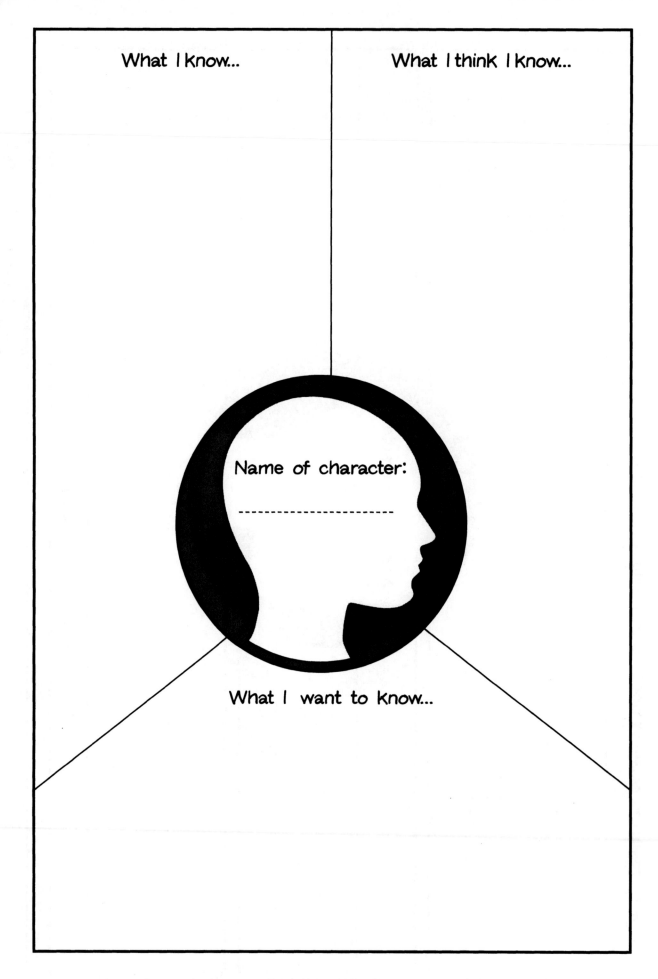

What I know...                          What I think I know...

Name of character:

------------------------

What I want to know...

What I know...                          What I think I know...

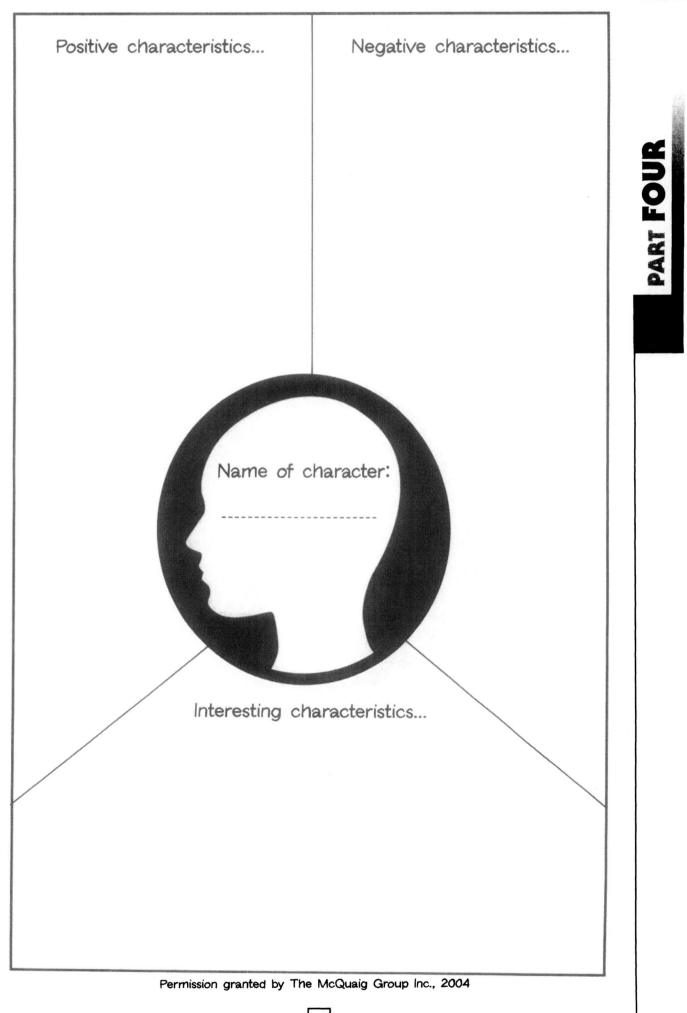

Positive characteristics...

Negative characteristics...

PART FOUR

Name of character:

-------------------------

Interesting characteristics...

Permission granted by The McQuaig Group Inc., 2004

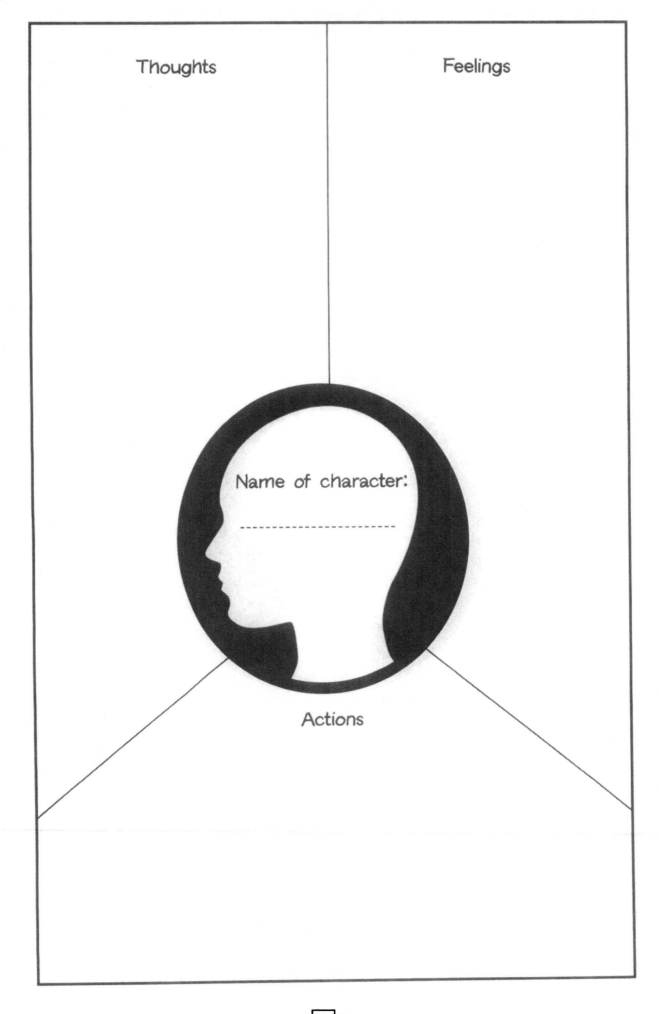

Thoughts

Feelings

Name of character:

------------------------

Actions

Thoughts

Feelings

The reality:

The steps that need to be taken:

The ideal:

How can you buy the sky?
How can you own the rain and the wind?

My mother told me,
Every part of this earth is sacred to our people.
Every pine needle. Every sandy shore.
Every mist in the dark woods.
Every meadow and humming insect.
All are holy in the memory of our people

My father told me,
I know the sap that courses through the trees
As I know the blood that flows in my veins.
We are part of the earth and it is part of us.
The perfumed flowers are our sisters.
The bear, the deer, the great eagle, these are our brothers.
The rocky crests, the meadows, the ponies – all belong to the same family.

The voice of my ancestors said to me,
The shining water that moves in the streams and rivers
is not simply water, but the blood of your grandfather's grandfather.
Each ghostly reflection in the clear waters of the lake
tells of the memories of the life of our people.
The water's murmur is the voice of your great-great-grandmother.
The rivers are our brothers. They quench our thirst.
They carry our canoes and feed our children.
You must give the rivers the kindness that you would give to any brother.

The voice of my grandfather said to me,
The air is precious. It shares its spirit with all the life it supports.
The wind that gave me my first breath also received my last sigh.
You must keep the land and air apart and sacred,
as a place where one can go to taste the wind
that is sweetened by the meadow flowers.

When the last Red Man and Woman have vanished with their wilderness,
and their memory is only the shadow of a cloud moving across the prairie,
will the shores and forest still be here?

Will there be any of the spirit of my people left?
My ancestors said to me, This we know:
The earth does not belong to us. We belong to the earth.

The voice of my grandmother said to me,
Teach your children what you have been taught.
The earth is our mother.
What befalls the earth befalls all the sons and daughters of the earth.

Hear the voice of my ancestors, Chief Seattle said.
The destiny of our people is a mystery to us.
What will happen when all the buffalo are slaughtered?
The wild horses tamed?
What will happen when the sacred corners of the forest are heavy with
the scent of many men?
When the view of the ripe hills is blotted by talking wires?
Where will the thicket be? Gone.
Where will the eagle be? Gone!
And what will happen when we say goodbye to the swift pony and the
hunt?
It will be the end of living and the beginning of survival.

This we know: All things are connected like the blood that unites us.
We did not weave the web of life.
We are merely a strand in it.
Whatever we do to the web, we do to ourselves.

We love this earth as a newborn loves its mother's heartbeat,
If we sell you our land, care for it as we have cared for it.
Hold in your mind the memory of the land as it is when you receive it.
Preserve the land and the air and the rivers for your children's children and
love it as we have loved it.

Chief Seattle (1854)

Chief Seattle No 1

*MSCA, University of Washington Libraries (neg. NA893)*

With Drama in Mind

Here stands a statue of:

# ■ References

Alexander R. (2000) *Culture and Pedagogy; International Comparisons in Primary Education*, Blackwell, Oxford

Arts Council England (2003) *Drama in Schools* (2nd edition)

Baldwin P. & Fleming K. (2003) *Teaching Literacy through Drama – Creative approaches*, Routledge/Falmer

Blakemore S.J. & Frith U. (2000) *The Implications of Recent Developments in Neuroscience for Research on Teaching and Learning*, ERSC Teaching and Learning Programme

Boal A. (1992) *Games for Actors and Non-Actors*, Routledge

Bolton G. (1979) *Towards a Theory of Drama in Education*, Longman

Bowkett S. (2001) *ALPS StoryMaker*, Network Educational Press

Bowkett S. (2003) *StoryMaker Catch Pack*, Network Educational Press

Bruer J.T. (1993) *Schools for Thought: A Science of Learning in Classrooms*, MIT Press

Carter, R. (1999) *Mapping the Mind*, Weidenfeld and Nicolson, London

Corrie C. (2003) *Becoming Emotionally Intelligent*, Network Educational Press

DfEE & QCA (2000) *The National Curriculum*

DfES (2002) 'Training materials for the foundation subjects', Key Stage 3 National Strategy

DfES (2003) *Excellence and Enjoyment – A Strategy for Primary Schools*

Dixon P. (2002) *Colour of my Dreams*, Macmillan Children's Books

Feuerstein R., Rand Y., Hoffman M. & Miller R. (1980) *Instrumental Enrichment: An Intervention Program for Cognitive Modifiability*, MD University Press, Baltimore

Gardner H. (1983) *Frames of Mind: The Theory of Multiple Intelligences*, Basic Books, New York

Gardner H. (1993) *Multiple Intelligences: The Theory in Practice*, Basic Books, New York

Gibran K. (1926) *The Prophet*, William Heinemann

Goleman D. (1996), *Emotional Intelligence*, Bloomsbury

Harland et al. (2000) *Arts Education in Secondary Schools: Effects and Effectiveness*, NFER

Harris J.R. (1998) *The Nurture Assumption: Why children turn out the way they do*, Free Press, New York

Heathcote D. & Bolton G. (1995) *Drama for Learning*, Heinemann

Iwanuik, Nelson & Pellis, (2001) 'Do big brained animals play more?', *Journal of Comparative Psychology*, 115:29

Jeffers, S. (1991) *Brother Eagle, Sister Sky*, Puffin Books

LeDoux, J. (1996) *The Emotional Brain: The Mysterious Underpinnings of Emotional Life*, Simon and Schuster, New York

Lipman M. (1991) *Thinking in Education*, Cambridge University Press, New York

MacLean P. (1989), *The Triune Brain in Evolution*, Plenum Press, New York

McGuinness C. (1999) 'From Thinking Skills to Thinking Classrooms: a review and evaluation of approaches for developing pupils' thinking', Research Report No 115, DfEE

Mercer N. (2002) 'New Perspectives on Spoken English in the Classroom', briefing paper for QCA conference, 27 June 2002

Mercer N., Wegerif R. & Dawes L. (1999) 'Children's Talk and the Development of Reasoning in the Classroom', *British Educational Research Journal*, 25, 1, 95–111

Moreno J.L. (1946) *Psychodrama* (2nd revised edition), Beacon House, New York

Mosely, J. (1996) *Quality Circle Time in the Primary Classroom*, Vol. 1, LDA

NACCCE (1999) *All our Futures: Creativity, Culture and Education*, DfEE

Neelands J. (1990), *Structuring Drama Work*, Cambridge University Press

NFER (2003) *Saving a Place for the Arts – survey of the arts in primary schools in England*, NFER, Report 41

Norman, John (1999) 'Brain Right Drama, Parts 1 & 2', *Drama: The Journal of National Drama* (Vol. 6, No.2), Dokumenta

Ofsted (Aug 2003) *Expecting the Unexpected – Developing creativity in primary and secondary schools*, E-publication (HMI 1612)

Perkins D. (1995) *Outsmarting IQ: The Emerging Science of Learnable Intelligence*, The Free Press

QCA (2003a) *Creativity: Find it, promote it!*

QCA (2003b) *Giving a Voice: drama and speaking and listening resources for Key Stage 3*

QCA (2003c), *Speaking, listening, learning: working with children at key stages 1 & 2*

Resnick L.B. (1987) *Education and Learning to Think*, National Academic Press, Washington

Rizzollati G., Gentilucchi M., Camarda R.M. et al. (1990) 'Neurons relating to reaching-grasping arm movements on the rostral part of area 6 (area 6a beta)', *Experimental Brain Research*, 82:337–50

Rockett M. & Percival S. (2002), *Thinking for Learning*, Network Educational Press

Seltzer K. & Bentley T. (1999) *The Creative Age*, Demos

Sharp C. (November 2002) *School Starting Age: European Policy and Recent Research*, NFER

Simard R. & Pratt P. (1998) *Mr Once-Upon-a-Time*, Annick Press Ltd

Smith A. (1998) *Accelerated Learning in Practice*, Network Educational Press

Smith A. (2004) *The Brain's Behind It* (revised edition), Network Educational Press

Smith A. (2003) *Accelerated Learning: A User's Guide*, Network Educational Press

Swartz R. & Parks S. (1994) *Infusing the Teaching of Critical and Creative Thinking into Content Instruction*, Critical Thinking Books and Software, Pacific Grove, CA

Sylwester R. (1995) *A Celebration of Neurons: An Educator's Guide to the Human Brain*, ASCD, Virgina

Vygotsky L.S. (1978) *Mind in Society: the development of higher psychological processes*, Harvard University Press, Cambridge, Mass.

Young J.Z. (1987) *Philosophy and the Brain*, Oxford University Press

# ■ Further reading

Ackroyd J. & Boulton J. (2001) *Drama for Five to Eleven Year Olds*, Fulton

Baldwin P. (1992) *Stimulating Drama – cross curricular approaches in the Primary School*, National Drama

Baldwin P. & Hendy L. (1994) *The Drama Box* and *The Drama Book – an active approach to learning*, Collins Educational

Baldwin P. & Fleming K. (2002) *Teaching Literacy through Drama – Creative Approaches*, Routledge/Falmer

Beetlestone F. (1998) *Creative Children, Imaginative Teaching*, Open University Press

Boal A. (1992) *Games for Actors and Non-Actors*, Routledge

Boal A. (1995) *The Rainbow of Desire*, Routledge

Bolton G. (1984) *Drama as Education*, Longman

Bolton G. (1992) *New Perspectives on Classroom Drama*, Simon and Schuster

Booth D. (1994) *Storydrama*, Pembroke Publishing

Bowell P. & Heap B.S. (2001) *Planning Process Drama*, David Fulton

Egan K. (1992) *Imagination in Teaching and Learning ages 8–15*, Routledge/Falmer

Egan K. (1999) *Children's Minds, Talking Rabbits and Clockwork Oranges*, Teachers' College Press

Fleming M. (1994) *Starting Drama Teaching*, David Fulton

Fleming M. (2001) *Teaching Drama in Primary and Secondary Schools – an integrated approach*, Fulton

Haynes J. (2000) *Children as Philosophers*, Routledge/Falmer

Heathcote D. & Bolton G. (1995) *Drama for Learning*, Heinemann

Hornbrook D. (1991) *Education in Drama: Casting the Dramatic Curriculum*, Falmer Press

Johnson L. & O'Neill D. (eds) (1984) *Dorothy Heathcote: Collected Writings on Education and Drama*, Hutchinson

Kempe A. (1996) *Drama Education and Special Needs*, Nelson Thornes

Kitson N. & Spiby I. (1995) *Primary Drama Handbook* (Franklin Watts)

Marson P. et al (1990) *Drama 14–16 – A Book of Projects and Resources*, Nelson Thornes

Morgan N. & Saxton J. (1987) *Teaching Drama*, Hutchinson

Murris K. & Haynes J. (2000) *Storywise: Thinking through Stories*, DialogueWorks (www.dialogueworks.co.uk)

Neelands J. (1990) *Structuring Drama Work*, Cambridge University Press

Neelands J. (1992) *Learning Through Imagined Experience*, Hodder and Stoughton

Neelands J. (1998) *Beginning Drama 11–14*, David Fulton

O'Neill C. (1992) *The Process of Drama*, Routledge

O'Neill C. & Lambert A. (1982) *Drama Structures – a practical handbook for teachers*, Hutchinson

Readman G. & Lamont G. (1994) *Drama: A Handbook for Primary Teachers*, BBC Educational Publishing,

Toye N. & Prendeville F. (2000) *Drama and Traditional Story for the Early Years*, Routledge/Falmer

Wagner B.J. (1972) *Drama as a Leaning Medium*, Hutchinson

Winston J. (1998) *Drama, Narrative and Moral Education*, Falmer Press

Winston J. & Tandy M. (1998) *Beginning Drama 4–11*, David Fulton

Woolland B. (1993) *The Teaching of Drama in the Primary School*, Longman

# ■ Index

# Titles from Network Educational Press

## THE SCHOOL EFFECTIVENESS SERIES

**Book 1:** *Accelerated Learning in the Classroom* by Alistair Smith

**Book 2:** *Effective Learning Activities* by Chris Dickinson

**Book 3:** *Effective Heads of Department* by Phil Jones & Nick Sparks

**Book 4:** *Lessons are for Learning* by Mike Hughes

**Book 5:** *Effective Learning in Science* by Keith Bishop & Paul Denley

**Book 6:** *Raising Boys' Achievement* by Jon Pickering

**Book 7:** *Effective Provision for Able & Talented Children* by Barry Teare

**Book 8:** *Effective Careers Education & Guidance* by Andrew Edwards & Anthony Barnes

**Book 9:** *Best behaviour and Best behaviour FIRST AID* by Peter Relf, Rod Hirst, Jan Richardson & Georgina Youdell

*Best behaviour FIRST AID* also available separately

**Book 10:** *The Effective School Governor* by David Marriott (including audio tape)

**Book 11:** *Improving Personal Effectiveness for Managers in Schools* by James Johnston

**Book 12:** *Making Pupil Data Powerful* by Maggie Pringle & Tony Cobb

**Book 13:** *Closing the Learning Gap* by Mike Hughes

**Book 14:** *Getting Started* by Henry Liebling

**Book 15:** *Leading the Learning School* by Colin Weatherley

**Book 16:** *Adventures in Learning* by Mike Tilling

**Book 17:** *Strategies for Closing the Learning Gap* by Mike Hughes with Andy Vass

**Book 18:** *Classroom Management* by Philip Waterhouse & Chris Dickinson

**Book 19:** *Effective Teachers* by Tony Swainston

**Book 20:** *Transforming Teaching & Learning* by Colin Weatherley with Bruce Bonney, John Kerr & Jo Morrison

**Book 21:** *Effective Teachers in Primary Schools* by Tony Swainston

## ACCELERATED LEARNING SERIES    General Editor: **Alistair Smith**

*Accelerated Learning: A User's Guide* by Alistair Smith, Mark Lovatt and Derek Wise

*Accelerated Learning in Practice* by Alistair Smith

*The ALPS Approach: Accelerated Learning in Primary Schools* by Alistair Smith & Nicola Call

*The ALPS Approach Resource Book* by Alistair Smith & Nicola Call

*MapWise* by Oliver Caviglioli & Ian Harris

*Creating an Accelerated Learning School* by Mark Lovatt & Derek Wise

*ALPS StoryMaker* by Stephen Bowkett

*Thinking for Learning* by Mel Rockett & Simon Percival

*Reaching out to all learners* by Cheshire LEA

*Leading Learning* by Alistair Smith

*Bright Sparks* by Alistair Smith

*More Bright Sparks* by Alistair Smith

*Move It* by Alistair Smith

# EDUCATION PERSONNEL MANAGEMENT SERIES

*The Well Teacher – management strategies for beating stress, promoting staff health & reducing absence* by Maureen Cooper

*Managing Challenging People – dealing with staff conduct* by Maureen Cooper & Bev Curtis

*Managing Poor Performance – handling staff capability issues* by Maureen Cooper & Bev Curtis

*Managing Allegations Against Staff – personnel and child protection issues in schools* by Maureen Cooper & Bev Curtis

*Managing Recruitment and Selection – appointing the best staff* by Maureen Cooper & Bev Curtis

*Managing Redundancies – dealing with reduction and reorganisation of staff* by Maureen Cooper & Bev Curtis

*Paying Staff in Schools – performance management and pay in schools* by Bev Curtis

# VISIONS OF EDUCATION SERIES

*The Power of Diversity* by Barbara Prashnig

*The Unfinished Revolution* by John Abbott & Terry Ryan

*The Learning Revolution* by Gordon Dryden & Jeannette Vos

*Wise Up* by Guy Claxton

# ABLE & TALENTED CHILDREN COLLECTION

*Effective Resources for Able and Talented Children* by Barry Teare

*More Effective Resources for Able and Talented Children* by Barry Teare

*Challenging Resources for Able and Talented Children* by Barry Teare

# MODEL LEARNING

*Thinking Skills & Eye Q* by Oliver Caviglioli, Ian Harris & Bill Tindall

*Think it–Map it!* by Oliver Caviglioli& Ian Harris

*Reaching out to all thinkers* by Oliver Caviglioli & Ian Harris

# OTHER TITLES FROM NEP

*The Thinking Child* by Nicola Call with Sally Featherstone
*The Thinking Child Resource Book* by Nicola Call with Sally Featherstone
*StoryMaker Catch Pack* by Stephen Bowkett
*Becoming Emotionally Intelligent* by Catherine Corrie
*That's Science!* by Tim Harding
*That's Maths!* by Tim Harding
*The Brain's Behind It* by Alistair Smith
*Help Your Child To Succeed* by Bill Lucas & Alistair Smith
*Help Your Child To Succeed Toolkit* by Bill Lucas & Alistair Smith
*Tweak to Transform* by Mike Hughes
*Brain Friendly Revision* by UFA National Team
*Numeracy Activities Key Stage 2* by Afzal Ahmed & Honor Williams
*Numeracy Activities Key Stage 3* by Afzal Ahmed, Honor Williams & George Wickham
*Teaching Pupils How to Learn* by Bill Lucas, Toby Greany, Jill Rodd & Ray Wicks
*Creating a Learning to Learn School* by Toby Greany & Jill Rodd
*Basics for School Governors* by Joan Sallis
*Questions School Governors Ask* by Joan Sallis
*Imagine That...* by Stephen Bowkett
*Self-Intelligence* by Stephen Bowkett
*Class Talk* by Rosemary Sage
*Lend Us Your Ears* by Rosemary Sage
*A World of Difference* by Rosemary Sage

**For more information and ordering details, please consult our website
www.networkpress.co.uk**

With Drama in Mind

Lightning Source UK Ltd.
Milton Keynes UK
171615UK00001B/13/P

9 781855 390942